ABOUT THE AUTHOR

Paul B. Kidd is a Sydney-based author, Radio 2UE talkback broadcaster, freelance *60 Minutes* researching producer and photojournalist who specialises in Australian true crime, humour, adventure and fishing.

Paul's articles, interviews and photographs have appeared in most major Australian outdoors and men's publications, in numerous magazines and on websites worldwide.

Paul B. Kidd is a recognised authority on Australian serial killers and criminals who have been sentenced to life imprisonment, never to be released. The author of fifteen books on Australian true crime and fishing, he lives in Sydney's eastern suburbs.

OTHER AUSTRALIAN TRUE CRIME TITLES BY PAUL B. KIDD

Never to be Released: Australia's Most Vicious Murderers

Never to be Released: Volume Two

Never to be Released: Volume Three

Australia's Serial Killers: The Definitive History of Serial Multicide in Australia

Australia's Serial Killers: The Definitive History of Serial Multicide in Australia Revised Edition

The Knick Knack Man: Inside the Mind of Australia's Most Deranged Serial Killer

Shallow Graves: The Concealments of Killers

Till Death Us Do Part: Australian Marriages That Ended in Murder

The Australian Crime File: A 'Best of' Collection of Notorious True Crime Stories

THE AUSTRALIAN CRIME FILE 2

More Stories from Australia's Best True Crime Collection

Paul B. Kidd

The Five Mile Press

The Five Mile Press

The Five Mile Press Pty Ltd
950 Stud Road, Rowville
Victoria 3178 Australia
Website: www.fivemile.com.au
Email: publishing@fivemile.com.au

First published 2006

Cover design by saso content & design pty ltd
Page design by Andrew Cunningham–Studio Pazzo

Printed in Australia by Griffin Press

Publisher's Note:
Aside from Newspix, Fairfax and AAP photographs, all pictures have been sourced by the author. The author takes full responsibility for the copyright responsibilities attached to the use of these photographs.

National Library Cataloguing-in-Publication data

Kidd, Paul B. (Paul Benjamin), 1945- .
The Australian crime file 2 : more stories from Australia's best true crime collection.

1st ed.
ISBN 1 74178 253 8.

1. Crime - Australia - Case studies. 2. Criminal investigation - Australia. I. Title.

364.994

To Tania.

My partner and the best assistant a bloke could have.

And, as always, for my son, Benny.

CONTENTS

INTRODUCTION

In light of the extraordinary success of *The Australian Crime File* I guess it's only logical that I would write a *Crime File 2*. After all, writing books is a big part of what I do for a living. And, let's face it, it wasn't as if the chapters were hard to put together, given that I read a 'Crime File' – one that I have written during the week – on the *Weekend Breakfast Show*, the show George Moore and I broadcast from 6am until midday on Saturday and Sunday on Sydney's Radio 2UE.

Having said that, I would like to point out that many of the stories in this book are a little more out of left-field than those that appeared in the first *Crime File*. That edition dealt mainly with Australia's better-known crimes, rather than the unusual or the bizarre. While a few of our more higher-profile cases – Lindy Chamberlain, Alan Bond and the Port Arthur Massacre come to mind – are in this book, you will also find many other yarns from our rich, unlawful history, a history that makes us one of the more unusual nations in the world.

While, sadly, it would have been impossible to write a *Crime File 2* without the cases of multiple, serial, mass and child murder, this book also looks at a huge variety of lesser crimes that make up this genre. You will read about illegal SP bookies, bent police commissioners and cops, the day the police went on strike, our first political assassination attempt, the world's best escapologists, bent entrepreneurs, Australia's leading abortionist and underworld murders. They are all in here. Plus lots of fascinating historical crimes.

A 'Crime File' that I present on air is usually about 1200 words long and takes about seven minutes to read. Lots of the stories included here are the length I wrote them for radio, and exactly as I read them out on air. Others you will find are a little longer and, in some cases, a lot longer. I have gone to the trouble to re-write these as I believe that they are interesting enough to bring them to you in much more detail. The persecution of Lindy Chamberlain is such an example.

I have also included several chapters that have arisen out of my own personal experience and that I would like to share with you. The opening chapter tells how I supported a very brave man named Sandy MacGregor who visited a jail to forgive the man who had murdered his (Sandy's) three daughters. In *The Deep-Sea Contract* I tell of my near-death experience at the hands of a marauding mako shark and a gun-totin' gangster's minder – both at the same time. And *A Trout to Die For* is the unusual story told to me about a couple of harmless crooks who try to outsmart the bigger crooks, with disastrous results. Fact or urban legend? You'll have to decide that one for yourself.

Which brings us to my masterpiece, if I don't mind saying so myself – *Celluloid Serial Killers: The History of Serial Killers in the Movies*. Years in the researching, it tells the history of serial killers on the screen throughout the ages and, as a bonus, I give my list of the top ten serial killer movies in history. Given that serial killer movies are either factual (*The Boston Strangler, Ten Rillington Place*), a mixture of fact and fiction (*Wolf Creek, Dirty Harry*) or just pure fiction (*Se7en, Manhunter*), there's something in here for everyone – even if it's just to assist you to make up your own list of favourites and compare them with mine, or to help you win a bet at the pub.

Paul B. Kidd
Sydney, 2006

1 'I FORGAVE MY DAUGHTERS' KILLER'

In 2001 Sandy MacGregor went to prison to confront the man who shotgun-blasted his three daughters to death. Author Paul B. Kidd was there as the drama unfolded.

'As I sat waiting to meet the man who murdered my children, I really didn't know what my reaction towards him would be,' says Sandy MacGregor. 'I was incredibly nervous and uptight. Not shaking or anything like that. It was all on the inside.

'In all of the months I had spent preparing myself for this moment I had never kidded myself that it was going to be easy. But I had imagined, or rather hoped, that it would be a lot easier than this. But now that it was actually happening I was apprehensive of the outcome, frightened of what I might do.

'I could have stopped it then and no one would have thought any the less of me,' he says. 'But there was no turning back now. I had to meet this man and forgive him for what he had done. Not for him, but for me. And then I could be completely at peace with myself and get on with my life.'

As he relaxes in the loungeroom of his Sydney home, Sandy MacGregor is the embodiment of what he teaches: how to manage your life through the powers of your own mind. He sits surrounded by photos of his family – his deceased daughters, their elder brother Andrew, now 36, his second wife Sandra and their family of Ian, 17 and Lara, 19. And this tall, gentle man speaks candidly about the murder of his daughters Lexie, 16, and twins Jenny and Kirsty, 19, and their 19-year-old girlfriend – and how he came to forgive the man who so callously took his loved ones from him.

The early hours of 24 January 1987, are deep-etched in Sandy MacGregor's memory forever. 'I was re-married with a young family and my daughters lived with their mother nearby,' he recalls. 'The kids and I were extremely close and I was in frequent contact with them. At 2am there was a loud knocking on the door and I answered it to two policemen, who ushered me through to the loungeroom and sat me down. They said they had some terrible news. They told me that my three daughters and a friend had been killed in their mother's home.

'My reaction was disbelief. My daughters couldn't be dead. Only the night before I had called to wish Lexie a happy birthday and talked about the camping trip they were going on the following day for the Australia Day long weekend. It had to be a mistake.'

As they drove Sandy to the scene, the officers explained that a male friend who was going on the camping trip had called several times during the evening and when there was no answer, although the lights were on, he had climbed through a window at 1.10am to find the carnage.

'When I arrived I embraced my ex-wife Beverley, who had arrived home to the chaos from a friend's wedding celebration, and we sobbed uncontrollably,' he says. 'Beverley wanted to go inside and see what had happened to her daughters but the police took me aside and explained that the girls had been "blown away" with a shotgun.

'They apologised for being so graphic but said that they had to tell me this as due to the horrific nature of the crimes they wanted my support to keep Beverley from going inside. They said that it was best that we remember our children as they were. Neither of us went inside. I am glad that I didn't.'

The following day police arrested unemployed student Richard Henry Lawson Maddrell, 27, as he sat on a cliff top contemplating suicide. He had thrown the shotgun in the ocean. A diagnosed paranoid schizophrenic and high on a cocktail of drugs at the time of the killings, Maddrell had met Jenny MacGregor when she was a student at Wollongong University, 100 kilometres south of Sydney. Maddrell had become infatuated, but over the previous 12 months she had rejected his advances.

Maddrell told police that he had gone to Jenny MacGregor's house at 9.30 that night with a loaded shotgun. After she answered the door, he marched her at gunpoint into the loungeroom where the other girls were watching television and allegedly said to her, 'You don't know how much you have hurt me and screwed me up, but I still love you', before shooting her in the head at point-blank range. Maddrell then killed the other three girls with five more shots to their heads after stopping to re-load twice.

'After the murders I was in two states of shock,' Sandy says. 'I was either like a zombie, wandering around in a daze, or I was consumed by loathing and hatred. I had a consultancy business in the city and I just abandoned it. All I wanted to do was kill Richard Maddrell. To me he was just vermin – and mad vermin at that – who should be put down.

'I was approached by a person who said that he could have him killed in jail for me as a favour. And I believe this person could have. But eventually I declined, though I must admit, I did give it a lot of thought.

'If anyone had told me then that there would come a time in my life when I would be able to forgive Maddrell, I would have said they were crazy.'

Sandy MacGregor's father was a major in the British Indian army. Sandy was born in 1940 and in 1947 the family migrated to Tasmania. Sandy was the top army cadet at school. After graduating from Duntroon he completed a civil engineering degree at Sydney University.

Sandy commanded the Royal Australian Engineers 3 Field Troop in Vietnam, the first 'tunnel rats' to discover the Viet Cong's secret underground cities in 1966. Back in Australia in 1967 to train young officers about Vietnam, he was awarded the Military Cross for bravery and leadership. He left the regular army in 1968 to work as an engineer, but stayed in the Army Reserve. His marriage to Beverley ended in 1976 and he married Sandra Dewhurst in 1979 and started a new family.

Sandy first encountered the healing powers of the mind when he encouraged his son, Andrew, then 17, to seek alternative treatment for the chronic asthma he'd had since infancy.

'A couple of bad attacks had landed him in hospital,' Sandy says. 'I took him to an Indian doctor who taught Andrew a simple mental relaxation technique, which helped him control the severity of the attacks. And, later on, when Andrew was seriously injured in a motorcycle accident and looked like losing a leg, he used the same techniques to cope with infection and pain and saved his leg.

'I was convinced there was something in this so Andrew taught me the techniques. I applied them to losing weight and I lost 22 kilograms in six months, without dieting, and could make my pulse disappear and bring my blood pressure down by 20 points,' Sandy says. 'Up to the time of the girls' murders I was meditating daily and had done a course on personal development.

'After the tragedy, even though I was in severe shock, I did another course and within two months I was meditating again. It was during the meditation that I realised that if I persisted in being consumed with anger, hate and revenge towards Maddrell I would become another of his victims,' he says. 'I decided to turn those negative thoughts into thoughts of acceptance, love and forgiveness. I worked on it for up to two hours a day and within six months my head was clear, I had forgiven Maddrell in my mind many times, I felt at peace with myself and I could get on with my life.

'By now I was convinced of the power of the subconscious and I decided to teach people about it. As a result of an interview on ABC Radio in 1990, when I said publicly for the first time that I had forgiven Maddrell, 300 people enrolled for my seminars. That was really the beginning of my new life.'

Since then he has conducted hundreds of seminars throughout Australia for many thousands of participants, recorded more than a dozen meditation tapes, written numerous books on personal development, one of which, *Piece of Mind*, has sold over 60,000 copies, and published his memoirs of Vietnam in *No Need for Heroes*.

'But in time Maddrell could be freed and it worried me not knowing how I would react if I bumped into him in the street,' Sandy says. 'Would I talk to him or would I avoid him? Would I abuse him? Would I react violently? I came to realise that until I found the answers I would go on wondering and he would always be like a monkey on my back.

'In late 2000, while consulting a spiritual teacher about my concerns, to my surprise he suggested that I could complete the process by seeing Maddrell in prison and forgiving him face to face. I was shocked. The thought had never crossed my mind.

'But after I thought about it I realised that it was also the opportunity to get all of my questions answered,' he says. 'Then the effect on my psyche would be gone and I would be free. But would he see me? I decided to find out.'

In March 1988, Maddrell had been found not guilty of murder by reason of mental illness and detained indefinitely in strict custody at Morisset Psychiatric Hospital for the criminally insane. After serving four years he was considered sane enough to live among mainstream prisoners and was now in Grafton Gaol, 620 kilometres north of Sydney.

'Maddrell was contacted through a New South Wales Corrective Services program called Conferencing,' Sandy says, 'which brings victims and offenders together for a multitude of reasons, such as venting their anger or giving the offender the opportunity to repent and ask forgiveness. Maddrell agreed immediately.

'During the four months it took to set up the meeting I worked hard at preparing myself with meditation, mental and physical exercise and prayer,' he says. 'With a friend to support me during the meeting, we drove to Grafton and discussed in detail what I wanted to talk about and the questions I wanted to ask. I wanted to get it right the first time as there was no going back and doing it over.'

The meeting's coordinator, Phil Hartmann from Corrective Services, met Sandy and Paul at the jail and took them inside to the tiny chapel, where six chairs had been set up in a circle in front of the altar. Sandy meditated for a few minutes to compose himself then indicated that he was ready. Psychologist Chris Drayden-Thompson and Reverend Richard Brown led a stony-faced Maddrell, his hands clenched in front of him, into the room. He looked as if there were a thousand other places he would rather be.

'When I looked up and saw him for the first time I thought: "So this is what he looks like. So this is the bastard who killed my kids,"' Sandy says. 'But rather than feel hatred or anger or want to abuse him, as I had dreaded I would when we met, I knew in that face-to-face instant that I *could* forgive him in the flesh and be free from ever having to wonder about those things again in my life. It was an enormous relief.'

Phil Hartmann introduced Maddrell to Sandy and Paul and they both remained seated. There was no shaking hands. Just nodding hellos. Maddrell was seated opposite Sandy.

At around 170cm, of medium build and dressed in a green T-shirt, tracksuit pants and runners, 42-year-old Maddrell looked younger than his years. He obviously worked out and looked trim and healthy. Atop his high forehead sat a crewcut. He had a pointed nose, no facial hair and his beady eyes gazed out from abysmal, ecliptic cavities. 'I noticed that there were red blotches around his eyes and I thought, "Good, maybe he's emotional, it looks as if he has been crying,"' Sandy says. 'To break the tension I told him that I was very nervous and asked how he felt. He replied that he was "scared witless".

'I told him that I was doing this on my own behalf and that my former wife and my son Andrew were not aware I was here,' Sandy says. 'I said that I would like to talk about what forgiveness is all about for me before I forgave him for the murders of my daughters.'

Sandy told Maddrell that he had already forgiven him many times in his own mind, had said it publicly on radio and published it in his book *Switch On To Your Inner Strength* in 1996. 'I explained that I teach that if you can forgive in your mind something that has been done against you, it prevents you from becoming hateful and angry. If you don't, then that hatred and anger will run your life, which would leave you wide open to sickness and disease of the body and mind.

'I made it clear that my forgiveness did not condone what he had done or trivialise the offence and that I was doing this for myself, not him. If he got some good out of it then that was his good fortune, though I said that I hoped that by forgiving him it would be a good outcome for us both.'

As Sandy spoke Maddrell sat bolt upright with his hands in his lap, not once taking his eyes from him. Apart from the occasional nod in agreement when Sandy asked him if he understood what he was saying, he remained silent and emotionless.

'I explained that I believed that all humans have an energy that runs through their bodies, which can be seen on a screen when it is measured by an electro-encephalograph, the machine that measures brain waves,' Sandy says. 'When you are brain dead the line is flat – the energy is gone. Sometimes that energy comes back in what is known as a "near-death experience" and then it is known as Life.

'When that energy has gone out of the body some people call it Soul, Spirit, Life-force, Prana, Chi, God or Spark of God. I choose to call it God. I firmly believe that this energy, this God, is in all of us and that we are all joined by it and therefore forgiving is a spiritual act.'

And then after a long pause, Sandy said: 'Richard Maddrell, I bring to mind that part of you which is joined to me, so whatever I do or say to you in this moment I am also doing and saying to myself. From the God in me to the God in you, I unconditionally forgive you for the murders of my three daughters, Jenny, Kirsty and Lexie.'

As he struggled saying his daughters' names, Sandy began to weep. If ever there was an opportunity for Maddrell to show any emotion, this was it. He didn't. Sandy sat and wept for a short time before composing himself. Then he asked Maddrell if he would like to say anything.

Maddrell said he was sorry (the first of six times that he said it) for what he had done and expressed gratitude at being given the opportunity to say it. He was softly spoken and appeared sincere. He said that he never imagined that he could ever hurt so many people so much and have so many people hate him.

'Then we discussed the things that I had struggled with in my mind and would have been doomed to live without the answers to, if I had not met with Maddrell,' Sandy says. 'Things about that horrible night that were deeply painful, but had to be answered so I would never have to wonder about them ever again.'

When he was satisfied that he had put his mind completely to rest, Sandy called an end to the meeting and Maddrell was taken back to his cell. It had been an hour and a half.

'I walked out into a perfect summer's afternoon,' Sandy says. 'The sun was beaming as if Jenny, Kirsty and Lexie were smiling down on me. I knew they would have been proud of their dad. As I walked from the jail a free man, it was as if I was floating on air. My 14-year sentence was over. The monkey was off my back forever.'

Sandy MacGregor conducts seminars all over Australia helping people to get on with their lives by understanding themselves better through the power of their minds and meditation. For information on Sandy MacGregor's seminars contact www.calm.com.au.

2 WHO MURDERED SALLIE-ANNE?

Just after dawn on the morning of 7 February 1986, a jogger noticed what he thought was a body floating face down in the lake known as Busby's Bore, situated on the westernmost corner of Sydney's Centennial Park. He notified the park rangers, who used a row boat to recover the corpse of a woman wearing blue jeans and a pink skivvy top, which had been rolled up to rest on the top of her breasts.

Police recognised the body immediately. It was one of the best-known underworld characters of the time, 32-year-old Sallie-Anne Huckstepp – heroin addict, prostitute, gangsters' moll and police informer. Huckstepp had a long criminal history for petty crimes and drug use, and was always in the company of one heavy criminal or another. It was said that she had also had affairs with police officers.

So no one was really surprised that Sallie-Anne had wound up dead, floating among the lilies. Over the years she had been an outspoken police informer on her criminal associates and, according to the underworld scuttlebutt, she was just marking time on the one spot waiting for any one of a long list of villains to see to it that she would never tell on them again. Sallie-Anne was known as a 'dead woman walking'.

Born Sallie-Anne Krivoshow into a respectable Jewish family in Sydney's up-market Bellevue Hill in 1954, she was educated at exclusive Moriah College, a private Jewish school. Sallie-Anne married young and had a daughter. After the marriage broke up she retained her married name and began hanging around Kings Cross, using heroin and selling herself to pay for it.

It wasn't long before Sallie-Anne's good looks and charismatic personality found her in the constant companionship of the notorious Sydney standover man, armed robber and heroin dealer, Warren Lanfranchi.

When Lanfranchi was gunned down and killed, allegedly in self-defence, in Woods Lane in the inner Sydney suburb of Chippendale in June 1981 by detective Roger Rogerson, Sallie-Anne made the fatal mistake of publicly condemning Rogerson and his criminal associate, underworld crime boss Neddy Smith.

Sallie-Anne told *60 Minutes* and the *Willesee* current affairs programs that when her lover had left home that day to meet Rogerson it was to give him (Rogerson) a $10,000, bribe which she saw him stuff down the front of his pants in $50 notes before he left home. No money was found on Lanfranchi's body.

At the inquest into Lanfranchi's killing Sallie-Anne was even more verbal and told the court about dealings that her dead lover had with Neddy Smith and the police. She told the court that Lanfranchi feared for his life after he had attempted to murder a police officer but the gun had failed to go off.

She said that Neddy Smith had arranged the meeting with Lanfranchi and detective Roger Rogerson, and Lanfranchi was to pay a $10,000 bribe and the matter would be forgotten. She said that Neddy Smith had driven Lanfranchi to the meeting with Rogerson at the secluded lane in Chippendale, where Rogerson had murdered Lanfranchi in cold blood and taken the money.

But despite Sallie-Anne's evidence and open outrage to anyone who would listen, Roger Rogerson was exonerated and she became a criminal pariah. For her own protection Sallie-Anne became the partner of another of Sydney's most feared and notorious drug traffickers, David Kelleher, whom she referred to as her 'Blond God' due to his muscular physique and bleached blond hair.

Together they became quite an item among the criminal milieu of Sydney's eastern suburbs and Sallie-Anne became what is known in criminal jargon as a 'koala' – a protected species. But that was only as long as she was with her Blond God. Without his protection, she was fair game.

So when Dave Kelleher was arrested, thrown in jail and ultimately sentenced to life imprisonment for trafficking huge amounts of heroin, Sallie-Anne was out in the cold. She went back to hooking for a living, only this time with more up-market clients. And being a celebrity of sorts herself, she liked to cater for the celebrities.

But that didn't dampen her newly acquired media profile as a walking authority on the underworld who wasn't afraid to say what she thought. She often appeared on current affairs programs and even had a regular column in *Australian Penthouse Magazine*. Blind Freddy could tell you that Sallie-Anne was long past her use-by date.

Around 11pm on the night of 6 February 1986, Sallie-Anne received a phone call at the apartment she shared with a girlfriend in Edgecliff Road, Woollahra. She left immediately, telling her flatmate she would only be a few minutes. The flatmate suspected that the call was from a drug dealer and that Sallie-Anne was going to collect some heroin.

Dimly lit Centennial Park at night is not the best of places to be on your own, especially if you are an attractive woman, but the lure of the heroin was strong enough for Sallie-Anne to park her car at the unlit Martin Street entrance, which allows pedestrian access, and she entered into the dark. It was also raining heavily. She never came out.

An inquest into Sallie-Anne Huckstepp's death concluded that she had been strangled by a person unknown. While police had their suspicions, no charges were laid.

Many years later while serving a life sentence for murder, Sallie-Anne's old adversary, Neddy Smith, began gobbing off to his cellmate that he had murdered her. The cellmate went to police and they wired him up and he recorded the conversations. Everything added up. Smith even said that he hated Sallie-Anne so much that, as he strangled her in the pond, he made sure that she looked into his eyes as she drew her last breath, so that his would be the last face she would ever see.

Smith was charged with Sallie-Anne's murder and sent to trial in 1995. So convinced were police that he had done it that they had Sallie-Anne's coffin exhumed in the hope that some of Neddy Smith's skin would be under her fingernails, which would give them the conclusive DNA proof that would wrap the case up. No such luck.

With only what he had said to his cellmate as evidence, Smith was found not guilty of murder. Neddy Smith has since been found guilty of the 1983 murder of brothel keeper Harvey Jones, and will never be released from prison.

The murder of Sallie-Anne Huckstepp remains open to this day, though police aren't looking too hard for the killer. They believe that the person who did it is safely behind bars as it is.

3 THE WICKED WITCH OF KINGS CROSS

Throughout the 1950s, '60s and '70s, Rosaleen Norton was Sydney's own real-live witch. An eccentric in the extreme, these days her antics would be treated for what they were, a bit of harmless fun. But, back in those archaic times, the authorities chose to look upon Roie, as she preferred to be called, as the devil's apprentice and treated her accordingly – to the point where she wound up in court for the most ridiculous offences that today would be laughable.

Like everything about her life, even Rosaleen Norton's birth was different. She claimed to have been born in the middle of a violent thunderstorm in October 1917, with two blue spots on her kneecap and a grisly strip of hard flesh running up from her waist to her armpit that, according to her, was the unmistakable mark of a witch.

She was born into a perfectly normal home to god-fearing Protestant parents in possibly the least devil-like place on the planet – beautiful Dunedin in New Zealand. When she was a girl the family moved to Sydney and she excelled at drawing and painting at the East Sydney Technical College. She claimed later on in her life that it was here that she became intrigued with the occult and Satanism. She satisfied her passion by reading macabre American paperbacks and classics of the occult by Bram Stoker, Mary Shelley and Edgar Allan Poe.

Rosaleen also had a flare for writing and, at age 15, her stories and drawings featured regularly in the most popular magazine of the time, *Smith's Weekly*. The first articles and illustrations were about normal topics of the day but they became more and more macabre and, when they got too over the top, she was sacked. After her mother died in 1935 she left home and hitchhiked around Australia with her boyfriend, making a living as a pavement artist.

By her late teens Rosaleen Norton could be best described as a bohemian, content to live day to day with her teenage husband in their tiny, dark bed-sitter in Brougham Street Kings Cross, where she would spend the rest of her life. The marriage didn't last long and now Rosaleen was alone to practise what was her life's calling – Satanism, black magic, voodoo and the occult.

She made a respectable living modelling nude for artists and privately selling her own paintings, which mainly depicted orgies in a setting that resembled her interpretation of hell. The works showed forbidden sex between naked devil-creatures with long tails, gargoyles intertwined with gargoyles, witches and hermaphrodites.

Before long, the Witch of Kings Cross, as she was now known, became notorious for the 'sex magic' parties at her tiny apartment. Those fortunate enough to have been to one told of wild orgies, drug taking and ceremonies where partygoers pledged themselves to the devil. It was rumoured that some of Sydney's more prominent people attended the orgies and had given themselves over to the dark side.

Rosaleen Norton was a sight to behold as she swanned through the Cross with her worshippers in tow. The flowing black cape with a huge Victorian collar, waist-length jet-black hair flowing in the slipstream, plucked arched eyebrows, pancake make-up, ruby-red lips, elf-like pointed ears, high cheek bones, that accentuated her lecherous smirk, and the pointed vampire's eye-teeth, made her a sight worth the drive to Darlinghurst just to say that you had seen her. Unfortunately the pong that came off Roie indicated that she didn't tub too often. But, maybe that was the way witches were meant to smell. I doubt that anyone was game enough to ask her.

In 1945 Roie took up with Gavin Greenless, a young up-and-coming poet from a respectable family of Sydney journalists. All the while she had been painting and, with help from Greenless, she had an exhibition of 47 pastels and sketches at Melbourne University's toffy Rowden White Library.

Given that the art world was still gasping in horror at William Dobell's 1943 Archibald Prize–winning caricature of Joshua Smith, it is little wonder that they fainted in shock at the sight of Satan, ghouls and werewolves having their way with naked nuns on the altar in front of the fires of Hades.

The vice squad arrived at the exhibition and took away four of Norton's works appropriately named *Lucifer*, *Triumph*, *Individuation* and *Witches' Sabbat* and charged her with having exhibited obscene articles. Norton went to court and won the case, but a ban placed on the exhibition saw to it that she didn't sell any paintings. We can only wonder just how much those paintings would be worth today.

In 1951 Norton and her husband jointly produced a book *The Art of Rosaleen Norton*, consisting of his poems and her illustrations. The book was declared obscene and was banned. In August 1955 Norton exhibited her works at the Kashmir Café in Kings Cross, only to have the vice squad take them away and charge her with breaching the Obscene and Indecent Publications Act. She was eventually found guilty of exhibiting three paintings that were deemed to be obscene and were subsequently destroyed. At the same time she and her husband were fined £25 for their part in taking obscene photographs of what the court classed as 'unnatural acts'.

In March 1956, Sir Eugene Goossens, the celebrated conductor of the Sydney Symphony Orchestra, was arrested as he stepped off a flight from London to Sydney. In Sir Eugene's bags customs officers found a swag of pornographic material, which consisted of 1166 explicit photographs, films, ribald books and three rubber masks. It was alleged that Sir Eugene was a regular at Rosaleen Norton's sex parties. He was fined and left Australia in disgrace, never to return.

By now Norton's reputation as High Priestess of the Witches of Australia was established and through the late 1950s and '60s she made a living consulting in witchcraft and allowing the believers to have their pictures taken with her alongside a life-size portrait of Pan, her favourite demon.

She did nothing to quash the stories of the sex orgies at her tiny apartment with as many as nine naked guests at a time in grotesque masks and capes lusting over her, naked but for a cat mask, black apron and black shawl, and smoking a hashish joint from a long cigarette holder.

By the mid-1970s Rosaleen Norton's novelty value had worn off and she was virtually alone, friendless and forgotten and dying a lingering death from colon cancer. Ironically, the ones who took her in to ease her into the next life were the once-dreaded enemy, the nuns at the Sacred Heart Hospice for the Dying. In 1979 the Witch of Kings Cross died, aged 62.

We can only imagine that when Rosaleen Norton knocked on the gates to hell and asked to come in, the devil would have opened them and said, 'Hello Roie. We've been waiting for you.' And that would have made her very happy.

4 'DARLING, YOU DO THE RENOVATING AND JUST GIVE ME THE BILLS'

When Coles Myer boss Brian Quinn bought a modest two-bedroom house on a generous block in leafy Templestowe, in Melbourne's fashionable eastern suburbs, for $440,000 in 1982 he said to his wife, 'Darling, you do the renovations and just give me the bills'. Little did he realise that the budget they set would be passed in a minute and the house would end up costing a fortune – even by today's standards – and he would wind up in the clink.

It seemed as though a lot of the money he used for the renovations came from the company Brian Quinn had so brilliantly managed for 36 years. But, loyal employee or not, the shareholders were far from impressed and off he went to the cooler.

At the time of the indiscretions, Brian Quinn was one of Australia's most liked and respected businessmen, who had started dirt poor at the bottom and ended up at the top delivering healthy profits year in and year out for the only company he had ever worked for in his life. He began sweeping floors in a

Coles store in Adelaide in 1956 and over the years worked in every facet of retailing until he was chief executive of a business with an annual turnover in excess of $10 billion per annum on a salary of $1.5 million a year. And worth every cent.

Along the way the boy from humble beginnings was elected to the Board of the Reserve Bank and collected an Order of Australia. When he retired in 1992 he did so with his reputation intact as one of Australia's most respected leaders of commerce. But there were a few unpleasant skeletons lurking in Brian Quinn's closet and they would be hung out to dry in the years to come.

When the Quinns bought the house in Templestowe it was with the intention of renovating it into a comfortable family home. Given that they had been described as the perfect couple in that he could earn money like no other and his wife Trenna could spend it as fast – if not faster – than he made it, it seemed like a marriage made in heaven.

And so, with a budget of $250,000, Mrs Quinn set about building their home for them and their young family. Once the shell of the house, which was described as resembling the Palace of Versailles, was finished, the fittings to the house and the external construction began. This included a tennis court and spa, a floodlit cricket pitch and an eight-car garage. More than $250,000 was spent on marble floors and walls and over $100,000 for glass in the windows, and the imported toilet suites cost around $5000 each.

Not happy with the new first floor of the house, Mrs Quinn had it demolished before anyone had set a foot on it and another floor more to her choosing was installed. The airconditioning system was removed and reinstalled at a cost of $242,000 because the vents were visible. The painting bill came to $1 million for a house that was almost entirely wallpapered. Mrs Quinn was said to have run her hand over a wall after a sixth coat of varnish had been applied, only to tell the workmen to rub it down and give it another coat.

Mrs Quinn was also unhappy with the ultramodern kitchen, when she saw a better one in a magazine, so she had it ripped out and updated without so much as a tin of Beluga caviar being opened in it. Unhappy with the shade of the imported marble in one of the guests' powder rooms, after the tradesmen had spent forever lovingly installing it, Mrs Quinn had it replaced with a different coloured marble more to her choosing and at a cost of more than $100,000.

For six years the trucks kept coming and going from dawn until dusk. At any given time during working hours there would be as many as 20 work vehicles in the street out the front. When it was finished the house and grounds took up five suburban blocks. All together it had cost $6 million. Such was Mrs Quinn's exquisite taste that eight years later the Quinn mansion sold for just $1.9 million. But for long before the sale of the house, tongues had been wagging that Brian Quinn didn't have that kind of money to throw around and an investigation into the origin of some of the money that had paid for the renovations was put in motion.

The suspicions were correct. Some of the payments had come from Coles Myer. Marble, granite, gold-plated taps, the marble-floored tennis pavilion, the flood-lit tennis court, guttering, plumbing, swimming pool and crystal chandeliers had been all charged to Coles Myer's account.

But proving that a man such as Brian Quinn was corrupt wasn't going to be easy and it wasn't until April 1997 that the former CEO of Coles Myer and a former Coles Myer national maintenance manager, Graham Lanyon, pleaded not guilty in court to defrauding Coles Myer of $4.6 million between September 1982 and October 1988.

The Crown alleged that on Brian Quinn's instructions Mr Lanyon was writing cheques and burying the costs in the company books for work allegedly done on Coles projects, when in fact they were payment for the army of workers and mountains of materials coming into the Quinn mansion. In his defence, Brian Quinn's counsel maintained that as a Coles Myer executive he was entitled to have some improvements to the house paid for by the company. In an act of good faith, Mr Quinn paid back $2.9 million to Coles Myer.

Brian Quinn's list of character witnesses looked like a who's who of Australian business and politics. The Victorian Premier, Jeff Kennett, spoke on his behalf, as did many leaders of commerce and the community at large. They spoke of Brian Quinn's generosity with both his time and money, his public spiritedness and his selflessness for the huge variety of causes that he supported. But it was all to no avail. He was sent to prison for four years.

Ever the retailer, while he was in central Victoria's Loddon Prison, Brian Quinn was granted permission to run the canteen, which he apparently did more efficiently and profitably than ever before. His salary was $5.50 a day. He was released after serving two and a half years.

Brian Quinn has always steadfastly maintained he did nothing wrong. Out of prison in 1999, he and his wife moved to Queensland to live. For both their sakes I hope they moved into a brand new apartment and not a run-down house that needed a lick of paint.

5 THE *AVOCA* GOLD HEIST

It was early August in 1877 when three heavy metal boxes were loaded onto the P&O steam ship *Avoca*, docked at Darling Harbour in Sydney, and captained by a seafarer named Pockley. The boxes held cloth bags, and inside those bags was £5000 in shiny gold sovereigns, a substantial amount of wealth back in those days. The bags sat amongst sawdust to protect their contents from being thrown around if they encountered rough seas on the journey that would eventually see them land in Ceylon, now Sri Lanka.

Notably, these weren't ordinary sovereigns, which featured an image of St George and his dragon foe on one side. Because they were intended for use in Ceylon, religious differences dictated that these specially minted coins depicted a floral wreath instead.

The three heavy boxes were carried on board the *Avoca* by two men from the Pitt Street offices of the Oriental Banking Corporation, who were then shown to the ship's office, where they were met by Chief Officer Elliston. Taking responsibility for the riches, Elliston signed for the boxes before they were stowed in a safe in a strongroom deep in the bottom of the ship, the hatch of which was located directly opposite Elliston's own cabin. The *Avoca* made its way out of Sydney Harbour that afternoon, steaming through the Heads and down to Melbourne, where the boxes would then be loaded aboard the mail steamer RMS *China*, bound for Ceylon.

Everyone involved in transporting the riches felt that the gold sovereigns were in safe hands. After all, the cabin in which they were left was below the lowest deck in the ship. It was also only accessible through one hatch – and Chief Officer Elliston was holding on to the only key to that hatch.

When the *Avoca* reached its southern destination, bank officials were on hand to witness the boxes' relocation to the RMS *China*, which reached the port of Galle in Ceylon just short of three weeks later, on 29 August 1877. With such tight security measures having been adhered to the whole time, it's little wonder that everyone on hand was shocked to find only sawdust when the boxes were finally opened.

No time was wasted in contacting the P&O offices back in Sydney, and they in turn got in touch with the authorities straight away. After discussing the situation, the police were sure that the gold had been stolen from the *Avoca* somewhere between Sydney and Melbourne, but how? Chief Officer Elliston was the most likely culprit, but detectives questioned him thoroughly and he seemed to be innocent. With that avenue leading nowhere, police decided to question each and every member of the *Avoca*'s crew – including the ship's resident carpenter, a quiet man named Martin Weiberg. Even though Weiberg's job meant that he had a set of keys for almost every door onboard the *Avoca*, he said he had no key for the strongroom. Indeed, the carpenter seemed put out that he would even be considered a thief.

The case dragged on for months, with the Sydney police having no luck in unearthing even a basic lead. In the meantime, P&O felt they needed to save face. They launched an inquiry, which resulted in Elliston being found guilty of negligence. The Chief Officer was dismissed from the company right away. Another employment casualty was Captain Pockley, who it was found had gone against company policy by disembarking in Melbourne while the *Avoca*'s precious load was still on board.

Just as the case was reaching its dead end a few months later, Martin Weiberg decided he'd had enough of life on the water. He quit his position as carpenter on the *Avoca*, telling his colleagues that he was marrying a barmaid and becoming a farmer. Indeed, the quiet, spectacle-wearing chippie had bought a 50-hectare property on the banks of the Tarwin River in South Gippsland, Victoria. The newlyweds soon settled into their rural existence and Weiberg even had his wife's mother and sister Emma and her husband move in with them. All was going well for Weiberg until one day when his sister-in-law needed some soap. She went to the property's laundry and found a 50-centimetre length of homemade soap and broke off a section. Emma was shocked to see some torn cloth sticking out the end of the hollow bar. She pulled out the cloth and found it to contain several gold sovereigns. On one side of the sovereigns was a picture of a floral wreath. Emma showed the find to her mother, who told her to take the gold pieces to the authorities. An arrest warrant was put out for Martin Weiberg in October 1878, more than a year after the robbery on board the *Avoca*.

It transpired that while Weiberg had been working on the steamer, the carpenter had made himself a virtual labyrinth of hidden passages and hatches, which gave him an easy and secret path around the *Avoca*. None of his shipmates had any idea of their existence, and he had even gone to the trouble of resealing some of them before he left the ship. Of further assistance in his robbery was the fact that he had stealthily made a copy of the strongroom key sometime before the sovereigns were stowed on board, in preparation for just such an opportunity. Realising, though, that the risk of entering the strongroom through the hatch opposite Chief Officer Elliston's room was too great, Weiberg had simply cut out part of the room's panelling, giving him easy access for whenever a suitable prize was placed on board. Once he set his greedy desires on the sovereigns, he had plenty of time to sneak into the strongroom, spirit them away, reseal the heavy metal boxes and hide the stash, cleverly waiting several months until the heat died down before leaving the *Avoca* for good.

But even though the plan seemed strong, it was about to come unstuck. After Weiberg's sister-in-law told the law of her find, four plain-clothes officers were sent to bring the erstwhile carpenter to justice. Led by Inspector Frederick Secretan, the posse also included Mounted Constable Mackay, who knew Weiberg by sight. Indeed, Mackay had no trouble recognising Weiberg as he trotted towards the group on a horse on a quiet bush track. The posse made out that they were looking to purchase property in the area. They subtly surrounded Weiberg while asking him innocent questions, then abruptly dragged him from his horse and told him that they believed he was a thief.

Perhaps expecting such a situation, Weiberg was quick with an excuse. He told the posse that a bearded passenger who he couldn't identify had handed him a heavy package out of the blue one day on the *Avoca*, telling him it was a present and asking that he remain quiet about it. Weiberg told the policemen that he was shocked to find 200 gold sovereigns when he eventually checked the parcel's contents.

But the story was too hard for the lawmen to believe, and Weiberg was taken into custody, with two members of the posse taking him to be detained at Griffiths Point, while the other two men conducted a search of Weiberg's property, where they soon uncovered further sovereigns – one stash in a carpenter's plane, another in a hollow log.

When Weiberg was confronted with the find back at Griffiths Point, he admitted the story of the bearded stranger wasn't totally true. What had really happened, he said, was that Chief Officer Elliston was the brains behind the whole operation, while Weiberg himself had been unknowingly roped into the theft.

After a brief check, it turned out that Elliston – angry at being fired from his position on the *Avoca* – had returned to London.

Scotland Yard were contacted and asked to pick up the former chief officer. They did so, and Elliston was soon bought before a London court, which declared that he was innocent due to a lack of evidence.

While this was going on, Weiberg told the police that he would take them to retrieve the rest of the gold sovereigns – around 1800 pieces, hidden in a sealed iron kettle that had been deposited in the Tarwin River.

Weiberg was taken to the spot where he said the gold was located by three officers – Inspector Secretan and detectives Mahoney and Duncan. Once they reached the river, Weiberg suggested Secretan and Duncan row into the middle of the waterway to help pinpoint the exact location of the sunken sovereigns. Having grown to trust the man in their custody, the pair did so without hesitation. While they were on the water, though, Weiberg punched Mahoney in the stomach and bolted into the surrounding bush, leaving the officer winded and embarrassed.

Months passed and Weiberg could not be found. Neither could the remaining sovereigns. In this time, Weiberg ventured into Melbourne, where he met up with his friend Joseph Pearce, who it is speculated was his accomplice in the heist. Weiberg had given Pearce 1000 of the gold sovereigns and the man had bought a rackety old cutter called the *Petrel*. The plan was for the pair to sail her to freedom in South America, but they only got as far as Port Phillip Bay before the *Petrel* began to take in water. Still, they managed to make it to Queenscliff before they beached the boat and disappeared into the bush.

Before long, the authorities caught up with Pearce, who had returned to his old place in Melbourne. When questioned, he told the police that he believed Weiberg was hiding out in the district of Waratah Bay. Wanting to make up for losing Weiberg so easily, Inspector Secretan despatched one of his best men, Detective Edelsten, to hunt down the thief.

Edelsten reached Gippsland in early May and, along with local policeman Mounted Constable Taylor, set out on an arduous trek, both of the men disguised as bushies. They spent more than two weeks venturing through harsh terrain, often on foot because it was too overgrown for their horses. Besides the frequent rain and lack of food, their job was made more difficult by the fact that what few settlers there were in the inhospitable region were sympathetic to Weiberg's cause.

Still, the officers pushed on, and on 16 May 1879 they finally got a break, coming across footprints on a remote beach near Cape Patterson, where they believed Weiberg had gone to ground. The men followed the footprints until they reached an inlet that was said to be filled with sharks. Deciding that it was too dangerous to risk crossing the waterway, the pair made their way around the inlet almost 50 kilometres until they found a solitary hut, but Weiberg saw the men first. The felon fled for some distance and then jumped off a four-metre cliff onto the beach. But the officers drew their firearms and shot them ahead of Weiberg, who threw his hands in the air and surrendered himself.

Weiberg was transported back to Melbourne by steamer and coach. When he arrived at Melbourne Gaol, there was a crowd of around 2000 people to greet him. Weiberg, it turned out, had become something of a sympathetic folk hero. When he was finally bought to trial, he reverted to his original story that a strange bearded passenger had given him the sovereigns. The jury believed it, and Weiberg and Pearce were both charged with receiving. As a result, Weiberg spent five years in prison, while Pearce received a lesser sentence of 12 months.

Once he was released, Weiberg went back to the South Gippsland area to be with his wife and their child. He later bought a yacht and told everyone that he planned to sail it across to New Zealand. But his wife – having already fallen in love with another man – said that she would have no part of the trip. Weiberg beat her and left on his own.

Just two days after he set off, though, the dinghy from his boat was found washed up upside down on a Waratah Bay beach. Nearby was Weiberg's cap. His abandoned boat also turned up offshore at the Glennie Islands.

No one knows for sure the fate of former carpenter Martin Weiberg, or the still-missing gold sovereigns. One story has him buying a hotel and settling down in Sweden, while many believe he drowned in the Tasman Sea.

Either way, it seems a fitting end to the mystery that to this day is known as 'The *Avoca* Gold Heist'.

6 | A TROUT TO DIE FOR

This tale was told to the author, Paul B. Kidd, by a local down the Snowy Mountains way and he believes it to be true. But, for all of his inquiries, he couldn't find anyone in the district who knew anything about a four-day fish festival involving tagged trout. Or, for that matter, of a mysterious dead body that became tangled in sash cord. Could our author have been deceived? You decide for yourself.

The annual four-day fish festival was shaping up to be a beauty. The big cash prizes on offer were attracting anglers from all over the country and although there were some notorious cheats among them, the organisers didn't seem to care.

With around 5000 anglers each paying a $10 entry fee, they stood to make a killing, so a little fudging here and there wouldn't hurt. In fact, the rules almost encouraged it; the boundaries were anywhere within 30 kilometres of the starting point, and they weren't policed. The area included four dams and several rivers.

The big prizes were for the capture of Terry, the Tagged Trout. There were four Terrys – one for each dam. They were trout of about a kilo brought in from a trout farm and had been branded with an identifying tag stapled to the tail.

Amid much fuss and press coverage, each year the Terrys were released into their new homes the day before the event. The release spots were kept secret so as not to give anyone an advantage.

The four Terrys were worth $50,000 each and even the village idiot could tell you that the organisers were in deep shit if they were all captured. For that matter, only one had to be taken to prove embarrassing. Plus there were prizes of $10,000 each for the biggest Murray cod and yellowbelly.

You didn't need a degree in mathematics to work out that the difference between the prize money on offer and the entry fees collected was minus $170,000 – and that was without running costs. There had to be some skullduggery afoot.

The organisers maintained that the prize money for a Terry was underwritten by a big insurance company. But it wasn't, because they knew that a tagged trout would never be caught.

In the five years of the Fish Fest no one had ever caught a Terry and the organisers had walked away with a bundle. To ensure that no one came up with the goods, the Terrys were all orally fed a slow-acting poison before release. While they looked healthy enough when photographed being thrown into the dam, they were as stiff as a board in a matter of hours.

What the organisers did not count on was one of their own being even more corrupt. He was known as 'the Moth' because he was attracted to the light. He would get legless at the fishing club or the local and stagger home. If he saw a light on, he would invite himself in for a drink and there was no getting rid of him. He was a dreadful pest drunk, but sober he wasn't a bad bloke at all.

Being an official assistant organiser and Terry-releaser, the Moth had been entrusted with the secrets of the villainy that went on. For his silence, he picked up a small share of the returns. But the Moth had got into big trouble on the punt and, with the heavies breathing down his neck for the money, he decided to out-cheat the cheats.

The only bloke he could trust with his life was an old mate of his from Sydney called Bill 'Dago' Oliver. They called him Dago because he never stopped whingeing about the fact that his missus spent her entire life in front of the TV watching the soapies. It had been going on for years and his constant grizzle was: 'There's not a day goes by without her watching that crap. There's not a day goes by when she does nothin' around the house. There's not a day goes by when I don't get a meal at home. Fair dinkum, there's not a day goes by ...' That was the Dago.

Rocket scientists they were not. But between them, the Moth and Dago devised a scheme that would scoop the pool ...

Admittedly the rules of the tournament were loose, but a couple were hard and fast. There was absolutely no berleying allowed before the event, and all fish had to be weighed by 6pm sharp. Apart from that, it was open slather.

'We'll wrap up the biggest cod and yellowbelly sections,' the Moth had told Dago on the phone. 'I know an old cod hole about 50 kilometres out of town. When you arrive a day before the comp, I'll have 'em boilin' on the surface. Oh! And don't forget to bring your snorkel and flippers. You'll need them to catch Terry.'

The Moth drove out to the cod hole, on a big corner in a bend in the river, and hung six sheep heads from the branch of an overhanging tree. He made sure to keep them hidden well within the leaves.

He returned a week later to find his self-berleying device working a treat. The sheep's heads were well and truly flyblown and the maggots were dropping into the water at a steady pace.

A week later every fish within 100 miles was waiting underneath with its head sticking out of the water and mouth open. The Moth knew that the smaller fish like the redfin and silver perch would attract the bigger cod and yellowbellies, which would eat them all, and then Dago could catch them the first day of the comp at his leisure.

Snookering Terry the Tagged Trout wasn't so simple. It wasn't until four days before the comp that the Moth and Dago devised a plan. And even then it was by a stroke of luck.

To add some authenticity to their shonky contest, the organisers announced that, due to being hounded by cheating anglers with binoculars, they would now secretly release the four Terrys without any press in attendance. The media spewed. 'How do we know that you will release any fish at all?' they barked.

Amid cries of deception and fraud, the organisers agreed to let the media photograph the four boats leaving with the Terrys on board and also arranged for a trusted observer to go out with each fish releaser.

The observers were selected from the town's most prominent and honest citizens – the police chief, the headmistress, the head of the chamber of commerce and the mayor. The Moth drew his old mate the mayor, alderman Clarrie 'Carbuncle' Carr. He couldn't believe his luck.

The mayor was as bald as Kojak and the locals called him Carbuncle because they reckoned he was shiny on the outside but inside he was full of shit. Carbuncle loved nothing more than a bottle of scotch and a friendly ear. The Moth had such an ear. It would be no trouble to get Carbuncle well and truly pissed and carry out his deception.

At the releasing of the Terrys on the eve of the comp, the cameras flashed as Carbuncle and the Moth held Terry up in his plastic bag for all to see.

'Take your time,' the organisers had told the Moth. 'Don't make it obvious where you're heading to let the trout go. And don't let Carbuncle see you give it the poison. Otherwise we'll be paying him blackmail forever.'

The Moth putt-putted a couple of kilometres around the lake before he pulled in at Knot's Pier for the couple of bottles of scotch he had hidden there the previous day. They sat and talked and the Moth primed Carbuncle with a bottle of Johnny Walker Black Label. It wasn't long before the mayor was dribbling and farting and talking about all the bribes he'd taken over the years.

The Moth then loaded on board a block of concrete with a wire handle, explaining to his drunken friend that it was a ballast in case a breeze came up. And off they went, straight to Mackenzie's Flats, the shallowest and sandiest part of the dam where no one had caught a fish in years. Here the Moth tied a hundred metres of sash cord to the concrete block and lowered it over the side.

When it hit the bottom a few metres down, he removed Terry from its bag, tied the other end of the sash cord through its gills, stuffed the poison capsule up its arse and threw it overboard for Dago to find in the morning.

Carbuncle was oblivious to all of this because he was out cold on the bottom of the boat. The Moth got stuck into the other bottle of scotch and, by the time Carbuncle woke from his drunken stupor, the Moth was skiting about the exact location of the maggot-berleyed cod hole, the tethered trout and how clever he and the Dago were.

The cunning old mayor, now sober, listened intently.

When the cops hauled the Moth in the following day and questioned him about the body they had found, the person having apparently drowned when he got tangled up in a length of sash cord at Mackenzie's Flats, the Moth denied any knowledge of it.

Apparently the victim, complete with flippers and snorkel, had been diving towards the bottom and had become entangled in the cord because whoever had tied the fish to the end of it had jammed something up its backside, causing it to blow up with air and float to the top.

'That explains why they told me ten times to shove the poison capsule down its gob,' the Moth thought to himself as he examined the trout the police had found attached to the sash cord.

'But that's funny,' he thought to himself, 'where's the tag?' The Moth was puzzled and upset. His partner in crime was dead and the tag was missing. What was going on? 'Did you seen anything that night?' the cops asked. After all, he and Carbuncle had headed out in that direction.

'No, sir,' the Moth replied, and Carbuncle backed him up.

The cops didn't connect the Moth with the drowned Dago Oliver and Carbuncle wasn't saying anything. By a strange coincidence, the brother of the guy who found Dago's body – who by an even stranger coincidence happened to be Carbuncle's nephew –

turned in a Terry that very afternoon and claimed the fifty grand.

Seeing as the tag was only just stuck to the tail and not stapled on like the originals, and the trout was only about a half a kilo instead of a kilo like the original Terrys, the organisers smelt a giant rat, but couldn't do a thing about it. They had to pay the winner out of the takings, which left them with not a cent left over to pay the huge debt of putting the competition together.

And, by an even more extraordinary coincidence, Carbuncle's son weighed in a huge cod and a yellowbelly that same day and picked up a cool twenty grand. No one could figure out why maggots kept dropping out of the fish's mouths at the weigh-in.

The organisers had to mortgage their houses to pay the bills and the cops had an unexplained corpse. Carbuncle came into a lot of money all of a sudden and the Moth left town. They say these days he's sighted from time to time around Bondi where the lights are on 24 hours a day.

7 AZARIA – HOW COULD THEY HAVE GOT IT SO WRONG?

From the moment that the frantically shouted words 'The dingo's got my baby' echoed through the still campsite near the giant monolith Uluru at around 8.30pm on the night of 17 August 1980, the lives of Seventh Day Adventists Lindy and Michael Chamberlain were changed forever. The disappearance of the couple's nine-week-old daughter Azaria (meaning 'blessed of God' or 'Whom God aids') would become a major talking point around the country – and indeed the world – for years to come, eventually becoming the subject of countless jokes and a major motion picture, *A Cry In The Dark* (or *Evil Angels*, as it was known in Australia). It would also see an innocent mother jailed, and break up a strong family unit, unable to withstand the obvious pressures of rumour, persecution and media scrutiny.

The Chamberlains – Michael, Lindy and their three children, Azaria, six-year-old Aidan and four-year-old Reagan – had left their home in the north Queensland town of Mt Isa on 13 August on a family holiday, to see the huge sandstone rock formation that draws so many tourists to Central Australia; a sacred site for the local indigenous Australians. Michael and Lindy had been married for a decade and Michael was a minister at his local church. The pair were understandably excited by the prospect of camping out with their children.

After a long, dusty drive the tired group arrived at their destination late at night on 16 August. They set up camp in the red sand and desert scrub just a few kilometres away from the massive rock, unloading their yellow Holden Torana hatchback with the help of their two boys and erecting their four-person tent. The next morning, after a breakfast of vegetable sausages cooked on the campsite's public barbecue, they started on their adventure in earnest, with Michael and the two young boys climbing portions of the famous rock while Lindy and her baby daughter visited a nearby formation named Fertility Cave. It was here that the soon-to-be-infamous woman first saw a wild dingo. The native dog was staring ominously at her and young Azaria. Lindy Chamberlain would later tell authorities that she sensed that the animal was 'casing the baby'.

Indeed, that very morning another camper in the area – a 12-year-old girl by the name of Catherine West who was on holidays with her parents – had been bitten on the elbow by one of the semi-tame creatures, of which there were about a dozen that regularly hung around that particular campsite in the hope of picking up an easy meal of leftovers. Catherine's mother Judy was forced to lunge at the dog twice before it let go of her daughter and wandered away.

As night fell and the temperature dropped, the Chamberlains gathered with other tourists at the campsite's barbecue area. Happy and relaxed after a day of exploration, Michael Chamberlain enjoyed a conversation with fellow holiday makers Greg Lowe, an amateur geologist, and his wife Sally. The two young couples struck up an instant rapport as the Lowes also happened to be travelling with an infant child – an 18-month-old daughter named Chantelle. Coincidently, Azaria's middle name was Chantel. While her husband talked about their day's exploration, Lindy held her baby lovingly in her arms.

Sometime around 8pm that evening Sally Lowe took the left-over scraps from the evening meal to a nearby rubbish bin. While she was doing so, she turned around to see a dingo stalking her just a few metres away. Not long after that, Michael Chamberlain saw a lone dingo near where the group of tourists were still talking. He threw a crust of bread to the native animal but was immediately admonished by his wife, who pointed out that he shouldn't be feeding the wild scavenger. Indeed, there were notices around the site instructing tourists not to do so. As she was saying this, the dog pounced upon a small mouse that their son Aiden had been watching and chasing with a beam of light from his torch.

After seeing the animal leap at the rodent and carry it off in its mouth, Lindy Chamberlain decided she should put young Azaria down for the night. She took the infant to their tent and lay her next to Reagan who had already fallen asleep, exhausted from the day's activities. Back at the barbecue area a short time later Lindy heard a baby's scream coming from the direction of their tent. Aiden heard it as well, and exclaimed, 'That was bubby crying.' Lindy raced back to the tent with her fear in her racing heart before bellowing out the words, 'My God, the dingo's got my baby!'

Greg Lowe immediately ran to investigate, with a startled Michael Chamberlain close behind him. Other campers also rushed to the tent, where they found Lindy pointing across the road yelling, 'Somebody stop that dingo!' As the gathering crowd peered into the dense blackness of the desert night Lindy cried out for a torch. Weak battery-powered rays tried to illuminate the area as Michael Chamberlain attempted to find his car keys in order to retrieve a stronger lamp. In his panicked state, though, he couldn't find them. Instead, he rushed off through the bushes in a vain attempt to locate his stolen daughter. Having no luck, he returned to the tent and his wife in shock.

Meanwhile, a Melbourne school teacher and experienced tracker by the name of Murray Haby was following a set of paw prints he had found wending their way up a sand hill in a diagonal direction. It was sheer coincidence that Murray Haby had arrived at the campsite earlier that day with his family. As he reached the crest of the sand hill he took note of an oval-shaped depression that looked to have been imprinted with a woven fabric of some sort. It would transpire that the indentation was caused by Azaria's clothing as the dingo lay the child down to rest. Haby continued on but the paw prints he was following were no longer visible once he reached the road. Having no luck locating the dingo or its human prey, Murray returned to the campsite, where Lindy Chamberlain was being comforted by Sally Lowe, Judy West and another camper named Amy Whittaker, who was a social worker from Melbourne. All three women would later be called upon to speak at Lindy's subsequent trial.

It wasn't long before the blue light of a police car flashing through the night heralded the arrival of the first official investigator to reach the scene, Constable Frank Morris, the more senior of the two police officers stationed at what was still known to many as Ayers Rock. Constable Morris shone his torch light at the Chamberlains' tent and noticed that there were some drops of blood on a rug in the child's bassinet near the still-sleeping Reagan. He also saw the paw prints going away from the tent's front flap and followed them until they disappeared at the edge of the road. He questioned Lindy Chamberlain about the recent events. The upset mother explained that she had seen a dingo trotting away from the tent. She also said that while she hadn't been able to actually see anything in the animal's mouth, its head was down and it looked to be shaking something from side to side.

While this was going on, Aidan was crying to Sally Lowe, pointing to the bassinet and saying, 'The dingo has our bubby in its tummy.'

Before long, between 200 and 300 people had formed a search party, the volunteer group of tourists and locals arranging themselves into a human chain and trekking through the darkness looking for little Azaria or a sign as to what may have happened. The search party was headed up by the chief ranger at Uluru, Derek Roff. Roff had been stationed at the rock for 12 years and had previously worked as a police officer in Kenya. Even when public opinion veered strongly against Lindy Chamberlain, he would always maintain that the mother was innocent.

While the search party combed the area, a visibly shaken Lindy was comforted by a nurse named Bobbie Downs. By now it was 9.30pm, almost an hour since Azaria had gone missing. Bobbie suggested that it may be for the best if Lindy and her young sons booked themselves into a nearby motel to get some rest, but Michael Chamberlain decided the family should stay at the campsite, in the slight chance that something would come of the search. Even then, however, Michael was becoming resigned to the tragic fate of his first daughter.

By this time, Murray Haby and Derek Roff had been joined by a local Aboriginal tracker named Nuwe Minyintiri, who made his own version of a torch by setting twisted strands of dried grass alight. Minyintiri observed the oval-shaped depression where the dingo had presumably set the baby down, and also noticed two more similar indents in the sand hill that Haby had overlooked. But once again the men were at a loss once they hit the roadway.

After the search party returned to the campsite with nothing to report other than the set of dingo prints, a seemingly defeated Michael Chamberlain thanked them all for their generous efforts, explained to the group that he was a pastor of the church and admitted that he had accepted that his baby daughter was dead, adding that he believed Azaria was already 'safe in the arms of Jesus'. At such an unfortunate time it seemed the deeply religious man could only find solace in his faith.

At shortly after midnight the Chamberlains heeded nurse Bobbie's advice, packing up most of their belongings, leaving their tent where it was and taking a room at the Uluru Motel. Lindy and the boys travelled to their new accommodation in a police truck along with all their gear, while Bobbie joined Michael in the Chamberlains' Torana, where she noticed the bereaved father was driving with a camera bag under his knees. She pointed out that there was room in the passenger side of the car in front of her, but Michael explained that it wasn't a problem, adding that he always kept the bag in that spot with him.

The bag would become important in the prosecution's case, with many believing it contained the body of the Chamberlains' dead child.

In the days that followed, the story of baby Azaria's disappearance swept through Australia via newspapers, TV, radio and word of mouth, and it wasn't long before doubts began to surface regarding the family's innocence.

It was a week after the incident when a Melbourne tourist named Wallace Goodwin, holidaying at Uluru with his family, headed along a trail through thick scrub with the motive of photographing wild flowers. Walking through the narrow track, around five kilometres west of the campsite from where Azaria was taken, Goodwin soon came across a shredded towelling baby's jumpsuit, singlet and torn nappy sitting near a boulder amongst the dense scrub. The press studs of the jumpsuit were open and there was blood drenched around the neckline. Constable Morris was informed of the find and, after arriving at the scene, he picked up the jumpsuit, much to the shock of Goodwin, who believed Morris should have let the evidence lay where it was so that professionals could examine the findings. The amateur nature photographer is said to have wished he had taken a shot of the jumpsuit and other clothing as it was when he had first found it.

Meanwhile, the Chamberlains' life was rapidly descending into a tabloid hell, with the incessant calls from journalists constantly breaking any peace they were able to achieve in their home near the Mt Isa Seventh Day Adventist Church where Michael presided. They also began to receive mail from the public. Some of the letters commiserated with the family. Others, however, could be scathing in their condemnation.

The deluge of press seemed to fuel speculation that the Chamberlains were somehow behind Azaria's disappearance, possibly as a result of some bizarre religious sacrifice connected with the parents' religion. At the time the Seventh Day Adventist church was viewed with suspicion by the general public and there was a widespread lack of understanding about their beliefs. As the wild theories escalated, there was even talk that the Chamberlains were linked to the mass suicide in Jonestown two years earlier. It didn't help the couple's case that they looked and sounded resigned to their loss in interviews and photos splashed across the nation's front pages, their faces seemingly devoid of emotion or the hysteria many members of the public believed they should be expressing following the tragic loss of their offspring.

As this was going on, four policemen assigned to the increasingly convoluted case met up at the Northern Territory's Red Sands Motel to discuss the situation over a few drinks. While Frank Morris kept his opinions to himself and Michael Gilroy said he fully accepted the Chamberlains' story, John Lincoln openly opposed the dingo theory. After Inspector Gilroy pointed out that there had already been a string of attacks by native dogs on children in the same park where Azaria was taken previous to the disappearance, Lincoln voiced his opinion that a dingo could not have possibly carried a 10-pound child over a large distance for an extended length of time. To back up his belief, he left the room and returned a short time later with a bucket holding around the same weight in sand. He tried to hold it by the handle in his mouth. He didn't even last a minute.

Less than a fortnight after the incident, on 28 August, Detective-Sergeant Graeme Charlwood of the Northern Territory Police took charge of the investigation. While his crew checked out the registrations of all vehicles in the campsite on the tragic night, hoping to find something suspicious that may lead them towards a human felon rather than what seemed to be an increasingly unlikely canine culprit, Charlwood went over Gilroy's initial report, picking through the information with a fine-tooth comb. He found several facts that seemed strange. One of these was that when Lindy Chamberlain had earlier taken baby Azaria to a routine check-up at the doctor's following the birth, the child had been dressed all in black, rather than the traditional pink often associated with newborn girls. The story goes that the examining physician found the sombre attire so out of the ordinary that he looked up Azaria's name and reportedly – and wrongly – found it to mean 'sacrifice in the wilderness'. Various similar tidbits of misinformation and speculation would become talking points in public discussions into Lindy's guilt or innocence for years to come.

Gilroy's report also indicated that the Chamberlain family had been in the area where Azaria's clothes were found earlier in the day she went missing. Could they have planted them at the time? The notes said that when Lindy had been seen with Azaria while Michael talked to the Lowes around the barbecue, people may have actually 'assumed she was holding a baby when they have seen her holding a white bundle to her breast'. It wasn't long before the official forensics examinations began. These tests would later become the backbone of the prosecution's case against Lindy Chamberlain. Dingoes shot in the Uluru region were cut open, with vets looking for traces of human remains. None were found. Tears in Azaria's clothing were examined to see if they had been made by animal teeth or an instrument such as scissors or a knife. An expert in hair fibres, Dr Harry Harding from the Institution of Medical and Veterinary Science in Adelaide, was flown up to the Northern Territory. He was given evidence from the local forensics unit – eight strands of hair collected with a vacuum in the Chamberlains' tent. The expert concluded that the strands did not belong to a dingo.

Bloodstains on Azaria's jumpsuit were examined by Dr Andrew Scott. He noted that blood was thick around the neck of the clothing, but could not confirm the presence of animal saliva – though he admitted that the science of the time meant that would be difficult anyway.

Scott then teamed up with an expert in dental analysis, Dr Kenneth Brown. The pair went to Adelaide Zoo. Wrapping the carcass of a small goat in clothing similar to that which Azaria had been said to be wearing when she went missing, they left the meat in the dingo enclosure overnight. When they returned the next day they found that the animal had buried portions of the clothing as well as bits of the dead carcass. Seeming to further damage the Chamberlains' case, the dog had taken the meat out of the jumpsuit having only opened the top two press studs, unlike the clothing found in the desert, where all the studs had been opened.

Detective-Sergeant Charlwood interviewed the Chamberlains

separately for several hours each on 1 October 1980 at Mt Isa. His aim was to build a precise timeline from the family setting out on their holiday adventure, leading up to Azaria's disappearance and for the days following the tragedy. While both went along with the interviews as best they could under the circumstances, Lindy seemed frustrated that seemingly damning forensic evidence had been leaked to the press and public, evidence that suggested her account of the details may be false.

Charlwood suggested the mother be hypnotised in an effort to uncover details of the night that may be locked inside her head or forgotten in the ongoing stress. At this point, even the smallest recollection may have helped sway the case in either direction, but Lindy was forthright in her refusal to undergo hypnotism, explaining straight away that: 'The church wouldn't allow it and I wouldn't do it. God slew Saul for that.'

They seemed to have reached an impasse. It was now down to the legal process to decide what happened on that fateful night. Few would be prepared for the controversy that would follow.

The inquest opened at Alice Springs Court on 16 December 1980, around four months after Lindy's cries pierced the desert night. The nation's reporters flocked to hear the local magistrate and coroner, Denis Barritt, begin what would become the first of three separate inquests into the death of Azaria Chamberlain.

Proceedings opened with Ashley Macknay speaking for the prosecution, pointing out that the evidence suggested human intervention in Azaria's death. Macknay argued that the clothing found by Wallace Goodwin had been placed there by human hands, not dragged to the spot by a dingo. He added that they had been removed by a person, not an animal, and that the damage to the separate articles was not consistent with the work of a native dog. The prosecutor questioned Lindy Chamberlain, but was not able to project her as a mother with either the motive or will to murder her own daughter.

Still, Lindy did herself no favours in the public's eyes with her blank demeanour and seeming lack of emotion. Much was made of the fact she wore many different outfits throughout the case. She later explained that her clothing was second-hand. In interviews she came across as objective and pragmatic about the situation. In the witness box she would often answer rhetorically.

Coroner Barritt made note of the fact that Azaria's name had nothing whatsoever to do with sacrifice, and listened as a string of experts presented their evidence. The public looked for signs of grief, but found little.

An obstetrician from the hospital where Azaria was born was brought in to clear up rumours that had begun to be regarded as fact. Dr Irene Milne testified that Lindy Chamberlain had not suffered from postnatal depression. Neither, said Dr Milne, had Azaria suffered brain damage in a fall, another supposed reason why the Chamberlains would kill their only daughter.

One expert on dingo behaviour, Dr Alan Newsome, pointed out that it was quite unlikely that a baby would be stolen by a dingo. But when asked about an animal's growl heard by the West family shortly before Lindy Chamberlain found her daughter to be missing, Dr Newsome admitted that the sound could have been a warning by one dingo to another to stay away.

Public interest in the case was so high that television cameras projected Coroner Barritt's final decision live around the country. Believing that the Chamberlains were innocent, the scientific evidence presented by the prosecution failed to sway him. He was also sympathetic to the family, stating that: 'You have not only suffered the loss of your beloved child in the most tragic circumstances but you have been subjected to months of innuendo, suspicion and probably the most malicious gossip ever witnessed in this country.'

In handing down his findings, Coroner Barritt announced that baby Azaria had 'met her death when attacked by a wild dingo whilst asleep in her family's tent'. Speaking about the Chamberlains, he said neither Michael or Lindy were 'in any degree whatsoever responsible for [Azaria's] death'.

Nonetheless, the coroner did contend that there were irregularities regarding the state of the clothing found, and said that he believed 'the body of Azaria was taken from the possession of the dingo and disposed of by an unknown method, by a person or persons name unknown'.

Feeling vindicated, but still persecuted, the Chamberlains moved from their home in Mt Isa to a Seventh Day Adventist campus at Cooranbong near Newcastle in New South Wales, to protect their children from public scorn and harassment. Little did they realise that the case was far from over. In fact, the Northern Territory Police had stepped up their efforts to pin the blame on Lindy Chamberlain.

Seven months after the inquest finished, on 19 September 1981, Detective-Sergeant Graeme Charlwood and a crew of local police officers visited the Chamberlains and conducted a search of their home. In that time they seized more than 250 items of interest, including scissors and clothing, as well as the yellow Torana Hatchback the family had driven on their fateful holiday.

Detective Charlwood then explained that part of the reason for the search was due to the findings of a British forensics pathologist who had examined Azaria's jumpsuit. When told that Professor James Cameron had looked into the matter and decided the evidence suggested that no dingo could have been involved in the disappearance, Lindy Chamberlain is said to have iced up, responding that: 'I didn't know there were any dingo experts in London.'

But what the Chamberlains couldn't know was that their world was about to fall down around them. After their car was airlifted back to Alice Springs and dismantled, a spray of what appeared to be dried blood was found on a panel under the passenger seat. As a result, in November 1981, the attorney-general for the Northern Territory, Chief Minister Everingham, filed a motion to ignore the findings of the first inquest due to the new evidence. The media circus was about to begin again.

A second inquest into Azaria Chamberlain's death began on 14 December 1981 in Darwin, with Northern Territory Chief Magistrate Gerry P. Galvin acting as coroner. He was assisted by Brisbane lawyer Des Sturgess, who made it obvious early in proceedings that the prosecution believed Lindy Chamberlain had cut her only daughter's throat in or near the front seat of the yellow Torana with a sharp instrument (probably scissors). It was suggested that the mother then told Michael Chamberlain to hide the deceased body in his camera bag, and that the parents later placed the child's clothing on the track where it was found by Wallace Goodwin.

Much of Sturgess' questioning related to the dried blood found in the family vehicle. 'Did you notice any blood staining inside or outside the car when you cleaned it?' the assistant coroner asked the Chamberlains. 'Do you recall cleaning blood off the seats?'

Biologist Joy Kuhl from the crime laboratory in New South Wales testified that the blood found in the car and on the zipper and compartments of the camera bag was that of a young baby as it contained high amounts of foetal haemoglobin.

Michael Chamberlain told Sturgess that his young sons often suffered from nose bleeds. He said that both he and Lindy were experienced at first aid and had more than once stopped at accidents to lend a hand. He also added that they had picked up a bleeding hitchhiker in North Queensland in June 1979. The man had been in an accident and the Chamberlains took him for treatment at Cairns Base Hospital.

Professor James Cameron was flown out from London to testify. Using photos and slides to explain his findings, he argued that it was unlikely the tear on Azaria's jumpsuit had been caused by dingo teeth, adding, 'It's more consistent with scissors.' All up, 60 witnesses were called to the second inquest. Australian taxpayers supplied the $1.5 million to fund the deluge of evidence and testimony. In the end, Chief Magistrate Galvin charged Lindy Chamberlain with murder. Michael Chamberlain was then charged with being an accessory after the fact.

By time the trial against Michael and Lindy Chamberlain commenced in Darwin on 13 September 1983, Lindy was seven months pregnant. Supreme Court Judge Henry Muirhead headed the case, with Ian Barker QC acting for the Crown. John Phillips QC lead the case for the defence along with his co-counsel Andrew Kirkham. The jury – selected from some 123 Northern Territory residents – was comprised of nine men and three women.

Opening proceedings, Ian Barker contended that the dingo story was 'a fanciful lie, designed to conceal the truth that the child Azaria died by her mother's hand'. He added that Michael Chamberlain became aware of the murder not long after it had occurred and became an accessory to the crime. Barker told the jury that the defence would argue that Azaria 'died very quickly because somebody had cut her throat'. He also said, 'The Crown does not venture to suggest any reason or motive for the killing. It is not part of our case that Mrs Chamberlain had previously shown any ill will toward the child.'

As he continued his address he spoke of the blood found in the car and said the Crown's theory was that Lindy had murdered Azaria in the front seat by cutting the child's throat.

The first witness to be called by Barker was Sally Lowe, but her testimony was also helpful to the defence. Speaking about the night the two families were gathered by the campsite's barbecue, Sally Lowe insisted that Lindy Chamberlain was only away from the group for a period of six to 10 minutes, giving her hardly any time to murder her child and conceal the body. Sally also confirmed the defence's case by stating that she had heard Azaria scream out before Lindy ran off, saying, 'I heard the baby cry; quite a serious cry.'

When cross-examined by the defence, Sally Lowe added that she was positive she had heard Azaria cry out, and that the cry 'definitely came from the tent'. Finally putting the postnatal depression rumours to bed, Sally described Lindy as having 'a new-mum glow about her' before her baby went missing.

Indeed, most of the prosecution's witnesses seemed to be of more use to the defence. When Greg Lowe was asked on cross-examination if he had seen the Chamberlains cleaning their car at the time they would have had to remove blood stains, he said he hadn't, adding, 'There were quite a lot of people around at that time at the tent site, and I'm sure if anything like that happened it would have been noticed.'

Another of the holiday makers at Uluru in August 1980, Judy West, told of her 12-year-old daughter being bitten on the arm by a dingo, and repeated her claim that she had heard a native dog growling between five and 10 minutes before Lindy screamed that a dingo had stolen her baby.

The prosecution's case was helped out, however, by Amy Whittaker, the social worker who helped comfort Lindy on the night. In testimony that seemed to confirm the public image of the Chamberlains as cold and calculating, the Melbourne woman said that Michael Chamberlain had turned up at their camper door just minutes after the incident, proclaiming, 'A dingo has taken our baby, and she is probably dead by now.' Amy Whittaker then spoke of a conversation she had with Lindy while comforting her, in which the grief-stricken mother reportedly said, 'Whatever happens, it is God's will.'

Amy went on to back up the prosecution's case by claiming she saw the Chamberlains heading into the bush alone together for between 15 and 20 minutes – enough time, the prosecution argued, for them to bury their baby's body.

Keyth Lenehan – the hitchhiker picked up in Northern Queensland whose blood Michael Chamberlain contended was found in his car – was next to take the stand. But while Ian Barker was hoping to show that the blood couldn't have been Lenehan's because the man didn't have high levels of foetal haemoglobin, all he managed to do was lend credence to what had at first seemed a fairly spurious claim. Lenehan testified that he was bleeding from a head wound after overturning his car when the Chamberlains picked him up. He added that, on the drive to the hospital, he had been laying down with his head facing towards the passenger's seat.

Still, opinion seemed to sway towards the prosecution when the forensics experts started to take the stand. Adelaide biologist Dr Andrew Scott explained that he had examined Azaria's singlet and that the blood on it flowed down from the neck region, from what appeared to be a cut mark made by a sharp instrument.

Australia's leading textiles expert at the time, Professor Malcolm Chaikin, then showed the jury how cutting a jumpsuit resulted in small loops of towelling. Such loops had been found in Michael Chamberlain's camera bag. However, the defence countered this in cross-examination by getting the expert to admit similar loops may have come from a brand-new jumpsuit, and the Chamberlains had already said they had previously used the camera bag to hold Azaria's clothing.

The prosecution's 35th witness was forensic biologist Joy Kuhl. In a strong argument for the prosecution, she again explained that her tests had shown the blood in the car had come from a baby. She went on to use slides to show how bloodstains were identified in relation to other stains, but when asked in cross-examination to produce the actual plates she had used in her tests, she had to admit they had been destroyed as 'standard procedure in our laboratory'. The defence then pounced on her, questioning the accuracy of the tests.

Continuing with the prosecution's case, London odontologist Bernard Sims took the stand to testify that the tears in Azaria's clothing were inconsistent with that of a dingo attack. Having investigated around two dozen dog attacks, he claimed that an animal would have caused 'copious' bleeding, and then added that a baby's head would not even fit into a dingo's jaw. Sims' testimony was weakened by the defence, however, who produced a photograph of a native dog holding the head of an infant-sized doll in its mouth, with its teeth up around the doll's ears. Sims was forced to admit he may have been wrong in his claims.

The final witness for the prosecution was British professor of forensic medicine James Cameron, who again contended that the bloodstains around the collar of Azaria's jumpsuit were consistent with 'a cutting instrument across the neck, or around the neck' held by a human. His belief was that if an animal had taken the child by the head, blood would have run down the suit in rivulets, which it hadn't. After Cameron went on to show slide evidence that supposedly showed bloodstained fingerprints on Azaria's clothing, the defence went on to point out that Cameron had previously acted on behalf of prosecution cases that eventually incriminated innocent suspects.

The defence then opened their case on 13 October, with John Phillips calling Lindy Chamberlain to the stand. The mother was in tears while describing what her daughter had been wearing on the night she disappeared. While cross-examining Lindy Chamberlain, Ian Barker hoped to weaken the accused's account of the events of the night, asking why, if she had indeed seen the dog shaking her baby, there was no blood in and around the family's tent. He also again called for the defendant to explain the foetal blood found in the car. Lindy, however, refused to even speculate.

Even after Barker suggested the Chamberlains' story was 'mere fantasy', there were still around two dozen defence witnesses to take the stand. Some of them were brought forward to speak about the family's strength of character and grief following their tragic loss. Others spoke of similar encounters with the wild dogs of the Uluru region. Eight other forensics experts were brought in to question the findings of the prosecution's scientific team. One if these experts was Professor Barry Boettcher, who refuted biologist Joy Kuhl's testimony about the blood in their car having high levels of foetal haemoglobin, believing that she may have used a flawed method to come to her conclusions.

Dingo expert Lee Harris then put a strong case forward for the defence, explaining that attacks in the wild produced very little blood, adding that the animals generally shake their heads to break the neck of their prey. As for prosecution claims that a dingo couldn't fit a baby's head in its mouth, Harris explained that a dingo intent on taking down something the size of an infant would 'make seizure, which would be of the entire head, and it would close its jaws sufficiently to render the mammal immobile'. The animal would also leave the scene with its catch immediately, the defence expert explained.

Michael Chamberlain was the among last witnesses called by the defence, and Ian Barker went hard against the father in cross-examination, calling into question his actions immediately following his daughter's disappearance. The Crown prosecutor implied that Michael failed to ask his wife pertinent questions because he already knew she had murdered their child. Michael said this was not the truth, but Barker pushed him, describing the defence's case as 'nonsense'. Chamberlain wouldn't budge. After several hours in the stand he sat back down next to his wife and the couple held hands.

In his closing arguments, John Phillips QC again pointed out that the prosecution had still failed to provide a motive for Lindy Chamberlain to murder her baby daughter. 'The prosecution has had two years and three months to think of a reason,' he said, adding that, 'they can't.' Ian Barker himself agreed that the prosecution had not supplied a reason behind what they believed to be murder, but declared that they hadn't had to. 'All the Crown says is that you should find the murder happened,' he told the jury before cunningly asking them if there was enough evidence to convict a dingo, pointing out the mostly undamaged jumpsuit and fact that no one actually saw the dog carrying off the baby. 'The case against the dingo would be laughed out of court,' Barker said in closing.

By the evidence presented, most reporters and experts seemed to believe an acquittal was on the cards, but that was not to be the case. At shortly after 8.30pm on 29 October 1984 the foreman of the jury announced that Lindy Chamberlain had been found guilty of murder, while her husband Michael was found guilty of being an accessory after the fact. Michael was shaken by the result. Lindy, meanwhile, remained steely in her gaze, though the colour is said to have ran from her face when Justice Muirhead decreed that she would be 'imprisoned with hard labour for life'. He added, 'I consider it not only appropriate, but in the interests of justice to do so.'

Lindy Chamberlain was then taken past the flashing glare of the media's cameras and driven to Darwin's Berrimah Prison, where she gave birth to her second daughter just 10 days later. She named the little girl Kahlia.

The day after Lindy was sentenced to life, Michael Chamberlain was back in court to hear the results of being declared guilty as an accessory after the fact, with John Phillips appealing for clemency on emotional grounds and pointing out that he had the duties of a father to attend to while his wife languished in jail. As a result, Michael was sentenced to 10 months in prison, but that was suspended and the pastor only had to provide a $500 bond and remain on good behaviour for three years.

Lindy was soon granted limited freedom when she was released on bail pending an appeal into her case. But the appeal was rejected. Then, 10 months later, yet another appeal was rejected by the High Court of Australia on a three to two count. Lindy remained in Block J of Berrimah while others championed her case from the outside. The 'Free Lindy' movement headed by the Chamberlain Innocence Committee managed to collect 100,000 signatures on a petition, despite the fact that the country still seemed divided down the middle in their opinion of the mother's guilt or innocence. One poll showed 54 per cent of the public in favour of Lindy remaining behind bars.

On top of this, though, new reports came to light showing that the blood found in the Chamberlains' car may have actually been paint emulsion rather than foetal blood.

November 1985 saw the Northern Territory solicitor-general reject an application into the inquiry, but just three months later Lindy Chamberlain walked free from Berrimah Prison following a bizarre tragedy.

Some five and a half years after baby Azaria went missing in the night, English tourist David Brett fell to his death during an evening climb of Uluru. On 2 February 1986, Brett's body was found by a search party with a broken back and neck. Animals had started to devour the remains. As authorities looked around the area for identification, they stumbled across Azaria's once-white matinee jacket, a jacket described in great detail by Lindy Chamberlain in her original interviews. The prosecutors who had been so sceptical of the jacket's existence during court proceedings had no leg to stand on. Five days after the discovery Lindy walked free from the prison that had housed her for more than three years. In a pink frock and sunglasses, she strode determinedly towards the limousine and drove off into yet another flurry of media attention – this time calling for an inquiry into her wrongful conviction.

Opening in front of Justice Trevor Morling in May 1986, the inquiry asked former prosecution witnesses to answer for their original findings. Justice Morling eventually issued a 379-page report into the matter, which was critical of experts such as Joy Kuhl and James Cameron.

Victorian forensics expert Tony Raymond spoke at the inquiry, explaining that the 'foetal blood' found in the Chamberlains' car that was believed to have come from Azaria's severed throat was actually a sound deadener commonly used in similar automobiles. A Victorian farmer told of how a dingo had attacked his three-year-old daughter at Uluru just six weeks before the Azaria Chamberlain incident.

Other experts again contradicted each other in relation to dingo behaviour, with one specialist remaining firm in their belief that a native dog could not possibly carry off an infant child, while another said they had seen a dingo cart around the body of a large baby kangaroo.

In the end, Justice Morling spoke strongly of the Chamberlains' fellow campers, saying, 'It is extraordinary that the persons at the barbecue area at the time of and immediately after Azaria's disappearance accepted Mrs Chamberlain's story and noted nothing about her appearance and conduct suggesting that she had suddenly killed her daughter ... I am far from being persuaded that Mrs Chamberlain's account of having seen a dingo near the tent was false.' He finished by saying, 'If the evidence before the Commission had been given at the trial, the trial judge would have been obliged to direct the jury to acquit the Chamberlains.' All up, the inquiry lasted nine months and saw 142 witnesses called upon at a cost to Australian taxpayers of $6 million. At one point during proceedings, Lindy Chamberlain let fly at her prosecutor Ian Barker QC, calling out against 'stupid courtroom lawyers'. Justice Morling was forced to threaten clearing the room after the gallery exploded in applause at her outburst.

When all was said and done, all convictions against Michael and Lindy Chamberlain were quashed. Lindy went on to write the book *Through My Eyes*, released in 1990 and telling her own side of the story. She would later receive $1.3 million from the Northern Territory Government as compensation for her wrongful imprisonment. Sadly, the Chamberlains' marriage could not withstand the ongoing pressure and they later divorced and are today married to different people while attempting to stay out of the limelight.

8 THE FAMILY LAW COURT MURDERS

Decreeing that a mother or father must lose visitation rights to their children, or in the least have them restricted, is something that no judge wants to hand down unless it is in the absolute best interests of the children. Where the kiddies are the pawns in a broken relationship, it is often up to a Family Law Court judge to do what he or she feels best for the sake of the youngsters. And it takes a special type of judge to do this. Overwhelming emotions are involved and it is gut-wrenching in the extreme for all concerned, including the adjudicator.

But there was a time in Sydney when Family Law Court judges were putting far more than their emotions on the line. It was a time when being a Family Law Court judge was a life-threatening occupation. It began on the winter evening of 23 June 1980. Forty-three-year-old Justice David Opas presided over the Family Law Court at Parramatta in Sydney's western suburbs.

He finished as usual at 5.30pm and was driven home in a Commonwealth car. He arrived an hour later in time for dinner as usual with his wife and two children. As the bespectacled, slightly built Justice Opas sat down to his dinner, the front security gate bell rang and he went to answer it. In doing so, he walked out through the front door of the house into the front courtyard and closed the door behind him to stop the two family dogs from going out with him. He walked another 12 paces and opened the thick wooden security gate and must have looked straight into the face of his killer.

Investigators believe that it was his same daily routine that allowed the killer to choose the right moment to strike. They believe that Justice Opas had a brief conversation with the person, but it will never be known whether he knew who it was. After a few moments Judge Opas collapsed backwards to the ground with blood pumping from a wound beneath his chest caused by a single .22 bullet fired at close range. Not having heard the shot, and with his dinner going cold on the table, after a few minutes Kristina Opas went outside to see what was keeping her husband, to find him lying flat on his back with blood flowing profusely from the bullet wound. Mrs Opus, a trained nurse, began emergency treatment and alerted a neighbour who rang an ambulance and police. Judge Opas died without regaining consciousness.

Immediately a combined team of federal and New South Wales' most experienced homicide investigators began a search for a lead on what was apparently a Family Law Court–related murder. At first they were optimistic of a quick arrest. Surely there would be someone who Judge Opas had visibly upset in the course of his decision making in the Family Law Court, who had made a threat somewhere down the line that they could follow up on. Perhaps there would be a disgruntled relative who had openly disapproved of one of Judge Opas' decisions and had threatened to do something about it? But, as the investigators dug into the mountain of cases of the families affected by the decisions made by Judge Opas and investigated each scenario on its merits, all they drew were blanks on all counts.

A ray of hope came when several witnesses came forward and said they saw two men in the vicinity of the judge's home around about the time of the murder, but even when the witnesses underwent hypnosis to jog their memories, police still couldn't come up with anyone who remotely resembled a suspect. But by now, anyway, they were convinced that it wasn't a professional hit. A hired assassin would have used a much more powerful weapon and fired a lot more than one shot to make sure the victim wouldn't live to identify his killer.

Countless thousands of federal and state police hours were spent attempting to track down the killer, but to no avail. A $100,000 reward, later increased to $250,000, failed to get a solid lead. The murder of Judge Opas remained unsolved. The inquest into his death caused a sensation when a man refused to give evidence on the grounds that he may be incriminated, but he was deemed not to be a suspect.

In 1984, four years after the murder of Judge Opus, the Parramatta Family Law Court and its employees encountered a wave of terror the likes of which have never been seen before or since. On 6 March, Judge Richard Walter Gee and his family were asleep in their northern Sydney home when a bomb exploded at the front door of the house. Judge Gee's family escaped with minor cuts and bruises, but it brought home in the worst possible way the fact that anyone who had anything to do with the Family Law Court was not safe.

Four months later the bomber struck again, only this time with much more devastating results. The wife of Judge Ray Watson of the Family Law Court was killed when a bomb exploded in their Sydney flat. Mrs Pearl Watson died almost instantly when she opened the front door of their apartment, after kissing her husband goodbye for the day, and triggered off a bomb left in a suitcase on the front doormat. Judge Watson was seriously injured but survived the explosion.

Also in 1984, the Family Law Court building in Parramatta was bombed, but no one was seriously injured. Then, amid the most extraordinary safety procedures ever seen in Sydney to protect the lives of the employees of the Family Law Court at Parramatta, the bombings stopped. While the investigation was the most comprehensive and thorough ever carried out in the history of New South Wales, no one was ever arrested and charged in connection with the crimes.

The murders of Judge Opas and Mrs Pearl Watson and the bombings of Judge Richard Gee's home and the Parramatta Law Courts have never been solved. If there has ever been a positive police suspect, it has never been disclosed to public. The cases remain open.

9 THE POSTCARD BANDIT

Brendan Abbott was a charismatic bank robber who escaped from two of the toughest jails in Australia. While on the run for years at a time he left a trail of crime that kept him in the news almost on a daily basis. It could be said that his catchy, but grossly exaggerated, nickname of the 'Postcard Bandit' may have had a lot to do with it.

Brendan James Abbott was born in Melbourne in 1962 and, as is typical of so many career criminals, he came from a broken home. His unhappy childhood resulted in rebellion and, in turn, poor schooling, boys' homes, juvenile detention and jail for minor crimes before he graduated to bank robbery. But Brendan Abbott was different from the other up-and-coming crims on the block. He had an IQ in the 140s and a real talent for crime that blossomed as the years passed.

Abbott pulled off his first bank job in Perth on 29 May 1987, when he and two accomplices escaped with more than $100,000. By then a habitual criminal with a long record for lesser offences, Abbott was quickly rounded up and sentenced to 14 years in jail. He copped another four years for his leading role in the Fremantle Prison riot of 1988. In 1989 Abbott and another prisoner, Aaron Reynolds, escaped from Fremantle Prison when they broke through a barred window and, dressed in tradesmen's overalls they had stitched together themselves, brazenly walked across the prison roof, jumped a few metres to freedom and calmly walked away.

A week later Reynolds and Abbott held up a TAB at gunpoint and fired shots at police as they made their getaway. When their stolen getaway car was located police found a roll of film which, when developed, showed the two bandits posing with shotgun shells and counting money outside a Western Australian police station. When Reynolds was arrested on his own in 1989, police found more pictures of him and Abbott at holiday spots all over the country, including one of them posing with a Japanese tourist at Uluru.

Thanks to a few grossly inaccurate stories about the origin and intention of the pictures, it became an urban myth that Abbott was sending photos of himself having a good time to the police and he was dubbed by the press the 'Postcard Bandit'. As is the Australian way – which is that you never ruin a good story by putting too much truth in it – the name stuck and now one of Australia's most dangerous men was a folk hero on the loose.

While on the run Abbott developed a unique style of robbing banks that would be the catalyst for many bank robbers in the years to come. During the night he made his way into the ceiling of the target bank – obviously one that was suited to his requirements – and lay in wait until the staff arrived in the morning. Then he would simply 'drop in', so to speak, and force the staff at gunpoint to open the vault and give him the cash. He was long gone by the time police arrived. While on the run Abbott robbed at least 38 banks all over Australia for an estimated tally of $4 million.

But his run came to an end when in March 1995, after six years of freedom, he was recaptured on the Gold Coast. And for bloke as smart as Abbott, it was a pretty dumb pinch. In a raid on Abbott's brother's home, police had found the number for a Gold Coast post office box and there they found a bill for a pager. From the numbers in its memory they located Abbott's girlfriend's home unit and arrested him there without a struggle.

Convicted of robbing three Queensland banks to the tune of $1.2 million, Abbott was sent to prison for 12 years. During his trial the court was told that Abbott was a self-taught expert on electronics and that, years earlier while in prison, he had done a course in acting where he specialised in learning about theatrical make-up and disguises. It was these disguises that had helped him repeatedly elude police in numerous close scrapes with the law during his years on the run. The court was told that Abbott was a strong possibility to escape again, given the opportunity.

For these reasons Abbott was manacled every time he appeared in court and kept in solitary confinement for the first year of his sentence, before being moved to the high-security Sir David Longland Correctional Centre. But rather than become bitter, Abbott remained in high spirits and, in time, his charming personality saw to it that he was given a trustees job as an education clerk, where he had access to a telephone. He didn't waste time in contacting some of his old friends on the outside to give him a lift on the off chance that he just happened to jump the wall.

In November 1997, Abbott, three murderers and a rapist sawed through prison bars using a fine diamond-encrusted wire known as angel wire, and made their bolt for freedom under the cover of outside snipers. Within days all of them except Abbott, who had left the main group immediately they were free, had been picked up. Abbott had a young friend, Brendan Luke Berichon, waiting for him. They had spent prison time together and Berichon hero-worshipped Abbott and would do anything for him. Abbott and Berichon moved into a house together in Carlton in early 1998 and police suspect they were the two bandits who held up an Armaguard truck in Dandenong and escaped with $250,000 around the same time.

On 20 April, Berichon and a young friend were questioned by two police officers at Box Hill as they were trying to score some heroin. Berichon produced a 9mm automatic pistol and shot one of the officers in the hip and the other in the arm, before forcing a woman to drive him at gunpoint to Carlton where he and Abbott gathered their belongings and fled five minutes before the police arrived. They were now the subject of a national manhunt. Police don't like those who shoot their own.

Abbott should have used his brains and given Berichon a wide berth, but instead he teamed up with him again when they reached Darwin separately. In May 1998 staff in a Darwin hotel alerted police after they recognised Berichon from police circulars. Armed tactical response officers sat at the pub waiting for their chance to grab him without anyone getting hurt. They couldn't believe their luck when they saw Brendan Abbott come out of the same hotel.

Abbott was nabbed quietly on his way to a local supermarket to get a pizza for dinner. Berichon also gave up without a struggle. The Postcard Bandit now sends heavily censored postcards to his friends from a Queensland prison where he will be spending the next 23 years under 24-hour electronic supervision. When he gets out Abbott could serve more time for other armed robberies around Australia. Brendan Berichon was extradited to Melbourne and sentenced to 13 years for the attempted murder of the two police officers.

10 THE DEADLY LOVE QUADRANGLE

Since the beginning of murder as we know it, the love triangle has been responsible for many murders. It's usually two men in love with the one woman, but not always – sometimes two women have fought for one man. To a lesser degree, women have been known to murder their lover so another woman couldn't have him, and men have killed their woman and faced the consequences rather than have their beloved fall into the arms of another man.

But rarely have there been love quadrangles, where three men were in love with – and competed for the favours of – the one woman. It is a circumstance that could only end hideously. Such was the case of what became known as the 'Mad Dentist of Wynyard Square'.

In 1860 the young Henry Louis Bertrand arrived in Melbourne from England and worked as a dental assistant before marrying Jane Palmer. Their young family moved to busy Sydney in early 1865, where Henry set up a thriving dental practice in busy Wynyard Square. Around the same time another young family, Henry and Ellen Kinder and their children, moved to Sydney from New Zealand and Henry Kinder took up work as a bank teller at the Wynyard branch of City Bank.

The Bertrands and the Kinders met and became friends, and it wasn't long before Henry Bertrand and Ellen Kinder were having a torrid affair right under their respective spouses' noses. While Henry Bertrand was a newcomer to infidelity, Ellen Kinder was an old hand at the game, having had numerous affairs with men in New Zealand. The most recent affair had been with a man named Frank Jackson, whom Ellen had been seeing up to the time she and her husband had left New Zealand for Sydney.

So when Frank Jackson moved to Sydney a few months later and took up with Ellen Kinder exactly where he had left off, and she made no bones about it to her new lover, Henry Bertrand, there seemed little else to do but make her choose between the two. Would it be Bertrand or Jackson, never mind the poor husband, who would be the only one savouring her wares? Ellen chose Bertrand, and Jackson was shown the door.

But, along the line somewhere, Bertrand had become friendly with Jackson and offered him lodging at his house in the hope that he (Jackson) would take up with his (Bertrand's) wife, so that he would be free to be with the woman he loved. Jackson wasn't interested. That aside, this left one minor problem, of course: what to do with Ellen Kinder's long-suffering husband.

But the dentist had that all worked out. He would murder Henry Kinder. He told Jackson of his scheme and Jackson, in fear of his own life, fled to Maitland. What Bertrand hadn't told Jackson was that he had found love letters between Jackson and Ellen Kinder, and he planned on murdering Henry Kinder and implicating Jackson with the letters. Then he would have everyone out of the way and be free to carry on with his mistress.

But while Henry Bertrand may have been good at pulling bicuspids, as a murderer he was a dismal failure. His first two attempts at murdering his mistress' husband were a disaster. On the first occasion he took Alfred Burne, his 20-year-old dental assistant, into his confidence and got him to row him across Sydney Harbour to where Ellen and Henry Kinder lived.

While the young man waited by the boat, Bertrand concealed a tomahawk beneath his coat and snuck up to the house, but was foiled when he saw Ellen (who knew nothing of the murder attempt) talking with her husband, who was in a drunken stupor. A week later Burne again rowed his boss at midnight and went with him up to the house to find the Kinder asleep. Bertrand didn't have the heart to axe Henry Kinder to death as he slept with his wife and, as it turned out, nor did his assistant, despite urging from his boss. They left with their mission unaccomplished.

Still intent on murder, Henry Bertrand decided on another method. He bought a pistol and practised with it by shooting at a pig's head as a target. On 2 October 1865 his opportunity came when the Bertrand family joined the Kinder family at the Milson's Point Hotel before adjourning to the Kinder home, where the children played outside, the women prepared lunch in the kitchen and the men played cards in the loungeroom.

A gunshot rang out and Henry Kinder slumped to the table, his head bleeding profusely. When the police and a doctor arrived to find Kinder barely alive, Henry Bertrand said that they were playing cards when Kinder, who was very drunk, suddenly produced the gun that now lay on the floor and shot himself in the head. Despite the huge wound and loss of blood Kinder survived, but when he recovered he was unable to recall the incident at all. Undaunted, Bertrand laced Henry Kinder's milk with poison and this time he died, and the cause of his death was accredited to the gunshot suicide.

With the widow Kinder seemingly up for grabs, Frank Jackson returned from Maitland and told Bertrand that he would go to the police and tell them that Bertrand had confided in him that he intended to commit murder, unless Bertrand paid him £20. Instead, Bertrand went to the police and Jackson was sent to prison for attempted blackmail.

But, with everything he wanted now his, Bertrand displayed enormous guilt and confessed his crime to his sister and numerous other family friends. He came under police notice when he threatened a relative with a knife and was sentenced to 14 days in prison. With Bertrand in jail, Bertrand's sister went to police and told them of his brutal behaviour to his wife and his confession to the murder of Henry Kinder. Bertrand, his wife Jane and Ellen Kinder were all questioned over the murder of Henry Kinder. The women were released on the proviso that they testify at his trial and Bertrand was charged with murder.

Henry Bertrand pleaded not guilty to murder and, in what was deemed as the trial of the century, Sydneysiders were shocked as every scurrilous, sordid detail of the affair was laid bare, with both women testifying against the man who was once their lover. Incredibly, the jury was undecided and Bertrand was ordered to stand trial again, where he was found guilty of the murder of Henry Kinder and sentenced to death.

Over the next couple of years Bertrand's legal council lodged appeal after appeal and eventually succeeded in having his death sentence reduced to life imprisonment. After serving almost 30 years in prison, Henry Louis Bertrand was released and returned to England where he disappeared and was never heard of again.

11 LIKELY TO OFFEND AGAIN

Brisbane labourer Robert Raymond Day was 37 years old in 1990 when he was sentenced to life imprisonment for the attempted murder of Danish tourist Hendrik Enevoldsen in December 1988. Explaining why he recommended that Day's papers be marked 'never to be released', Justice Shepherdson said that a psychiatric report described Day as being capable of extremely violent behaviour.

Day was described as a 'dangerous man', and Justice Shepherdson believed there was an extremely high risk that he would reoffend in the same manner. The judge went on to order that jail authorities be informed of his remarks 'for the protection of fellow prisoners'.

Two years earlier, on 23 December 1988, Day had appeared in the Cleveland Magistrate's Court charged with the attempted murder of 21-year-old Enevoldsen. Seven days later, on 30 December 1988, he was also charged in the Brisbane Magistrate's Court with the murder of 22-year-old Japanese tourist Noriyuki

Oda. Oda had last been seen buying tickets for a bus trip to Alice Springs on 4 December.

Day entered no plea to charges of murder (of Oda), attempted murder (of Enevoldsen) and assaulting a police officer, and was remanded in custody. It was alleged in court that detectives found Japanese-brand items – including shampoo, conditioner, tissues and a pen – in a flat used by Day. A friend of Oda's was flown in from Japan and identified the pen as similar to one she had given Oda when they worked together in Japan. The witness also identified an unusual brand of tissues found at Day's apartment as the same ones she had sold Oda before he left for Australia. On top of this evidence, authorities found an oriental amulet, alleged to have been Oda's, in a rubbish bin at Day's flat. They also found a pair of handcuffs.

During the case, Hendrik Enevoldsen told the court he had travelled with Day to Redland Bay, and that Day had attacked him there from behind with a piece of timber. Enevoldsen was taking pictures of a hollow tree near a bushland swamp at the time. He said Day then tried to drown him in the swamp, but he managed to escape and flag down a passing motorist.

At his trial for the murder of Oda, it was alleged that Day had confessed to the murder to two Brisbane Gaol inmates. And there was more: it was said that he had asked one of the men who was about to be released if the man could murder another Japanese person as a way of helping Day's defence case.

In his alleged confession to the two prisoners, Day is said to have told them he had handcuffed Oda to a tree before pouring petrol at his feet and taunting him, saying, 'You burn, you burn.' As Oda was set ablaze, Day said he pleaded and cried out in Japanese. Day was alleged to have buried the dead body in a 44-gallon drum full of chemicals.

During the trial, Justice Shepherdson ruled that a Japanese handwriting expert could only give evidence according to a particular basis of comparison with Japanese characters on documents accepted as Oda's, and characters written on a cassette case found in Day's flat. But the expert went further in his evidence.

Acting for Day, Bill Cuthbert then submitted that his case had been prejudiced because he could not cross-examine on evidence that the jury had heard, but the judge had then ruled inadmissible. The trial was aborted after 20 days of legal argument. It had heard from 20 witnesses, including 13 flown in from Japan. In discharging the jury, Justice Shepherdson said that regardless of the hundreds of thousands of dollars in costs incurred, if he allowed the case to continue he would be left with a strong sense of unfairness to Day.

Day was finally retried for Oda's murder in June 1990; he was acquitted, but he remained in custody facing the attempted murder charge. On 1 November 1990, he was found guilty on that charge. This time, Justice Shepherdson said that he was concerned about similarities in the evidence about the death of Oda and the attempted murder.

'I heard sworn testimony in that [the Oda death] trial that certainly suggested this man killed the Japanese man Oda,' Justice Shepherdson said. 'I realise that Day has been acquitted, but what concerns me is [that] this offence involving Enevoldsen occurred two to three weeks after Oda disappeared when it was said, in Oda's case, the accused had killed him.'

On 7 December 1990, Day was sent to prison with the recommendation that he never be released. In the psychiatric report that played such an important role in the judge's sentence, it was revealed that at the age of 18, in 1971, Day had entered a block of flats one afternoon and raped a 55-year-old crippled woman at knife-point. The report stated that Day had attacked and sexually assaulted the woman as she was crawling across the floor to change the television channel. Day was released in 1982 after serving 11 years for the crime.

On 8 April 1993, the remains of Noriyuki Oda were found in a bush grave in the Beerburrum State Forest on Queensland's Sunshine Coast. He had died from severe head injuries administered by an 'instrument of some kind'. Day still maintains his innocence in relation to that crime.

12 'JOCKEY' SMITH – COP HATER

Of all that is sacred to the police, killing one of their own is the cardinal sin. So when an evil little gunman named 'Jockey' Smith specialised in attempting to murder police officers in the course of their duties, it was only a matter of time before he would die by the sword.

Born in rural Victoria in 1942, all James Edward Smith wanted to do was become a jockey and as a teenager he became an apprentice to a local trainer. Although still a diminutive man, it wasn't long before Smith was too heavy and the rides were few. With a passion for horses and the racecourse, Jockey, as he was now known, turned to crime to fund his gambling. And, somewhere along the way, he picked up a seething hatred of police officers.

As a juvenile, Smith chalked up a formidable police record and, by age 19, he was doing his first stretch in 'big prison' for shop breaking. It was in Pentridge that he met Ronald Ryan, who would later become infamous as the last person to be hanged in Australia. On the outside Ryan and Smith teamed up and committed burglaries until one night they were caught red-handed; Smith produced an old gun that jammed when he aimed it at police and pulled the trigger.

In 1973 Smith was again saved from murdering a police officer by a faulty gun when he came up from behind on a St Kilda constable who had stopped him and was searching the boot of his car. Smith aimed the gun at the back of the policeman's head and pulled the trigger but, again, it failed to go off.

Smith fled to Sydney but was soon charged with a series of armed robberies. Miraculously he got bail and was re-arrested in Melbourne two months later on a public beach. This time there was no bail and he was locked up back in Pentridge, pending extradition back to New South Wales to face the armed robbery charges. Smith was in Pentridge less than two days before he used a visitor's pass to walk out of maximum security unchallenged.

Rather than lay low, Smith decided that he would like to carry out his lifelong ambition of becoming a horse trainer so, under the name of Tom Cummings, as in Tommy Smith and Bart Cummings, he settled in Nowra on the New South Wales south coast and somehow – though it is not clear how – forged a new identity and life for himself as a rural horse trainer.

Incredibly, it was so brazen that it worked. For three years he trained his horses on a small farm and raced them at country meetings, occasionally going to Sydney with an entry in a minor race. But Blind Freddie could tell you that it couldn't last and, in 1976, he was eventually recognised by a police officer. When confronted, Smith produced a gun and wounded Constable Jerry Ambrose before making off.

In 1977 police alleged that it was Smith who broke into bookmaker Les Tidmarsh's home and, when interrupted in the middle of the burglary, shot Mr Tidmarsh dead and escaped. When confronted in a phone box in Nowra, Smith held a gun at close range on the arresting officer, Detective Bob Godden, but the officer saved his life by jamming the gun's firing mechanism by sticking his thumb between the hammer and the breech. At last they had their man.

Smith was sentenced to life imprisonment for the murder of the bookmaker Tidmarsh and wounding Constable Ambrose. Both of the convictions were thrown out on appeal when Smith's counsel alleged that police fabricated Smith's confessions.

Smith was then tried for attempting to murder Detective Godden and was sent to jail for 14 years. But someone had a long memory and the day after he was released from Long Bay in February 1992, as he was returning to his flat near Bondi Beach after taking a stroll with his wife, someone opened up on him with a shotgun at close range in the stairwell of the building, hitting him full blast in the chest, stomach and leg. Miraculously, Jockey survived and within a month was back on the streets.

Not long out of hospital, Jockey Smith was caught shoplifting a steam iron and some cutlery from Grace Brothers at Erina. When confronted in the car park he pulled a gun on the store detective and forced a terrified couple to drive him away at gunpoint. Once safe he fled the car and disappeared. But police knew it would only be a matter of time before he surfaced.

In December 1992, near Daylesford in rural Victoria, local constable Ian Harris noticed a white Ford panel van being driven unnecessarily slowly in an 80kph-limit stretch of highway and checked out the registration. Sure enough, it had been stolen. Constable Harris followed the van until it stopped at the front of the Farmers Arms Hotel in Creswick, where drinkers in the public bar watched as the drama unfolded.

Jockey got out of the van and walked back to where the policeman was sitting in his marked vehicle, talking on the radio. After a quick chat, Harris asked for proof of ownership of the vehicle; Jockey walked over to the van and returned with a pistol and a can of mace, then shoved the gun in the policeman's stomach.

Smith ordered Constable Harris to hand over his gun but the policeman refused. Smith fired a shot into the ground and screamed at the officer to give him his gun, get out of the car and lay on the bonnet or he would blow him away. Instead, the policeman called to the drinkers in the pub to ring the police for help.

A passing motorist saw what was happening. He pulled up and pushed Smith away from the officer. Smith responded by again shooting into the ground to let them know he wasn't fooling around. To the cheers of the drinkers in the pub, the motorist jumped back in his car and, with his two little boys sitting in the back, amid a hail of bullets, gunned the car straight at Smith and knocked him down.

Jockey Smith struggled to his feet and pointed the gun point-blank at the brave motorist's head. the policeman seized the opportunity and pulled his service revolver and emptied it into his chest. Jockey Smith fell to the ground dead.

If you're ever down Creswick way call in for a cold beer and hear all about the shoot-out at the Farmers Arms Hotel.

13 THE STRATHFIELD MASSACRE

Unable to cope with what most of us consider the hardships of everyday life, Wade Frankum was a human time bomb, ticking away waiting to explode in the worst possible way. And, in August 1991, when he did, he did it in a fashion that would be remembered for a long, long time. But it was, sadly, for all the wrong reasons. When Frankum went, he took seven innocent bystanders with him. And, as is often the way of the cowards who go out in a blaze of infamy, he turned the gun on himself to save the humiliation of a trial.

Born in Sydney in 1958, Wade Frankum's childhood was an unhappy one brought about by parents who strictly monitored the way he dressed and who he associated with. It wasn't helped by the fact that the other kids at the exclusive Newington College he attended nicknamed him 'Piggy' because of his chubby face. Frankum became shy and withdrawn and no one was surprised when he was expelled at 16 for regular truancy. He completed his education at nearby Homebush Boys' High.

Frankum maintained work in the retail clothing industry, dressed neatly and conducted as busy a social life as he could, given his shy nature. His father died in 1987 and in 1990 his mother gassed herself in her car. Who is to say if that was the catalyst for the events that lay ahead? But having to cope with his mother's death, and a broken engagement the year before, seemed to be more than Wade Frankum could cope with.

Soon after his mother's death Frankum quit his job at a Bondi store and began work as a casual taxi driver. He shaved his head, stacked on the weight and dressed in sloppy clothes. He spent most of his time hanging around Kings Cross spending his inheritance on prostitutes. It was as if he was living a real-life existence straight out of the Robert De Niro movie *Taxi Driver*. His actions and dramatic change in character indicated to his friends and family that he was going off the rails.

On the advice of friends, in 1991 Frankum went to see a psychologist and told him he was depressed about his mother's suicide. Diagnosis revealed that Frankum was emotionally insecure and abnormally dependent on his mother, although he despised her and felt she did not love him. For these reasons he was unable to form a normal relationship with a woman. Obviously unimpressed with the diagnosis, Frankum stopped going after just four visits.

Later that month Frankum bought an assault rifle and a large Bowie knife at a Sydney gun store, explaining to the shop assistant that he was going pig hunting. When he returned home to the family unit, which he shared with his sister and her boyfriend, he said that it was his intention to use the gun to 'protect himself' and if need be to 'wipe people out'. With that he put the gun away until that horrible day seven months later.

Wearing a denim outfit and a grey beanie over his shaved head, at around 2pm on the afternoon of Saturday, 17 August 1991, Wade Frankum boarded a train for Strathfield in Sydney's inner-western suburbs. In a black bag over his shoulder was a large Bowie knife in a leather sheath, a fully loaded Chinese-made SKK semiautomatic military rifle and a copy of Fyodor Dostoevsky's 1866 classic *Crime and Punishment*.

From Strathfield station Frankum made his way to the busy Strathfield Plaza shopping centre, where he sat down at the Coffee Pot coffee lounge and ordered a coffee. He looked like any other shopper taking a breather and relaxing before getting on with the rest of the shopping.

At about 3.30pm Frankum got up as if to leave and, as he did, he produced the huge knife from his bag. Laughing, he plunged it into the back of 15-year-old Bo Armstrong, who was sitting in the booth behind him. The pretty young lady, who seconds earlier had been laughing with her friend, was killed instantly.

Taking the assault rifle from his bag, Frankum shot and killed 61-year-old Joyce Nixon and her daughter, 37-year-old Patricia Rowe, both of whom stood in the way of the gunman and Mrs Rowe's children, 14-year-old Kevin and eight-year-old Nathan. They would surely have been killed if the women hadn't sacrificed their lives.

Hearing the shots from the kitchen, the Coffee Pot's owner, George Mavis, ran to see what was happening and was shot dead. Next to die was 17-year-old Rachelle Milburn, shot at close range in the head. Carole Dickinson, 47, jumped over a table and grabbed her daughter Belinda by the hair and dragged her out of the way, at the same time putting herself between her daughter and the gunman, who shot her in the stomach. She died later in hospital. Belinda fled with Frankum in hot pursuit, shooting at her as she ran. She took several bullets, but escaped serious injury.

Shoppers fled as Frankum walked through the mall shooting at anything that moved. As 53-year-old accountant Robertson Kan Hock Voon walked out of a photographic store and made his way to the escalator, unaware of what was going on, he was shot dead in his tracks.

Frankum made his way to the ramp in the car park, shooting at anything as he went. He stopped Catherine Noyes, who was driving her car down the exit ramp and had no idea what was going on. Frankum jumped in beside her and aimed the gun at her head and demanded that she drive him to nearby Enfield. 'Don't panic,' Frankum told the petrified woman. When he said

'I'm sorry', while Catherine Noyes was looking into the barrel of his gun, she thought he was apologising for what he was going to do next – kill her.

Instead Frankum ordered her to stop the car and he got out. As she drove off still in fear for her life, Catherine Noyes watched in the rear-view mirror as Wade Frankum put the gun to his head and pulled the trigger. More than 50 bullets had been fired. Eight people, including Frankum, lay dead. Six others were wounded and would recover.

So was Wade Frankum insane? If so, then surely there could be some logic to such a pointless waste of life. Incredibly, that does not appear to be the case. In his book profiling Wade Frankum titled *Profile of a Mass Killer*, leading Australian forensic psychiatrist Dr Rod Milton concluded:

> Taking Wade Frankum as a whole, I would not regard him as being seriously outside the 'normal' range of persons, apart from the act of killing. Had he survived and stood trial, he would not have qualified for an insanity defence or for the defence of diminished responsibility.

14 'LAST RESORT' LAURIE CONNELL

Of all of Australia's corporate crooks of the opulent '80s, none was as brazen with other people's money as the Western Australian banker 'Last Resort' Laurie Connell. He made Gordon Gecko look like Mother Teresa. Connell got his nickname because there was nothing he wouldn't resort to in order to get what he wanted. And at the end he used the ultimate last resort to avoid going back to prison.

Born in 1947, the short, stocky Laurie Connell left school at 15 and worked as an office boy and a part-time boxer in the carnival tents around the Western Australian countryside. By the time he was in his early 20s Connell had gathered enough entrepreneurial skills to put himself into the promotions business, and had gathered a bunch of up-and-coming cronies around him who could help him gather in his new generation of investors. One of those contacts was a journalist named Brian Bourke, who would one day become the Labor premier of Western Australia and wind up in jail for fraud.

By the time Brian Bourke had fought his way up through the Labor Party ranks to become premier in 1983, Laurie Connell had formed his fledgling Rothwells Bank and was looking for investors. And what better customer could he have than the Western Australian government, courtesy of his old mate who had pledged that he was keen to promote local entrepreneurs. Hundreds of millions of dollars of public money poured into the coffers of Rothwells and the chairman of the board couldn't believe his luck.

Shortly after, as if by magic, Laurie Connell was said to have a personal wealth of around $350 million. No one bothered to ask where his newly acquired fortune had come from. Truth be known, it was his investors' money that he illegally 'borrowed' from his own bank and was spending in a fashion that made Iranian oil sheikhs and Greek shipping magnates look like paupers.

Apart from the huge sums deposited by the government, the mum and dad investors also trusted the little man in the Italian suits and left their money with him – many of them their life savings – on the promise of inflated interest rates that he could never possibly pay in the long term. But Laurie Connell didn't care whose money it was – just as long as he could get his hands on it and spend it on himself.

Connell built a palace on seven blocks of land on the Swan River, flew everywhere in his private $30 million Lear jet, had a fleet of limousines at his disposal wherever he and his entourage were anywhere in the world, sailed on his luxury yachts and built his own private racetrack for his stable of racehorses, which was said to be the biggest in Australia. His list of associates was the who's who of politics and business, and he was known to take Prime Minister Bob Hawke deep-sea fishing off north Western Australia.

A keen punter, Connell was said to keep a cash float in his office of around $3 million and outlaid up to as much as $1 million a week with the bookies. But gambling was nothing new. Connell had always been a gambler, and not always an honest one. On 3 September 1975, Connell and his associates hit the Kalgoorlie betting ring with a series of large last-minute bets on an unfancied horse named His Worship in a Melbourne race. His Worship won easily.

The bookies smelled a giant rat and, when stewards investigated the matter, they discovered that while the broadcast of the race was supposedly aired live on a Perth radio station, it was actually recorded and broadcast several minutes after the event was over. Lucky to escape without a conviction, Laurie Connell was banned from racecourses anywhere in the world for two years.

But Laurie Connell's biggest race fix was in the 1987 Perth Cup at Ascot where one of his horses, the stayer Rocket Racer, was heavily backed to win. Rocket Racer headed out from the barrier as if its tail was on fire and kept up the bewildering pace for the whole 3.2km until it crossed the line nine lengths in front. But anyone watching could tell that Rocket Racer wasn't feeling real flash as he wobbled off the track, aided by an army of attendants who stopped him from dropping dead in his tracks.

It was a time when horses were suspected of being doped with elephant juice, a sedative powerful enough to stop an elephant in its tracks, but if used in small doses it had the opposite effect and caused horses to run flat out until they dropped dead. This was the case with Rocket Racer, who, despite being attended to by vets, died not long after. Mysteriously, the horse was never drug tested. While Rocket Racer lay fighting for its life, Laurie Connell celebrated his Perth Cup win long into the night at an expensive Perth restaurant and shouted for everyone in the place, running up a bill in excess of $50,000.

When the stock market crashed in late 1987, the reality of Laurie Connell's excesses and theft were revealed. It was estimated that between 1983 and 1987 he had embezzled up to $500 million from Rothwells, none of which could be recovered due to an intricate and complicated business structure he had set up that kept him living like a king, even after he was declared bankrupt.

In 1994 Laurie Connell was found guilty of conspiring to fix the 1983 AHA Cup at rural Bunbury, when he bribed jockey Danny Hobby with $5000 to throw the race by jumping off

Connell's mount Strike Softly to stage a fall. The court found that Connell had conspired to pay Hobby $1 million over the years to stay out of the country, away from police who were investigating the matter. Hobby was jailed for three years and Connell was sent to jail for five years.

In 1996, Connell was brought before the court on fraud charges relating to the collapse of Rothwells Bank and $300 million that had gone missing. He died of a heart attack before a judgement could be reached. He was 49.

15 AUSTRALIA'S FIRST BANK ROBBERY

As you can imagine, given the history of most of the residents, Sydney in convict times was a place where the slightest opportunity of easy money was seized upon by a huge variety of sundry and assorted villains, most of whom had been experts in their field back home. Until they got caught, that is, and sent to the colonies.

And so, one day in 1828, while part of a road gang was digging a drain to run beneath George Street and across to the Tank Stream, a convict named Charles Dingle couldn't help but notice, not that he was looking out for it of course, that where they were digging provided access to the foundations of the Bank of Australia.

Dingle recruited the services of another convict, William O'Farrell, and together they devised a plan to rob the bank. But they would need three others to help them. There were thousands to choose from. Thomas Turner was ideal because two years earlier he had been employed on the building site of the bank and knew exactly where the strongroom was located. Another was William Blaxstone, a former London safe cracker and pardoned convict who was known in the trade as 'Sudden Solomon'. The third was the colony's most notorious fence of stolen property, Thomas Woodward, who would help them get rid of the loot.

Turner explained that the bank's construction was made of inferior mortar and he drew a map showing exactly where the strongroom was. From there the more experienced Blaxstone took charge of the operation. As there would be fewer people about, they planned to begin their digging late on Saturday night and work through until Sunday when there would be no one at all to hear them. Blaxstone figured that under the cover of darkness, digging through to the strongroom would take a few weekends to complete.

As the plan progressed Thomas Turner, the man who drew up the plans, elected to drop out for fear that he would be arrested after the robbery because of his inside knowledge. Turner then went about making himself very conspicuous in public as the digging went on. Another convict named Clayton was recruited to take his place and, as the workload became harder, yet another convict, Val Rook, was let in on the secret and took part in the digging.

On the evening of Sunday 15 September 1828, they finally punched a half-metre hole into the bank vault and the smallest of the men, William O'Farrell, was pushed through. After an agonising wait Farrell whispered that he was indeed in the right room and, most importantly of all, it was full of money. By the time Farrell had finished passing the loot through the hole, the bank robbers were in possession of almost £15,000 in banknotes, £750 in British silver, 2000 gold sovereigns and more than 2000 Spanish dollars. A king's ransom for the Sydney of 1828.

Before leaving with their prize stuffed into carry sacks, all of the looters entered the bank vault and trashed the bank's records, ledgers, mortgage documents and bills of sale, and left them scattered and destroyed in the slime of the water drain they had been working from the past month. When Sydney's Chief

Constable, George Jilks, arrived at the scene the following day he found the implements of the robbery – rock hammers, a crowbar, a stone saw, a broken lantern and half a dozen empty rum bottles. It wasn't determined if the robbers drank the rum while working or if they used it as a celebration.

Now you would think that with five convicts involved in a robbery as big as that, there would be some scuttlebutt as to who did it and where the money was. But, incredibly, there wasn't a word. Perhaps those who might have known something hated the bank so much they were glad that at last someone had committed Australia's first bank robbery and glad it was that bank in particular. But if anyone knew, no one was saying a word.

In desperation the bank manager appealed to the bank's customers to bring their notes into the bank and have them marked as 'good' in an attempt to isolate the stolen ones. Few responded. Then the bank offered a paltry £100 reward, which was hardly worth the risk of getting your throat cut should you attempt to claim it. Governor Darling offered an absolute pardon and free passage back to England to any informers, but there were still no takers. The *Sydney Gazette* published the numbers of the stolen bank notes, but neither the cash nor the notes ever came to light.

The only glimmer of hope came when an anonymous note was pushed under the front door of the bank. It said that the robbers could be found at an address at Millers Point. The police raided the place and arrests were made, but it never came to anything due to lack of evidence.

It wasn't until three years later that the Bank of Australia robbery was in the headlines again. One of the convicts at Norfolk Island, deemed 'a place of the extremist punishment, short of death' and the most evil place on God's earth outside of Hell's Gates in Tasmania, a William Blaxstone, reported to the commandant that he had important information about the robbery. It seemed that several months after the robbery Blaxstone and another convict had attempted to rob a house in Sydney and the other man was killed and Blaxstone was wounded. He was sentenced to death, which was commuted to 14 years on Norfolk

Island. They agreed that if Blaxstone told all he would be released from Norfolk. He did and was.

Only Dingle and O'Farrell could be found and, along with Blaxstone, they were found guilty of robbing the bank. It seemed as though their money was lost gambling and the recipients of the winning bets weren't going to tell the police where it came from. Blaxstone told the court that in one circumstance he gave the fence Woodward £1133 for which he was to receive £1000 in new banknotes. The pair went to the Bank of New South Wales and Woodward told him to wait around the corner and watch out for police while he got the money. Blaxstone never saw Woodward or any of the money again and it wasn't as if he could go to the police and complain.

Dingle, O'Farrell and Blaxstone were sentenced to 10 years in jail, but Blaxstone was released soon after for giving evidence against the others. He was in and out of prison for minor offences for the rest of his life until he was found murdered in a swamp in Woolloomooloo in 1844. Ironically, that same year the Bank of Australia declared itself in financial difficulties, having lost a fortune on the real estate market. The bank had to offer a vast slice of their assets in a lottery for £4 a ticket. The man who won the huge parcel of property, Mr Angus McDonald, died soon after.

16 BODILESS MURDER CONVICTIONS

It is extremely unusual that anyone is charged with murder when the alleged victim's body hasn't been found, because it is almost impossible to prove that a murder has been committed at all. It is a prosecutor's nightmare. So much so that after the jury had retired to consider their verdict in the December 2005 trial of Bradley Murdoch for the murder of Peter Falconio, one of the jurors returned soon after and asked the judge if they could actually convict Murdoch of murder, given that Mr Falconio's body had never been located. The judge assured them that they could.

But the evidence against Bradley Murdoch was so overwhelming that a body wasn't necessary to get him life in jail with a minimum parole period of 28 years. Mr Falconio's partner, Joanna Lees, positively identified Murdoch as the man who pulled them over in the middle of nowhere in 2001, shot her boyfriend and then tried to abduct her. Murdoch's DNA was found on the cable ties, Mr Falconio's kombi van gear stick and in a smudge of blood on Ms Lee's T-shirt. It was found to be 150 quadrillion times more likely to be from Murdoch than from any other person. Goodnight, Mr Murdoch.

Sadly this wasn't the case in Australia's greatest travesty of justice, in which the alleged murder victim's body had disappeared. It began when nine-week-old Azaria Chamberlain disappeared from the family tent at Uluru on the evening of 17 August 1980. Her body was never found, although her heavily bloodstained singlet, jumpsuit and nappy were discovered a week later. Azaria's mother, Lindy, alleged that a dingo had taken the baby. No one believed her and she was eventually charged with murder.

With no body, no evidence of motive and no eyewitness evidence that even vaguely incriminated the Chamberlains, the Crown case was wholly circumstantial, and supported in the main by the claims of expert witnesses to the effect that the state of Azaria's clothing was inconsistent with a dingo attack; that there was a bloody handprint on the jumpsuit; and that substantial quantities of blood, including the blood of an infant, had been found throughout the Chamberlain car. This 'blood' in the car was ultimately proved to be rust proofing.

The jury was asked to believe that in a space of five to ten minutes, during which Lindy returned to the tent with the baby and her six-year-old son Aidan, she had cut Azaria's throat and stuffed the body into Michael's camera case while her son watched. She then raced Aidan back to the barbecue area, where normal life was resumed, and displayed no signs of unease or distress until the opportunity presented itself for blaming a dingo for the baby's disappearance. The Chamberlains were said to have later buried the body, then exhumed it so that the clothing could be placed in a strategic location to lend further credibility to the dingo tale. Incredibly, the jury swallowed the lot.

Lindy Chamberlain was convicted of murder and sent to prison for life. Her husband, Michael, was convicted as an accessory. Appeals to the Federal Court and the High Court were unsuccessful. After the chance discovery of Azaria's matinee jacket in 1986, while rescuers were retrieving a suicide victim who had jumped from Uluru, the Northern Territory Government released Lindy Chamberlain after she had served four years in prison. In what was arguably the most shameful case of wrongful imprisonment in our history she was awarded $1 million compensation.

Fifty-three-year-old Daryl Francis Suckling already had 138 convictions for various offences dating back to the age of 11 when, in March 1988, he was arrested on an isolated property at Pooncarie, in southwest New South Wales, for the sexual assault and false imprisonment of a woman. She told them that Suckling had told her he had killed another woman and buried her body nearby, though he didn't specify where.

Police searched the area for a corpse but could only find jewellery, clothing and a set of dentures belonging to Jodie Maree Larcombe, a 22-year-old prostitute and heroin addict who had gone missing the day she was released from Pentridge Prison the previous December.

But when they discovered explicit photos of a battered, bruised and apparently drugged or drunk Jodie Larcombe in Suckling's car, police came to believe that she was the woman Suckling had boasted of killing and burying. On 3 April 1989, police charged Daryl Suckling with the murder of Jodie Larcombe but the charges were eventually dropped through lack of evidence.

While in prison for another offence, Suckling boasted to a cellmate about the abduction and murder of Jodie Larcombe. The cellmate went to the police, who wired him up with a recorder and he gathered more incriminating evidence, although Suckling never told where he had concealed Jodie Larcombe's body. A jury found Suckling guilty of killing Jodie Larcombe on or about 27 December 1987 at an unknown place in New South Wales. In sentencing him, Justice Bruce James said that the murder was a horrendous crime in the worst category.

On 2 September 1996, Daryl Francis Suckling, by now 60, was jailed for the term of his natural life for abducting, sexually assaulting, murdering and dismembering a woman whose body has never been found.

There is also the case where a trial without a body went awry. Although already serving life for murdering a child near

Rockhampton, police believed that Leonard John Fraser had murdered another schoolgirl, 14-year-old Natasha Ryan, who had disappeared in September 1998. They also believed that Fraser could help them with their investigations into the disappearances of three other women who knew Fraser and who had gone missing throughout Queensland between September 1998 and April 1999.

Police got lucky when Fraser started talking to his cellmate who they wired up with a secret recorder. When confronted with the confessions, Fraser led police to the remains of Beverly Doreen Leggo, 36, Julie Dawn Turner, 39, and the partial remains of 19-year-old Sylvia Maria Benedetti.

At Fraser's trial the jury was told Fraser had boasted to his cellmate that he had killed schoolgirl Natasha Ryan by knifing her because she was pregnant to him. In April 2003, the case took a sensational turn when police found the now 18-year-old Natasha Ryan, hiding at her boyfriend's house. Natasha Ryan appeared in the packed court and said she had never seen Fraser before in her life and the charge of her abduction and murder was dropped as Fraser obviously had no case to answer.

But not so with the other three charges. On 9 May 2003, the jury convicted Leonard John Fraser of the murders of Sylvia Benedetti and Beverly Leggo and the manslaughter of Julie Turner, and he was sentenced to three indefinite life terms.

17 | NOT YOUR NORMAL TOURIST

Josef Schwab was known to have a fondness for guns and violence from an early age, and had developed a reputation as a troublemaker in the small German village of Pocking even before he came to Australia in 1987. An active member of a local criminal gang in his home town, the 23-year-old was believed to be responsible for as many as 30 car thefts and numerous house burglaries in his village.

A police informant later told authorities that Schwab had carried a pistol from the age of 16. The informant believed that Schwab wouldn't hesitate to use the weapon if the situation came up. The informant also believed that Schwab had entered Australia as a tourist when he did because of increasing heat on him in Pocking.

Schwab arrived in Australia on a tourist visa on 18 April 1987. Before long he had checked into Brisbane's Atcherley Hotel, on Queen Street. He also defrauded the ANZ bank, conning them into believing he'd had his traveller's cheques stolen during the flight to Australia. He was issued with replacements worth $1000.

Five days after his arrival in this country, Schwab cashed his ill-gotten cheques at two separate Brisbane banks. He then went to Fiveways Firearms Store in the suburb of Woolloongabba and bought a Winchester 12-gauge shotgun, three rifles, a Ruger 223, a Sako .308 and a Bruno .22. He loaded his deadly cache into a Toyota 4Runner he had hired from the Avis depot at Brisbane airport and headed towards the Northern Territory.

Authorities who later tracked his movements know that Schwab bought petrol at the Shire of Diamantina on 6 May, and was given a parking ticket at Mt Isa on 9 May. He was in Darwin getting the front end of the Toyota repaired on 20 May. He was then spotted northeast of Darwin, at Carmon Plains, Point Stuart, on 4 June. It's believed he did some buffalo shooting there, as 10 sets of buffalo horns were later found in the back of the rented Toyota.

Then, on 9 June at Timber Creek in the Northern Territory, Schwab shot and killed the first human victims of his senseless murder spree – 70-year-old Marcus Bullen and his 42-year-old son Lance. The Bullens, from Western Australia, were on a camping and fishing holiday when Schwab shot them both in the back. He then buried the two men in shallow graves and set fire to their vehicle.

On 15 June, almost a week after the murder of the two men, Schwab came across three campers at a picnic area on the Pentecost River, south of Wyndham in north Western Australia. Julie Anne Warren, 25, her husband Phillip Charles Walkemeyer, 26, and Terry Kent Bolt were all from the Kimberley district. After shooting them in the back, Schwab stripped them, and left their naked bodies to flow down the river. The corpses were carried away by the strong tide. One of the victims was found in shallow water about three kilometres downstream from the burnt-out 4WD, which contained their clothes. Not long after that, another was found four kilometres further down from the Pentecost Creek crossing. The last body was found on rocks in shallow water nearby.

Due to the similarity of the murders, authorities had no trouble linking them to the same serial killer, despite the fact that they took place hundreds of kilometres apart. The problem was that the police had no idea which direction the heartless murderer had headed after the second group of murders. And the man they were after had a 24-hour head start. In the vast Kimberley region, that meant he could turn up anywhere – and could randomly murder again at any time.

Members of the police's elite Tactical Response Group (TRG) were flown in to join what had become the biggest manhunt in Western Australian history. On 19 June, local helicopter pilot Peter Leutenegger reported spotting a vehicle camouflaged in the scrub about 10 kilometres west of Fitzroy Crossing. Seven members of the TRG were driven to the scene. Local police surrounded the area. Police aircraft kept up surveillance on the vehicle. Camouflaged, and armed with high-powered rifles, police marksmen moved in on foot. They positioned themselves in scrub behind tall anthills about 50 metres from the vehicle. The police aircraft then flew in low to flush out anyone inside the car. A shirtless man wearing camouflage trousers suddenly appeared and started shooting at the aircraft with a rifle. He missed. The leader of the TRG shouted, 'Police. Stop shooting.' The man turned his rifle in the direction of the voice and opened fire. 'He's shooting at us – engage him,' was the TRG leader's response to the hail of bullets. Police returned fire. Schwab was hit on the left thumb, the bullet splintering the stock of the deadly .308 rifle he was armed with.

Schwab raced back to his vehicle and climbed in. Authorities bombarded him with tear gas grenades in an effort to flush him out peacefully, but the grenades sparked a scrub fire. Schwab left the vehicle and fled through the mounting flames, still firing at police as he tried to escape. Ammunition he had left scattered on the ground exploded in the heat as the fire spread quickly through the dry scrub, and Schwab disappeared through the smoke and flames.

Authorities could find no trace of the murderer until the light aircraft spotted him lying face down in nearby undergrowth. A single bullet wound to the heart had killed him; there were also bullet wounds to his shoulder and right buttock.

Police proceeded to search the rented Toyota. Inside they found a toolbox, credit cards, fishing rods, and bank books which had belonged to the Kimberley trio Schwab had recently murdered.

It wasn't until the next day that authorities identified missing German tourist Josef Schwab as the vicious serial killer they had been forced to gun down. Police still had no idea why he had turned on his five innocent victims. The most accepted theory is simple robbery. The fact that he stole the victims' possessions and tried to cover his tracks by stripping them and burning their clothes in their cars seems to support this idea; so do his methods of disposing the bodies. Schwab buried his first two victims, and threw the next three into a tidal river, perhaps believing the region's vicious saltwater crocodiles would eat the evidence.

18 | THE OUTLAW FOLK HERO

Over the years there have been many Australian outlaw folk heroes – bank robbers and murderers who captured the public's imagination – such as Ned Kelly, Squizzy Taylor and Darcy Dugan. In more modern times there was Russell 'Mad Dog' Cox – the only man to escape from Long Bay Jail's impenetrable fortress, Katingal, and stay on the run for 11 years. And then there was Brendan Abbott, who was chased all over Australia under the guise of the Postcard Bandit – which was all very romantic, but try telling that to someone who had looked down the barrel of Abbott's shotgun while he was holding up a bank in a balaclava and screaming at them.

But for sheer bravado and defiance of authority, few come close to the bank robber and escapologist Raymond John Denning. Songs were written about Denning, his prison diaries were published and a tape of him telling of prison authority's brutality in jail appeared on *60 Minutes*. Throughout the 1970s and '80s Denning was seen by some respected criminologists as a lone crusader in exposing to society the corruption and entrenched mutual hatred between authority and prisoners within the New South Wales prison system.

For his troubles, time and again Denning was savagely beaten by the guards and thrown into solitary confinement. But, though he probably never knew it at the time, his one-man campaign against a clandestine system of endemic violence within our prisons did society a favour in paving the way for the modern-day, violence-free approach. But along the way Denning made a bad mistake. He bashed a prison official almost to death in one of his escape attempts. And in the end his bravado didn't count for zip and he went the way of most of his ilk, only in a much less dignified manner.

Ray Denning didn't have much of a chance from the beginning. At age 10 and with his father in prison, he stood and watched as his mother committed suicide by pouring kerosene on herself and setting herself alight. 'I went to my mother's room and she was burning on the bed,' Denning wrote later in his memoirs. 'I got a saucepan full of water and threw it over her but it was no good. She died a day or two later.'

In and out of institutions and jail for a multitude of offences that ranged from drunken driving and vagrancy to malicious assault and carrying a gun, in 1973 Denning graduated into the big league when he was sentenced to prison for 13 years for a series of violent assaults and robberies. Denning first reached public notoriety in 1974 when he battered prison overseer Willy Karl Faber with a carpenter's claw hammer during an abortive escape attempt from Parramatta Gaol.

Faber spent months in hospital where he was treated for brain damage and underwent several major operations, one to remove bone from the top of his skull. Subsequently he suffered epilepsy attacks and then heart attacks, and he died from his injuries four years later. Denning received a life sentence on top of the term he was already serving.

Denning next grabbed headlines in September 1977 when he escaped from Maitland Jail, but was recaptured a few hours later. At his Sydney Central Court appearance on escape charges,

Denning's head was shaved. 'I object to being called Denning,' he told the magistrate. 'A Tibetan spirit has taken me over and I am now to be called Lob-sang Rampa.' No doubt taking his new calling into consideration, the judge gave Lob-sang another five years on top of what he was already serving, to meditate his dilemma.

Denning's next escape was from Grafton Jail on 2 April 1980 when he became the first prisoner to break out of there that century. His 19 months on the run were a media and crime circus. A videotaped interview with Denning, now Australia's most wanted man, was shown on Channel Nine's *60 Minutes*, he was interviewed for the Australian edition of *Playboy* magazine and tape-recorded interviews were aired over the ABC's 2JJJ. Denning had a 200-page book called the *Ray Denning Diary* published by the Prisoners Action Group, which outlined his philosophy on escapes: 'The only people who escape or try to escape from jail are that sick of jail sadism that they are willing to die rather than suffer the tortures that go on in jail every day,' he wrote. He made no mention of how they got there in the first place.

But while on the run making a martyr of himself, Denning also had to live. On 18 December 1980 he took part in an armed robbery of $9300 from Sydney Mechanical Services at Glebe, and on 21 April 1981 he was involved in the armed robbery of $20,260 from the Bank of New South Wales at Summer Hill. Denning teamed up with Australia's other most wanted man, Russell 'Mad Dog' Cox. On 22 September 1981, in Queensland's biggest payroll robbery, they held up Brisbane's Transurety Ltd and stole $327,000. On 8 November 1981 Denning was recaptured and sentenced to a further 10 years' jail to be served at the expiry of his life sentence and all of the other sentences on top of it.

On 15 July 1988 Denning escaped from Goulburn Jail with another convict, Les Carrion, and took part in the armed hold-up of the Zillmere branch of the Commonwealth Bank in Brisbane. After a wild shoot-out with police on 22 July 1988, Denning was recaptured in a Melbourne shopping centre car park in the company of Russell 'Mad Dog' Cox. On 10 February

1989 Denning was sentenced in the Melbourne Supreme Court to five years and two years on using firearms to prevent apprehension and 'going equipped to steal' charges.

Given that Denning was only given a concurrent two-and-a-half year sentence for escaping from Goulburn, sceptics claimed that he was deliberately allowed to escape so he would inadvertently lead them to Cox (which he did), who had been on the run for 11 years, but there was never any substance to the allegations.

Extradited to Sydney to serve out his original sentence, Denning found a way of getting his seemingly impossible sentence reduced and make a future release a possibility: he became a police informer. After dobbing in his mates from inside the prison, which saw him give evidence in such high-profile cases as the Sydney Hilton bombing and testify against his old mate 'Mad Dog' Cox, Ray Denning was finally released in 1993 after spending 20 years – less his escape time, that is – behind bars.

Two months after his release he was found dead in his run-down rented Darlinghurst semi from an apparently accidental self-inflicted overdose of heroin. It was no secret that Denning, sick of the low-grade heroin available in jail, had promised himself 'the shot of a lifetime' when he got out. Seems as though he got it. But from whom will always remain a mystery. Raymond John Denning's funeral wasn't a very big one.

19 REX 'BUCKETS' JACKSON AND THE PRISONER EARLY-RELEASE SCHEME

We all have our suspicions that people in high places could be on the take and over the years in *Crime File* we have looked at a few cases where corruption in the police force has reached the highest level. But while there is always talk that a politician here or there is taking money underhandedly, you would have to go back a long way to find a case where one has actually been caught and punished for his crimes against the position we entrusted him with.

One such crook is Rex 'Buckets' Jackson, a knockabout bloke who rose to high places in New South Wales' Wran administration in the 1980s. From all accounts Rex Jackson was a likable enough fellow who enjoyed a drink and a bit of lunch and was generally liked by just about everyone who knew him. As it turned out, he was also very popular among a lot of blokes who never got to meet him at all.

In Sydney in early 1982, the New South Wales Minister for Corrective Services, Mr Rex 'Buckets' Jackson, initiated an early-release scheme for prisoners. Mr Jackson said it was based on the most enlightening principles of penology. But something about the scheme wasn't right from the word go. Up until the scheme was initiated prisoners were released on licence at a rate of about one a month. Now they began getting out of jail early at the astonishing rate of about 50 a month. Something stunk somewhere.

A fluke brought the rort unstuck. In April 1983, while using authorised phone tapping during an attempted probe into drug trafficking, Australian Federal Police stumbled on some conversations that were related to the early-release scheme. In May 1983 the AFP commissioner advised his minister of the conversations who, in turn, advised the Prime Minister, Bob Hawke, who informed the New South Wales Government.

The documents containing the evidence about the information heard in the phone taps was handed over to the New South Wales Police Commissioner, Cecil Abbott. Coincidentally, in June 1983, five New South Wales judges complained bitterly about the early-release scheme. The judges queried the purpose of sending criminals to prison for lengthy terms if they were going to be released long before their time was due.

Rex Jackson and the New South Wales Attorney-General, Paul Landa, arranged to meet with the judges and hear their grievances. At this meeting Rex Jackson rejected any criticism and claimed that the scheme had a 95 per cent success rate. He said that given a second chance – and in some cases a third, fourth, fifth, sixth and many, many more chances – prisoners had rehabilitated themselves and were now worthy members of the community. Only a few reoffended. As Mr Jackson didn't have any figures to prove this they had to take his word for it. And that was that.

Also in June 1983 the leader of the New South Wales Opposition, Nick Greiner, criticised the extremely early release of three former Griffith police officers who had been sentenced to lengthy terms for their part in marijuana growing. It seemed as though the officers had bought their way out of jail. It was claimed that the going rates were from $2500 upwards, depending on the length of the term. Mr Greiner said that by now up to 640 prisoners had been released under the new scheme and the circumstances of some of the releases were appalling. Sixty of those prisoners had been serving life sentences for murder.

Mr Greiner told the parliament that the scheme had seriously undermined confidence in the government and that in the past months some of the prisoners released had committed serious offences. But Mr Greiner also pointed out that many of those released were genuinely entitled to be released under the provisions of the scheme.

In October 1983 it was raised by the Liberal Opposition in federal parliament that the AFP had detected, by the use of phone taps, the payment of money to people in authority, including a New South Wales government minister, to ensure the early release of prisoners.

The minister in question, Rex Jackson, was asked for a 'please explain' to confirm or deny the allegations in the tapes. He issued a statement in which he denied any knowledge of taking money to allow certain prisoners out early on license. The statement was read out in the New South Wales Parliament, and at a press conference Mr Jackson also denied any involvement in the taped allegations.

The following day Rex Jackson changed his mind and sent a letter of resignation, which was read out in parliament. It said in part: 'Having examined a particular matter in more detail [the tapes], I now have to advise you that my statement to the House was incorrect. I sincerely regret that I have therefore unwittingly misled the House. I have no other course to follow but to submit my resignation.'

After a public inquiry by Justice Slattery of the Supreme Court, five people were charged with conspiracy relating to the early release of prisoners from Broken Hill Jail between October 1982 and June 1983. Those charged were Rex Jackson, solicitor Howard Hilton and businessmen Keith Godfrey Harris, Morres George and Fayez Hakim.

In November 1984, Cabinet decided that the government would pay all of Rex Jackson's legal costs. The decision was kept secret, but it emerged in March 1985. Following a public outcry, the government decided to pay the $59,000 incurred to that date, but no more. Jackson said that he needed to put his $300,000 superannuation towards his $600,000 legal costs.

In November 1984, Hilton and George were found guilty. In sentencing them Justice Carruthers said from the bench that the community's grave and abiding concern about corruption in New South Wales called for an appropriate response from sentencing judges. He sentenced Keith Harris and Howard Hilton to nine years' jail and Morres George to five years.

In September 1987, Rex Jackson was sentenced in the New South Wales Supreme Court to seven-and-a-half years' jail, with a nonparole period of 45 months, for accepting bribes to arrange for the early release of prisoners.

20 THE MOUNT RENNIE RAPE CASE

While we are quick to condemn the gang rapes in recent years by young men of Middle Eastern origin, it is easy to forget that the majority of our most heinous crimes and gang violations against women have been perpetrated by Australians whose families have been here for many generations. So hideous were some of these crimes that they are deep-etched into our culture forever.

The 1973 torture, rape and murder of Mrs Virginia Morse after she was abducted from her lonely farmhouse in rural New South Wales by the beasts Allan Baker and Kevin Crump; the 1986 rape-murder of nursing sister Anita Cobby by five men in Sydney's western suburbs; and the abduction, rape and murder of bank clerk Janine Balding by a gang of teenagers as she made her way home from work in Sydney's western suburbs in 1988, come immediately to mind.

The killers had typically Australian names; Murphy, Baker, Crump, Elliot, Blessington, Jamieson, Travis and Murdoch. Nothing Middle Eastern about them. And it's not news that vile crimes against women by packs of men have been going on since the new settlers began arriving.

But among them, there is one crime that stands out for its initial ferocity and then, to pander to a public demanding justice, the punishment of some of its perpetrators. It happened a long time ago, in Sydney, and became known as the 'Mount Rennie Rape Case'.

On 9 September 1886, 16-year-old orphan Mary Jane Hicks left home on the outskirts of Sydney headed for the city in search of work as a domestic servant. So innocent was Mary to the ways of the world that she had never been kissed by a boy, let alone been aware of what else went on between consenting adults.

When the child was offered a free ride by a hansom cabbie, Charles Sweetman, Mary thought nothing of going with him because cabbies were trusted and respected members of the community. Not so Mr Sweetman. He pulled the cab over to the side of the road into the disused area of a rope factory in Waterloo, climbed down from his perch and sat next to Mary.

As Sweetman was attempting to assault the lass, a small gang of teenagers from the notorious local Waterloo Push arrived on the scene and saved her. Glad to be away from Sweetman, Mary was only too happy to go with the youths, who led her along a bush path heading towards Randwick Road. Once in the cover of the undergrowth they threw her to the ground and, while two of the teenagers held her down, the others had their way with her.

A labourer working nearby, Bill Stanley, heard Mary's screams for help and as he ran through the bushes to her rescue the gang fled. As Stanley was comforting Mary, covering her up and making her as comfortable as he could so he could carry her to help, he looked up to find the gang was back, only this time with a lot of their mates. Now there were about 20 of them.

Stanley did his best against the gang but he was beaten and kicked to the ground, where he was set upon and belted with rocks, tree branches, fists and boots. Mary was ripped from Bill Stanley's grasp and dragged screaming to a sandy hill nearby, which stood in what we know now as the Moore Park Golf Course. The hill was the highest part of the reserve and was known as Mount Rennie.

When Bill Stanley, who had fled to the nearby Redfern police station, returned with help, they found Mary lying naked and covered in blood, battered, bruised, barely alive and soaking wet. It turned out that she had tried to commit suicide by drowning herself in a drain rather than face the humiliation of the brutal mass assault.

She was rushed to Sydney Hospital but was so badly injured both physically and mentally that it was almost a week before she could give police a full account of what had happened, including descriptions of her assailants and the names they called each other by. The police knew them all.

The police dragnet rounded up 15 teenagers who were charged with 'carnally knowing and ravishing' Mary. By the time police broke it all down, as the youths gave each other up in an attempt to save themselves, 11 of them were charged and sent to trial.

In the meantime, the trusted cabbie, Charles Sweetman, was found guilty of attempted rape and given a public flogging on two separate occasions and sent to prison for 14 years.

Nine of the defendants claimed they were not at the rape scene and provided alibis. Two admitted having had sex with Mary, but said it was with her consent. But the prosecution had little trouble identifying the offenders, thanks to eyewitness accounts from Mary and the man who had tried so desperately to save her life, the brave Bill Stanley.

After a trial that lasted six days, during which the court heard from almost 100 witnesses, the jury retired and, in just two-and-a-half hours, returned a guilty verdict on nine of the 11 charged, content that the other two had watertight alibis.

Mr Justice Windeyer was damning in passing sentence. 'This poor, defenceless girl, friendless and alone, is like some wild animal hunted down by a set of savages, who spring upon her and outrage her until she lies a lifeless thing before them ... I warn you to prepare for death.' With that he sentenced all nine of them to be hanged.

All of the condemned men lodged appeals against the severity of the sentence and after their lawyers lodged one appeal after another, five of the youths were successful and had their sentences commuted to life imprisonment.

The four that remained – George Duffy, Joseph Martin, Robert Read and William Boyce – all of whom were under the age of 20, went to the gallows at Darlinghurst Gaol at 6am on the morning of 7 January 1887.

The remaining five rapists who narrowly escaped the noose were released after 10 years of hard labour. Little is known what became of them except for one – Mick Donnellan – who devoted his life to social work in the Waterloo district near where the rape had taken place. Later in his life he became a city alderman and earned great respect among those who knew him, and they forgave him for his crime.

21 THE CHARISMATIC CROOKED COP

Think of crooked cops and it's all but impossible not to think of Roger 'the Dodger' Rogerson. It seems that Rogerson has been in the headlines for one thing or another over the past 30 years and as recently as February 2005 he was sent back to prison. It all seems such a terrible end for a man who really was one of New South Wales' finest and bravest police officers.

Roger Caleb Rogerson joined the New South Wales police as a cadet in 1958 and from the very beginning showed signs of having the dedication and qualities to make an excellent investigator. Rogerson joined the force in an era when police officers were held in high profile by the media and the likes of Fred 'Froggy' Krahe and the Ray 'the Gunner' Kelly – who had shot and killed two men in course of apprehending them – were like folk heroes.

But Rogerson was going to be much more than a cop who claimed fame through killing villains in the streets of Sydney. He had much more to offer than that. He was handsome, charismatic, a proficient touch typist, took excellent shorthand, was a prolific joke teller and orator and played a good piano. To top it off he was as tough as nails and fearless in leading his troops into battle. Roger Rogerson was the perfect all-round cop the media was looking for to lift the New South Wales police out of the terrible reputation it had gathered through the Akin Liberal government's years of corruption at the highest levels.

Under the wing of Fred Krahe and colourful superintendent Don Ferguson, Rogerson learned all the tricks in the book – some of them certainly not in the police manual – and by 1974 he was moved to the armed hold-up squad. He witnessed his first killing two years later when his squad shot dead armed robber Phillip Western at Avoca Beach.

In 1977 Rogerson gained celebrity status from the press when he shot and killed an armed man who was trying to rob a courier of $60,000. In 1979 Rogerson was one of the police officers present when armed robber Gordon Thomas was shot dead in Rose Bay. In 1980 Rogerson was awarded the prestigious Peter Mitchell Award for the most outstanding performance of 1980 when, armed with a pump-action shotgun, he had taken on a car load of bank robbers and shot out the tyres of their vehicle at close range as they tried to make their getaway.

The image of Rogerson in his bulletproof vest blazing away with his shotgun at the villains was the image that the press needed to make him the new face of the allegedly incorruptible New South Wales police. They gave Rogerson as much press as he wanted and made him the police hero the public was looking for. Sadly, they were very much mistaken. The force was rotten and Rogerson was going to make the most of it.

By the early 1980s Rogerson was seen more and more associating with the likes of hit man Christopher Dale 'Mr Rentakill' Flannery and the head of the street gangsters, the most notorious gangster of his time, Neddy Smith. Rogerson claimed on TV that he hung out with the criminal milieu because they kept him informed about underworld events and so he could keep them under his control. But it was really for much more sinister reasons. They were his business partners.

The public beginning of Roger Rogerson's fall from grace was when he shot heroin dealer Warren Lanfranchi twice at point-blank range in a lane in suburban Sydney, killing him instantly. The gangster Neddy Smith had driven Lanfranchi to the meeting allegedly to give Rogerson a $10,000 bribe to get him (Lanfranchi) off charges of shooting at a police officer. Instead Rogerson killed Lanfranchi, allegedly took the money, planted a 90-year-old faulty gun in Lanfranchi's hand and claimed he shot the drug dealer in self-defence.

While a coroner's jury found that Rogerson had shot Lanfranchi while endeavouring to make an arrest, they refused to find that it was in self-defence or in the course of duty. The whole thing stunk of corruption and, for the first time, the public could see another side of Roger Rogerson.

At the same time rumours were rampant that Neddy Smith had been granted a 'green light' by corrupt New South Wales detectives led by Roger Rogerson, which gave Smith the right to commit armed robberies, sell heroin and kill whoever he wished, as long as it wasn't a police officer. Naturally the police got their cut. According to the rumours they even set up some of the armed robberies carried out by Smith.

In 1985 Rogerson was implicated in, although eventually found not to have had any involvement with, the 1983 attempted murder of undercover police officer Michael Drury. Drury was shot in his Chatswood home by the hit man Chris Flannery. In 1987 Rogerson was charged with conspiracy to pervert the course of justice when he was caught on camera closing a bank account and receiving cheques to the value of $111,000. The cheques were in turn paid to an associate in return for a false contract to justify the money.

Rogerson was found guilty on the conspiracy charges, sentenced to eight years in jail and booted out of the police force. He was released in December 1990 after a successful appeal against his conviction, but the Crown successfully appealed to the High Court and in 1992 Rogerson was sent back to jail where he served three years and nine months.

But that was not the end of it. In February 2005 Roger

Rogerson, 64, was jailed for two-and-a-half-years for giving one count of false evidence to the New South Wales Police Integrity Commission in May 1999, when he was called to give evidence to a commission whose objective was to weed out corruption. Rogerson faced a maximum of five years' jail for the offence, but judge Peter Berman took into account Rogerson's guilty plea, his age, evidence of good character in recent years and the mental hardship Rogerson would suffer in custody. Judge Berman ordered that he serve just one year of his sentence.

Roger Rogerson was released on 17 February 2006 and within days was doing the pub circuit with a highly successful on-stage comedy act comprising himself, author and self-confessed murderer Mark 'Chopper' Read, and ex-Aussie rules bad boy Mark 'Jacko' Jackson. From last reports it was bringing the house down.

It also inspired the joke: What's got four teeth and seven thongs? The front row at a Chopper, Dodger and Jacko gig.

22 MURDER BEYOND BELIEF

Child murder is considered the most despicable of all crimes. There was a time when it was an automatic death sentence. Many believe that still should be the case today. And, while all child killings are deemed to be the worst imaginable by the families and loved ones of the deceased, there are some that are so terrible that they defy belief. Such is the senseless and brutal murder of Nicole Hanns. And, as if the murder of their precious little girl wasn't enough for Nicole's parents, Gwen and Peter, to cope with, years later they had to stand by and watch as her killer was released from prison.

In 1972, John David Lewthwaite watched through a window as nine-year-old Anthony Hanns had a bath at his parents' home in Greystanes, in Sydney's west. He fantasised about killing the boy's parents and abducting, raping and murdering the boy. Two years later, on the night of 26 June 1974, the 18-year-old Lewthwaite returned to the house, but attacked Anthony's sister Nicole Margaret Hanns instead, stabbing the five-year-old 17 times. He used such force that some of the blows went right through her tiny body, injuring her heart, lungs and liver. At the time Lewthwaite was on parole after serving 15 months of a six-year sentence for arson.

When he arrived at the house, Lewthwaite silently cracked a window pane and removed the jagged glass. He then selected a long sliver to stab his intended victim with; he later exchanged it for a carving knife from the kitchen. Lewthwaite then went to young Nicole's bedroom and turned on the light. Nicole woke up. Lewthwaite motioned to her to keep quiet, then rolled her onto her stomach and stabbed her repeatedly in the back and on the arms. The attack was so violent that the knife buckled into the shape of a horseshoe.

Nicole's screams woke the family. Lewthwaite fled. Still wearing his blood-soaked clothing he took a train to North Sydney, where he exposed himself to a group of schoolboys the next day. He visited three churches, trying to make a confession, then contacted a parole officer he knew. 'I think I have hurt a little girl,' Lewthwaite said. Police were called. He confessed to the murder.

At his trial, in December 1974, Lewthwaite pleaded not guilty to murder but guilty to the manslaughter of Nicole Hanns. Court-appointed psychiatrists agreed that he was sane at the time of the murder, and said he was a danger to society.

It took the jury 90 minutes to find Lewthwaite guilty of murder. In sentencing him to life, Justice Slattery stated that he had the utmost concern as to whether Lewthwaite should ever be released. 'Regrettably, there is no future for you in society, and unless medical science can come up with a solution, there appears to be no solution to your psychiatric problems,' he said. 'The ferocity and extent of the particularly savage killing of the child indicate that you are not capable of ever leading a normal life in the community.'

In 1975, Lewthwaite escaped from Morisset Psychiatric Hospital, but he was soon recaptured. He escaped again in 1985 after being allowed out of Long Bay Jail on day leave to see his psychiatrist. The Hanns' house was put under surveillance – police feared he would return to kill Anthony – but he was caught two days later.

Lewthwaite's escape brought to the public's attention the fact that he was allowed to leave jail unaccompanied, even though he had committed one of Australia's most appalling crimes only 10 years earlier. Gwen Hanns sobbed when she heard of Lewthwaite's escape. She expressed her disgust with the prison system and demanded to know why a child killer was allowed to wander the streets alone.

'It [Lewthwaite's escape] brought back everything – the agony we have tried to keep at the back of our minds all these years,' she said. 'If the people who let him out had to go through what we have been through, they would be the first to throw away the key.'

In December 1986, Gwen and Peter Hanns were awarded the maximum $20,000 criminal injury compensation for Nicole's death. Justice Slattery commented that since the child's murder, the couple had led a secluded life. 'The couple had recovered to a degree until Lewthwaite's escape,' he said. 'They have undoubtedly suffered great trauma.'

Then, in July 1992, Lewthwaite's life sentence was reduced to a minimum of 20 years. Lewthwaite, by now a devout Christian, would be eligible for parole after 25 June 1994. He was reclassified as a C3 level prisoner at Cooma jail, making him eligible for day release.

The New South Wales Liberal government's attorney-general, John Hannaford, vowed to make amendments to the Sentencing Act, giving the Crown the ability to appeal such decisions. Other politicians pledged their support. The conservative Independent MP for Tamworth, Tony Windsor, said that Lewthwaite should be kept behind bars; Labor MP Carl Scully pledged his support to stop Lewthwaite being given parole or day release. Gwen Hanns said Mr Hannaford's intended reforms didn't go far enough: she would accept nothing less than a guarantee that Lewthwaite would be kept imprisoned for life. Mr Hannaford said he didn't believe Lewthwaite's release was in the community interest, but that vetoing his parole would leave the system open to political abuse.

Gwen Hanns lobbied against Lewthwaite being granted parole. On 29 August 1994, the Offenders Review Board denied his application, but allowed him to participate in a monthly day-release program.

With Mr Scully's support, Gwen Hanns opposed Lewthwaite's day release. Their cause was backed by Bob Carr, then the leader of the New South Wales Labor Opposition. Mr Scully alleged that psychiatric reports on Lewthwaite suggested he would kill again. Prison informants alleged that he had raped an inmate in jail.

Lewthwaite was again refused parole on 6 October 1995 and 19 July 1996. Again, Gwen Hanns had campaigned against his release. She was also there in 1997, demanding psychiatric assessments of Lewthwaite in her ongoing battle to keep him behind bars. 'I don't want the public to think I'm out for vengeance,' she stressed. 'My main worry is other kids, other parents' children who may become Lewthwaite's next victims. What I'm saying is I'd rather he got me than someone else's baby. If he's cured, if he has been treated and tested, then let the doctors tell me – and prove to me he is no longer a danger to society. While I get sick and tired of fighting to keep Lewthwaite in jail, I'm never going to give up. While there's breath in me, I'll never stop this fight.' She also compiled a list of 22 criminals who had committed murder after being released from jail, where they had served time for serious crimes.

On 2 May 1997, with Bob Carr's Labor government now in power in New South Wales, Lewthwaite's application for day release – the first step on the road to parole – was rejected. Instead, he was transferred to the new Metropolitan Reception and Remand Centre and placed on an in-jail work program.

In June 1997, Lewthwaite wrote a letter to the *Sydney Morning Herald* claiming that politics – not the fact that he had viciously murdered a child – was keeping him in prison. He said he wanted to be accepted as a man who has come to terms with his homosexuality. He stated that he had a long-term partner and had overcome the urge to sexually abuse boys. He added that he had taken God into his life not simply to improve his chances of parole, but to provide spiritual guidance.

'I am not an evil, cold-blooded killer,' he said. 'If I knew 23 years ago that the torture of uncertainty I would be put through when I finally was eligible for parole, the light at the end of what seems to be a tunnel that goes on forever and is all but extinguished whenever a politician who knows nothing about me except a 23-year-old crime decides to jump up and down for his votes, if I knew that I would be made to feel like the most despicable person alive by people who generate nothing but hatred, then I would never have applied to be released from jail.'

He went on to say that he felt eternal remorse for his crime, but believed he had earned a future out of prison. 'If there had been a death penalty in 1974, I would have gladly placed the noose around my own neck,' he said. 'What's done can't be undone.'

Gwen Hanns didn't believe him. 'He had over 20 years to say he's sorry – why now?' she asked. 'Because he thinks it will get him out.'

On 2 March 1998, the parole board rejected Lewthwaite's annual application for parole, saying, he 'should remain in jail because he would not be able to adjust to normal lawful community life, there was a risk that he would reoffend, he needed further participation in a pre-release program and his release would not be in the public interest.'

Lewthwaite was given the chance to present his case for release at an open public hearing held on 27 April 1998. At this hearing the board heard arguments against his release from Gwen Hanns and Dr Rod Milton, a forensic psychiatrist. The board announced that Lewthwaite would stay in prison.

At another parole application in 1999 he was successful and, on 21 June 1999, he walked from prison – under the strictest parole conditions the law would allow, but nevertheless a free man. John Lewthwaite lives in rural New South Wales with his long-time male partner, who he met inside prison.

23 THE SUITCASE KILLER

Edwin Street's murders went largely unnoticed by the press, but that didn't make them any less evil. Given the 42-year-old invalid pensioner's record of crimes against women and girls, it seemed only a matter of time before he committed murder and was locked away forever.

On 17 December 1993, Street's wife, Dawn Rebecca Street, 42, a charity worker who cared for quadriplegics, was found dead in a park in Wollstonecraft, on Sydney's north shore. She had been buried in a bag. Although there was no sign of violence, the post-mortem revealed that the woman had been suffocated.

When police checked out Street's record he immediately became a suspect. He had a number of convictions for carnal knowledge and indecent assault. In 1989 he was sentenced to four years' jail for attacking a young woman who had rejected his sexual advances.

But he steadfastly denied any knowledge of his wife's murder. He alleged that he had last seen her when she left their home and went for a pint of milk at 8.30pm three weeks earlier, on 29 November. He apparently hadn't thought to tell the police that his wife had gone missing.

Appearing emotionally distraught after the discovery of his wife's body, Street made gut-wrenching appeals to the general public on radio and TV for any clue that may solve the mystery of the murder of his loved one.

Street sobbed uncontrollably as he begged: 'Anyone with any information should let somebody know, because if I have to come out and do my own little investigation I will.' As one detective said later, 'It would have brought a tear to a glass eye.'

With the investigation going nowhere, detectives decided it might be a good idea to collect a few of the dead woman's things to help the investigation along. As it turned out, this was an excellent idea, but the result was not in the least what they expected.

On 23 February 1994, detectives called on Street's home in Enmore, in Sydney's inner west. He ushered them in and suggested they have a good look around and take whatever of his late wife's clothing and personal effects they wanted, if it might help them solve her murder.

Having collected various items, the detectives asked Street if they could use the suitcase sitting in the bottom of the wardrobe to take them back to the police station. Street hesitated, but it was too late. Before Street could stop him, a detective had opened the suitcase.

Inside was the body of Ms Linda Whitton. Ms Whitton had been living with Street for less than a week.

Street explained that during a ferocious fight Linda Whitton produced a knife and stabbed herself seven times before he could wrestle the knife from her. The detectives weren't convinced: one of the stab wounds was in Ms Whitton's back.

Under questioning, Street broke down and confessed to stabbing Ms Whitton to death in a fit of rage and hiding her body in the suitcase. He then also confessed to the murder of his wife. He told police that he had a short temper when it came to women and he had snapped when his wife had told him that one of her ex-boyfriends was a better lover than he was.

Street said that in a fit of rage he'd held a pillow over his wife's face until she was still. He then had a few drinks and went to sleep. The following morning he awoke to discover that his wife was dead.

He panicked then, he said. He put Dawn Street's body in a bag, packed it neatly into a suitcase, rang for a cab and bundled the suitcase into the boot. He instructed the cab driver to take him to the park at Berry Island Reserve where, when there was no one around, he dug a hole in the shrubbery and buried the bag with the body in it. He then caught a cab home.

Street was found guilty of the murders at his trial in the Supreme Court. Justice Dunford said Street's original story about Linda Whitton stabbing herself was 'obviously absurd, as the jury has found' and described the murders of the two women, who were both small and both epileptic, as brutal in the extreme.

'I regard the prospects of rehabilitation as only slight and the risks of his reoffending as significant,' he said.

At Street's sentencing, on 29 June 1995, Justice Dunford said Street had a 'terrifying record of physical violence', particularly towards women.

Justice Dunford told the court: 'The maximum penalty is intended for the worst category of cases, and I regard the quite separate murders of two women some 12 weeks apart as amongst the worst category of cases.' He then imposed the maximum sentence – life without the possibility of parole.

As he was led from the court, Street uttered Ned Kelly's final words: 'Such is life.'

But that final flippancy was the only thing that Edwin Street and Ned Kelly had in common. For all his shortcomings, even Ned Kelly's detractors would concede that Ned's principles wouldn't allow him to prey on women.

Edwin Street has no principles. He is a killer and basher of defenceless women and a molester of children. The remainder of his life will be spent in jail.

24 EDDIE 'THE FIREMAN' BIRCHLEY

Few punters have set Sydney racetracks alight the way that the appropriately nicknamed Eddie 'the Fireman' Birchley did in the 1970s. Birchley achieved his nickname because he had once worked as a fireman, but even more so because he loved backing horses that were long-odds on – or, as they say in racing parlance, well and truly in the red. Birchley was fearless and his betting duels with Sydney's leading rails bookies are the stuff legends are made of.

Birchley was not a criminal. Rather he was a thoroughly decent bloke who punted with his own money in cash or building society cheques. The only reason that he has wound up here in *Crime File* is because in the end – as has been the case with many famous punters over the years – he had to resort to crime, albeit petty crime, not to gamble, but merely to live.

Little is known about Birchley's early life except that he was born in 1931, was a fitness fanatic who specialised in long-distance swimming and had been a successful boxer with 13 professional wins to his credit. The legend goes that at 17 he won £700 on a greyhound named Good Silk and bought prime waterfront real estate with the winnings. A short man with a crew cut, he lived at Surfers Paradise, where he actually worked as a fireman for 17 years. He invested his savings wisely over the years in then cheap Gold Coast real estate and built up a healthy portfolio, which he used as collateral for his sojourn into big-time punting.

During the 1960s the Brisbane papers referred to Birchley as a 'mystery Gold Coast punter' and went on to describe him as 'a bloke who'd been punting in thousands for 25 years and had kept building up his bank with his winnings from backing long odds-on favourites over the years on Brisbane racetracks'. Birchley's really big plunges began in the 1960s when the Queensland Government guaranteed a profit in the early days of the TAB. There was a guaranteed profit of 10 per cent – or 10/1 on – on all winning bets, irrespective of the odds. Birchley made a fortune backing unbeatable favourites and soon the government had to change the law.

By the early 1970s Birchley's plunges on short-priced favourites became too big for the Brisbane on-course bookies to handle and he flew south for the Saturday meetings in Melbourne and Sydney, where he consistently laid bets of $100,000, mostly on short-priced two-year-olds. 'I'll always be happy to lay 4/1 on (that's outlaying $4 to win just $1 plus your outlay back) if I think the correct price should be 100/1 on,' the Fireman, as he was now known in the papers, told a reporter. And he wasn't frightened to put his money where his mouth was.

The Fireman wreaked havoc with the Sydney and Melbourne bookies: he placed mammoth bets in cash from his plastic carry bag or with building society cheques that, in today's money, would be in the high hundreds of thousands and, in some cases, over a million dollars. In December 1973 he invested more than $50,000 and backed the Melbourne filly Elle from 2/1 to even money at Moonee Valley to collect $127,000 profit.

The Fireman grabbed the nation's attention when he plunged $208,000 on the two-year-old colt Caboul at Flemington in

November 1974. In doing so Caboul's odds of 3/1 on firmed to a ridiculous 6/1 on and, for his staggering outlay, the Fireman won just $45,000. The same month he outlaid $50,000 to win $25,000 on Debbie-Jo at Rosehill and $60,000 to win just $15,000 on St Louis Blue at Warwick Farm.

The Fireman was on a roll and Australians sat back and watched in delight. If there was anything that Aussies punters loved it was to see the bookies taking a pounding. In 1974 the Fireman won over $200,000 during the three-day Autumn Carnival at Flemington when he won $80,000 on Cap d'Antibes at short odds, lay $100,000 to win just $20,000 on Roy Higgins mount Leilani in the Queen's Plate, and collected $70,000 on Cuban Crisis and $40,000 on Better Draw. He also had a plonk on Lord Dudley in the Sires Produce Stakes and the terrified bookies couldn't register the price on their boards because they only went as high as 1/10. Lord Dudley won and the Fireman cleaned up again – albeit not much given the short starting price of 1/15 on.

But as they say in racing, 'You bet backwards, you eventually end up going backwards', and it was only a matter of time before things turned sour for the Fireman. It all began to go pear shaped when he plunged $105,000 on two-year-old Danish Dancer at 1/4 to win just on $25,000. Danish dancer was beaten by Sheil Sail. Two weeks later the Fireman had a plonk on the short-priced Sheil Sail only to see it beaten by – wait for it – Danish Dancer. Later that day he bet $70,000 on another loser, Princess Thalia.

Embittered by the reversal of fortunes by Danish Dancer and Sheil Sail, the Fireman claimed that the fix was in and alleged that there was a signalling system between jockeys and bookies to ensure that heavily backed favourites got beaten. He threatened to put in a report to the AJC, but nothing came of it.

In 1975 Birchley lost $75,000 on Cap d'Antibes in the AJC Oaks in April, outlaid $50,000 to win $16,000 on the filly Gay Nineties at Randwick in May, won $62,000 on Bilgola Boy at Randwick in July but lost $60,000 on the Melbourne filly Juanita Gay in August. From there on, with his good fortune on the decline, the Fireman disappeared from the headlines.

In July 1980, 49-year-old Edward Albert Granville Birchley was fined $225 in the Tweed Heads Court after pleading guilty to several charges. He was convicted of stealing a packet of sausages, pork chops, a packet of peas, a chocolate, coffee whitener, and a packet of bacon, all from Woolworths, and of stealing a pair of single sheets valued at $5.99 and a packet of Pollyfilla valued at $2.75 from Target.

Today he lives a quiet life on the Gold Coast with his memories of once being Australia's biggest and most brazen punter.

25 THE FRANK BUTLER MURDERS

Despite the fact that gold has never been found in the scenic but sleepy Blue Mountains area of New South Wales, the lure of instant riches was all it took to draw three men to their deaths in the quiet region west of Sydney back in 1896. The ensuing hunt for the cold-blooded murderer would reach around the globe.

The story began on the night of 12 August 1896, when a man in his late 20s by the name of Burgess answered an ad in the *Sydney Morning Herald* looking for a helping hand on a gold-prospecting expedition. Burgess arrived at Gilham's Hotel on Pitt Street in Sydney's central business district looking for the man who had placed the ad – Frank Butler, a resident of the establishment.

The next morning, the pair set out by horse and wagon for the long and tiring journey west along Parramatta Road and beyond. Butler was in charge of the horses, while Burgess rode shotgun. In the rear of the red buggy sat all of their luggage and mining equipment. A lone bushie trekked past the pair 11 days later when they had set up camp at a spot roughly 65 kilometres out from the rural town of Parkes. Not long after that another person ventured past their lonely campsite. But, ominously, only Frank Butler could be seen. Just a few days later, Butler sold the wagon and horses and went back to his Pitt Street hotel. It would be several months before Burgess' tragic fate would be revealed.

Butler, however, still seemed set on his get-rich-quick gold-hunting scheme and placed another ad looking for help. But finding an applicant who was suitable – whatever his specific requirements may have been – proved too hard. Instead, Butler answered an ad himself, this one placed by a man named David Yates. According to Yates, gold had been found in the fields of Manning River, north of Sydney. He wanted an offsider with prospecting experience to help him strike it lucky.

Butler convinced Yates he was the man for the job, and the pair soon caught a train to Grafton together. They hit the yellow jackpot just a few short days later. Even though the nugget was only small, the men were ecstatic; luck was with them. Butler, though, revealing a somewhat shifty side to his nature, wanted to hide their find from the many other prospectors set up in the region. Yates refused to do so, explaining that it was an unseemly idea. As a result, the partnership quickly dissolved and Butler once again returned to the big smoke to round up volunteers for an expedition of his own. He interviewed one gentleman by the name of Michael Conroy, but he backed out unexpectedly before the pair could set out. It was only a matter of months before Conroy would realise just what a smart – and life-saving – decision he had made.

Not to be disheartened, Butler set up his operations in the Railway Dining Rooms in Sydney and was eventually called upon by three chaps – a 20-year-old geology student named Arthur Preston, and two of his friends from the inner-city boarding house where he was staying. Preston came from a wealthy family and Butler was soon trying to impress the young group with tall tales from his various fossicking adventures. Preston fell for the lofty spiel and even offered to front for half of the expenses to fund their expedition. The financial offer was music to Butler's greedy ears and he told Preston that the pair of them would be leaving within the next few days.

Preston's mates waved the two men off from Redfern station the following Monday evening, with Butler yelling back to them from the moving train that it would be as long as six weeks before they returned to the city.

Butler and Preston alighted from the locomotive at Emu Plains station, where they were bid goodbye by Elias Thomson, the owner of the Railway Dining Rooms, who coincidentally happened to be travelling on the same train. Butler told Thomson that he and Preston would be camping in the area overnight. He then set off down the road with Preston by his side, the men hiking into the sunset with their equipment-laden packs heavy upon their backs.

But the idea of anyone actually prospecting in the mountains struck many of the locals as utter foolishness, and news of Butler and Preston's foolhardy expedition spread quickly. Three days after their arrival in the region, they were seen camped near the village of Linden, a fair distance up the mountains. Labourer George Campbell walked past the pair and told them that he thought it was a strange place to be looking for the precious mineral. Sitting down and cleaning a gun that was resting across his knees, Butler informed Campbell that they had already found traces of gold in the grass. His claim was backed up by an eager Preston, and Campbell continued on his way.

Alone again, and with their camp set up, Butler told Preston to dig a trench. He specified that it should be at least half a metre deep. Once Preston had performed the duty, Butler shot him through the back of the head with his rifle and buried the young man.

Two days later Butler left the region, returning to Sydney by train, where he was once again spotted by Elias Thomson on 25 October. The hotel keeper asked why the prospector was back in town so soon after heading out to find his fortune, and Butler explained that Preston had taken ill. He added that he had returned to Sydney to find another offsider. Indeed, Butler had already placed another ad in the *Sydney Morning Herald* seeking a 'young male' to help him on his quest. He specified that no previous prospecting experience was necessary, and that any find would be split evenly.

It wasn't long before Butler set off in search of gold once again. This time his partner was Lee Weller, a one-time ship's captain whose beloved wife had recently passed away. Dwelling on his loss, Weller had been drinking a lot. He saw the prospecting expedition as a way of putting his troubles behind him and possibly starting a new and better life. It was a common story in those tough times.

For some reason, though, Weller refused to tell his friend Bob Luckham – with whom he had been staying while trying to get his life back together – the name of his partner in the venture. All he told his close mate was that he and his mysterious partner would be setting up their first camp at Glenbrook, a fairly low region of the Blue Mountains.

After packing up his belongings – including a British Bulldog service revolver – Weller wrote a letter to his solicitor in London, explaining that he was going on an expedition in the hope that it would turn his fortunes around. He added that he was putting no money into the venture.

When Butler and Weller finally alighted at Glenbrook station, loaded with the necessary tools of the prospecting trade, they presented quite a sight. Such a sight, in fact, that the station master would distinctly recall the pair. Weller even returned to the town from their campsite about a kilometre away that evening, asking the station master for directions to a local store. The last person to see Weller alive – besides Butler – was the station master, who remembered the short, bearded man waving him farewell as he returned to the campsite loaded up with provisions from the store.

That night, Butler tricked Weller into digging his own grave, the same as he had with Preston. He then used Weller's own revolver to shoot him dead just before dawn. After committing the murder, Butler went through the former sea captain's belongings, discovering a ticket to reclaim a chest that had been left for safekeeping at Central Station in Sydney.

Some time later that morning, Butler went to a pub at Emu Plains and struck up a conversation with a down-on-his-luck swagman by the name of Peter Farrell. Butler gave Farrell a bag full of food and told him he could find clothes and provisions at his abandoned campsite. He then drew a map to help the bushie find his way to where he had killed his short-time partner.

Back in Sydney, Butler went to redeem the ticket for Weller's chest, and could hardly believe his luck when he saw its contents. He had hit an unexpected jackpot. Besides clothing and books there were guns, as well as a selection of jewels. Butler quickly offloaded everything but the jewels at a nearby secondhand shop for 45 shillings. He left town a short time later, making his way to the shipping port of Newcastle north of Sydney and signing into the local Sailors' Home under Captain Lee Weller's name.

Within a week, the *Swanhilde*, a four-masted ship in Newcastle to source a load of coal, contacted the Sailors' Home looking for five worthy seaman. Captain Colin Fraser was surprised that someone with the experience of 'Captain' Lee Weller was willing to take a job as a deckhand, but he welcomed the experienced sailor on board and they soon set sail, bound for the bay of San Francisco, on the west coast of America. Still, if Butler thought he was making a stealthy getaway he would be in for a sound surprise.

Two days before the *Swanhilde* made its way out of Newcastle, authorities in Sydney received a letter from the real Weller's friend Bob Luckham. It seemed Luckham was worried about the safety of his mate who had gone off prospecting with a stranger. Detective John Roche wasted no time in contacting Glenbrook police station, where a Detective McLean soon went out looking for the men who everyone presumed were lost in the rugged bush of the Blue Mountains.

With the help of two indigenous Australian trackers, McLean searched the abandoned campsite near the station, finding a suit jacket, trousers with the initials 'FJ' printed inside, and the remains of a wallet that had been burnt in the fire. The find quickly made the Sydney papers, where the story was read by one of Arthur Preston's friends, Robert Fielding, who had seen

Preston and Butler off from Redfern station. Fielding went to the authorities on 27 November, telling Detective Roche all he knew about Butler and his missing friend.

But Fielding wasn't the only person whose interest in the case was piqued by the newspaper article. Mr Gilham, the owner of Gilham's Hotel where Butler had stayed, told the police that Butler had given a photo of himself to his daughter. The *Evening News* paper ran a follow-up story explaining how Butler had made many friends among the staff at the hotel, even shouting drinks for the waiters.

Meanwhile, as many as 200 locals joined police teams to search the Blue Mountains in pouring rain, looking for any trace of the missing men. After dragging a lagoon and trekking through hectare after hectare of dense bush, a blue silk shirt was located in an old mine shaft. The shirt was wrapped around 18 rifle cartridges. Further investigation revealed a half-burnt legging that was later identified as belonging to Arthur Preston. Preston's landlady would later explain that the young man had been wearing the item when he left for his ill-fated trip.

Sensing something was now amiss, the police issued a reward of £25 for anyone who could find Captain Lee Weller. They also issued a description of Frank Butler, stating that he was around 40 years old, well muscled, 175 centimetres tall with a dark moustache and dark hair that was peppered with grey. They also noted that he had a distinctive nose, explaining that it pointed to the left at the end and was flat on its bridge. The description struck a chord with Detective McHattie in Newcastle. A man fitting the bulletin had been a lodger at the local Sailors' Home. He made inquiries but found out the man he was talking about went by the name of Captain Lee Weller, and he had already shipped out for San Francisco. Nonetheless, he reported the news and it made its way into the press.

At the same time, the team of searchers combing the Blue Mountains stumbled across part of a shirt in a section of scrub. Closer investigation revealed the initials 'ATOP' inside the collar. They were Arthur Preston's initials. Concentrating their efforts around the village of Linden, authorities soon stumbled upon Peter Farrell, the swaggie Butler had offloaded his spare food on before returning to Sydney. Speaking to the loner, they quickly realised that Preston had probably met a sticky end at Butler's hands. But without a body, they had little proof. Despite ongoing bad weather, the searchers doubled their efforts, and it wasn't long before two police officers made the find they had all been waiting for.

Constables Delaney and Hardiman were making the lonely trek back to Linden, after a day of looking for signs as to the whereabouts of Arthur Preston, when Delaney happened to notice a patch of freshly turned dirt sitting beneath a rock ledge, which had protected it from the rain. Delaney approached the mound and poked a stick into it. The smell that erupted from the patch turned the men's stomachs immediately. And it only got worse the further they burrowed into the pile. They soon uncovered what remained of a human skull.

Delaney was quick to return to Linden to alert the others and it wasn't long before the bush grave site was teaming with experienced police officers and experts in forensics. Arthur Preston's friend Bob Fielding was also taken to the area so that he could identify his dead mate. He confirmed what everybody had already supposed, and Preston's body was laid to rest the next afternoon at Sydney's famous Rookwood Cemetery, where a large crowd gathered to watch the spectacle, having kept up with the story in the media.

Delaney's find spurred on the sagging spirits of the team of searchers. As they renewed their efforts to find the body of Captain Lee Weller, the government raised the reward to a substantial £125. They lure of the cash brought large groups of would-be searchers to Linden the next weekend, and it was only a short time later that Weller's remains were uncovered in strikingly similar circumstances. Bob Luckham was brought in to identify his friend at the makeshift mountain grave. He easily recognised Captain Lee Weller's pipe, also buried in the soil. An arrest warrant was soon issued for Frank Butler, though – seemingly in the clear on the high seas under an assumed name – he could have no idea of the controversy he had stirred up, or the trouble he was in.

As Weller, Butler had earned himself the nickname 'the Preacher' during his time on the *Swanhilde*. This was because he had been acting the part of a man with strong morals who went as far as to point out when his fellow sailors were using foul language. But his days as Weller were numbered.

When the *Swanhilde* passed the Kermadec Islands, almost 1000 kilometres northeast of North Zealand, they were approached by a steamer named the *Taupo*, which soon sent a long boat holding their second officer and four sailors to speak to Captain Fraser. The *Taupo* had been in Auckland two days earlier, where the Blue Mountains murders were all over the local papers. Fraser was shown clippings about the case, but didn't see any connection, despite the fact his ship was named in the articles. After all, they had no crewmember by the name of Butler. As the longboat pulled away, however, they threw a bunch of full newspapers onto the deck of the *Swanhilde*. Captain Fraser took them to his cabin to read about the strange murders in peace. It was here that he saw a name he did recognise – Lee Weller.

Fraser decided to discuss the case in confidence with his first mate. The *Swanhilde* was still seven weeks away from their destination of San Francisco. The crew were working well together and, besides, their Captain Weller hardly seemed capable of murder. Then there was the problem that if they did do something about the situation, and the man calling himself Weller turned out to be legitimate, the shipping company could be liable for damages for false arrest. The decision was made to keep quiet about the matter until they reached their final port of call.

Meanwhile, news of the grisly finds in the mountains spread across Australia like wildfire, and it wasn't long before the licensee of the Courthouse Hotel in Orange came forth to tell of a man fitting Butler's description passing through the region some months earlier, in August. The man had been travelling in a red wagon, with a younger man riding beside him.

Authorities throughout the area started looking into the matter but it was a man and his son out looking for wild beehives who would soon discover the putrid remains of Burgess, buried under some dirt some 45 kilometres from a small hamlet called

Waroo. The decaying corpse was taken to nearby Parkes where it was found to carry Frank Butler's murder signature – a bullet through the rear of the skull. The Sydney authorities contacted the San Francisco police department and they prepared for the *Swanhilde*'s arrival. New South Wales Attorney-General John Want asked the local law keepers to arrest Butler as soon as his ship docked. In Washington, the British Ambassador arranged a warrant for one Lee Weller to be arrested for murder.

As these preparations were under way, Australian police officer Detective McHattie set out for San Francisco on the fastest steamer possible. Accompanying him was Michael Conroy, who had earlier made a last-minute decision not to go searching for gold with Butler. The pair made it to the western Californian city ahead of the *Swanhilde*, and the story was soon all over the local media.

With the *Swanhilde* still three days from its destination, Butler – or Weller to the crew – approached Captain Fraser and made a request, captain to captain. When the ship docked, he wanted to be allowed to leave it straight away, without having to go through the customary rigmarole. He explained that, holding the rank of ship's captain, he would find it embarrassing to be seen working at the level of regular seaman. Fraser told him that would be fine. But Butler's precautions would come to no avail.

The *Swanhilde* made its way into San Francisco's famous bay just before 4am on the morning of 2 February 1897. Joining Detective McHattie and Michael Conroy on the customs boat that went out to meet it was Detective Roche, who had also been sent from Australia to attend to the matter. Conroy wore a false beard, just in case he was recognised by Butler.

Once the customs vessel reached the *Swanhilde*, Fraser ordered his crew on to the deck for a medical inspection. The captain spoke to the man in charge of proceedings for a short time in private, then the group walked down in front of the assembled men, standing on deck with their hands out to be inspected.

They soon reached the murderer passing himself off as Lee Weller, at which point Captain Fraser indicated that they had the man they wanted. As Butler looked into the barrel of a pistol, the Australian contingent boarded the *Swanhilde*. Conroy approached the man who had surely planned to kill him, removed his false beard and asked Butler if he recognised him. The game was up. As the ship headed towards the dock, the authorities searched Butler's belongings. They found the jewels that had belonged to the real Weller, as well as photos of the dead sea captain's wife.

Butler was taken ashore and questioned at City Hall. But all those waiting for him to face justice back home in Australia would have to be patient; the offender had to go up against a local district court judge before the Americans would pass him on to another country.

Butler, meanwhile, relished his new-found and bizarre celebrity status. A natural actor – as shown by his ability to lure three men to their deaths, as well as the tricking of the *Swanhilde*'s crew into thinking he was far more forthright than he really was – he delighted in entertaining visitors with stories of his exploits (some of which were true, others of which bordered on the ridiculous).

The famous San Francisco boxer Gentleman Jim Corbett was just one of many who passed through the local jail to speak with the famous murderer. Indeed, several of the crew from the *Swanhilde* visited, if only to see if it were true: could the pious man they dubbed the Preacher really be capable of cold-blooded murder?

When Butler finally found himself on the stand in front of a judge, Michael Conroy was called upon to tell his story of almost going on a prospecting expedition with the accused. Former shipmates of the murdered Lee Weller also took the stand to assert that Butler was indeed an imposter.

Though it seemed obvious to all involved that this was an open and shut case, it took a month before the Secretary of State finally signed the extradition request, though appeal requests by Butler's defence team added another three weeks to the wait to bring him to justice in Australia. By the time he was due to make the long trip home, though, Butler was a changed man. No longer boastful, proud and full of tall stories, he boarded the *Mariposa* with bandages covering his wrists, grim reminders of a failed suicide attempt. With Conroy and detectives McHattie and Roche by his side, Butler looked a lonely and beaten man.

Still, with the help of brandy and sea breeze, he brightened up considerably during the journey. It's even said he sang a duet during the trip with a famous actress of the day named Maggie Moore.

Butler's trial kicked off at Sydney's Central Criminal Court on the rain-drenched morning of 14 June 1897, amid a flurry of press damning him as a brutal murderer. Chief Justice Sir Frederick Darley presided over the case, with Attorney-General John Want acting for the prosecution, and Walter Edmunds, a local barrister, doing what he could for the defence. The court was stunned as Lee Weller's skull was produced, with the fatal bullet hole in the back of it.

Because of his earlier suicide attempt, Butler was kept under constant watch while housed at Darlinghurst Gaol during the trial. Despite the surveillance, though, he managed another attempt, slashing at his own throat with a piece of metal from a tobacco tin. He finally took the stand to speak in his own defence the next afternoon, his voice barely audible because of the deep cut.

Butler told his version of the events, which was that Weller – deeply depressed, no doubt because of the death of his wife – had died by accident. He contended that Weller had taken out his revolver with the intention of shooting himself. Realising what his companion was about to do, Butler wrestled with him and the gun discharged, killing Weller in the process. John Want laughed off the idea as fanciful. It only took the jury 80 minutes to decide that Frank Butler was a murderer.

Butler went to the gallows at 9am on the Friday morning of 16 July 1897. As the hood was placed over his head and he prepared to drop to his death with the noose around his neck, he screamed out, 'Let's go! Let's go!' Then he went.

26 A MURDER LIKE NO OTHER

Unless the killer confesses – and that is highly unlikely given the nature of her crime – it will forever remain a mystery as to whether or not the murder of John Price included cannibalism. What is for certain is that what his spouse, Katherine Kright, did with his corpse is a horror story of Gothic proportions unprecedented in Australia, probably the world.

In an attempt to draw any sort of comparison to this extraordinary crime we must first take a look at some atrocities of a similar nature throughout history.

In Wisconsin, USA, in 1957, after having sex with decomposing cadavers and skinning them, Ed Gein ate the body parts. When local police eventually caught up with the mild-mannered hillbilly on his farm, they found the headless body of a woman hanging from the rafters. It had been gutted and dressed like a deer. A human heart was sizzling away in the frying pan in preparation for lunch. The refrigerator was stocked with body parts neatly wrapped in newspaper.

Investigators also found lampshades and facemasks made out of human skin, a soup dish made from a hollowed-out human skull, a belt made of nipples and human skin slippers.

Ed confessed that he liked dancing around in the farmyard by the light of the moon with a real women's torso, tanned like shoe leather and oiled to keep it supple, strapped around his middle. Needless to say, farmer Ed was locked away in the rubber room at the state mental facility until he died in 1984.

In Philadelphia, USA, in 1986, 42-year-old army pensioner Gary Heidnik kidnapped women and kept them chained up in his cellar as sex slaves, eventually murdering some of them and eating their remains. Heidnik kept as many as five women in his cellar at a time, until one escaped and called the cops.

What police found in Heidnik's cellar defies imagination. Four young women who had been repeatedly tortured, raped and beaten, sat chained in filth and squalor in the dungeon. There was a young woman's head stewing in a pot on the kitchen stove and human ribs in a roasting dish that was presumably going to be their – and Gary's – dinner.

But long before Ed Gein and Gary Heidnik shocked the world with their culinary preferences, people had been murdering, violating corpses and eating each other. Back in 1570, an evil bit of work named Peter Stump roamed the German countryside, faithfully aided and abetted by his mistress and daughter, in search of young women to tear to shreds to satisfy his bloodlust for human flesh.

Stump had also eaten a freshly born baby that was the result of his incestuous relationship with his daughter. Urged on by the two women, in five years Stump murdered 15 women and children and ravenously ate their hearts while they were hot, along with other delectable body parts.

When caught, the law's retribution for the evil trio was almost as barbaric as their crimes. Stump was tied to a cart wheel and the flesh was pulled from his bones with red-hot pincers. Still alive, his arms and legs were then broken with a wooden hatchet and he was beheaded. His headless corpse was then burned alongside his mistress and daughter.

Australia's dark past isn't without a taste of human flesh, either. In 1822 convict Alexander Pearce escaped from the Hell's Gates penal settlement in southern Tasmania with seven other prisoners. After a few days in the freezing conditions, three of the escapees returned to prison, leaving the others to systematically murder and eat one another to survive.

Finally it came down to two men, Pearce and Robert Greenhill, who stalked each other until Pearce outwitted Greenhill, killed him with an axe and ate him. Pearce was eventually captured and returned to prison where, incredibly, he wasn't sentenced to death for escaping or for the ensuing cannibalism.

But the next time Pearce wasn't so fortunate when he persuaded fellow convict Thomas Cox to escape with him. Once on the outside Pearce killed Cox and ate him too. Alexander Pearce was hanged in Hobart in 1824.

The 'Werewolf of Hannover', Fritz Haarmann, delighted in killing his victims by biting through their throats while raping them and gorging on the meat and blood. In cohorts with another deviant, Hans Grans, the pair abducted, sexually assaulted and murdered as many as 50 transient young men in Germany between 1919 and 1924.

In his lucrative profession as a dealer in second-hand clothes and meat, Haarmann was in a perfect position to capitalise on Germany's recent crushing defeat in World War One by giving his starving fellow Germans exactly what they wanted ... fresh meat.

His black-market customers, who were delighted with their lovely cuts of veal and hindquarters of lamb, must have wondered where they came from in such grim times, but not in their wildest dreams did they think that they were from the two youths a week that Haarmann and Grans were raping, murdering and cutting up for sale. Haarmann was beheaded in 1924.

No crimes in history were more abhorrent than those of deranged 64-year-old house painter Albert Fish. Passing himself off as an innocuous, benevolent little old man, Fish abducted, molested, tortured, castrated and ate at least 16 children in New York and all over the USA between 1928 and 1934. What made

Fish's crimes even more ghastly was that he was a prolific writer and his jottings included a letter to the parents of a little girl telling them in detail how he had murdered, dissected, cooked and ate their daughter. This letter would be his undoing.

Born in 1870, Albert Fish was a devout Christian who married in 1898, fathering six children. When his wife eloped in 1917, Albert's latent perversions boiled to the surface and he began indulging in coprophilia (eating human excreta), inserting alcohol-soaked cotton-wool balls in his anus and lighting them, getting his children to beat him bloody with a nail-studded paddle and inserting needles into his genitals.

In 1928, in response to an advertisement, Fish, calling himself Frank Howard, called on the Budd family in New York, taking with him cheese and strawberries. While their 12-year-old daughter Gracie was sitting on the cuddly old man's lap he was fantasising about eating her. Fish convinced the Budds to let him take Gracie to a local children's party. That was the last they would see of her.

Six years later, in 1934, the Budd family received a letter, which read in part:

> *I took Gracie to an empty house in the country. I grabbed her and she said she would tell her mamma. First I stripped her naked. How she did kick, bite and scratch. I choked her to death, then cut her into small pieces so I could take my meat to my rooms, cook it and eat it. How sweet and tender her little ass was roasted in the oven. It took me nine days to eat her entire body. I did not fuck her though I could have had I wished. She died a virgin.*

The letter was traced to Fish and hardened police retched as Albert described to them how he had cooked and eaten another little boy's buttocks: 'I put strips of bacon over each cheek and put it in the oven,' he said. 'When the meat was roasted for about a quarter of an hour, I poured a pint of water over for gravy and put in the onions. At frequent intervals I basted with a wooden spoon so the meat would be nice and juicy. In two hours it was nice and brown. I never ate any turkey that tasted half as good as his sweet, fat little behind did. I ate every bit of the meat in about four days.'

Albert Fish was delighted to die in the electric chair, describing it as the 'ultimate experience in pain', and went to his death like a man going to a picnic, even helping them strap him in.

And no doubt to Albert Fish's eternal pleasure, the metal pins and needles self-embedded in his genitals and scrotum caused the electric chair to short circuit and the first charge failed to kill him. Amid wisps of blue smoke Albert was sent smiling to his maker with the second charge.

Over a 21-year period, from 1955 to 1976, Joachim Kroll murdered, mutilated and had sex with the corpses of at least 14 young women and children throughout Germany. After he had had his way with their bodies he would cook them up and eat them, the younger the better. When captured, he told police that he loved the meat of young children as it fell off the bone, and he said it was of much better quality than the meat available in the West German butcher shops.

When police searched Kroll's foul-smelling apartment, in the refrigerator they found pieces of human flesh on a plate. Scattered around the loungeroom were putrefying bags of human flesh, stripped from his victim's bones with a butcher's knife. On the stove was a simmering vegetable stew with a tiny human hand in it. Joachim Kroll was declared a mental defective, placed in a mental asylum and never to be released under any circumstances.

Of all of the modern-day cannibal killers, 56-year-old Andrei Chikatilo, who, in a 24-year killing career in Russia through the '70s, '80s, and '90s that saw the horrific deaths and cannibalisation of 53 victims, mainly children, was by far the most prolific. Like Kroll, Chikatilo was a necrophiliac in that his victims had to be dead before he could have sex with them.

Blaming his lust for human flesh on the fact that as a boy he witnessed his younger brother being eaten alive by villagers in a famine, Chikatilo selected his victims from the runaways and young prostitutes that hung around bus and train stations. Once he had lured his victims into the nearby woods on the promise of a meal or money, he would set upon them and hack them to death, rape the corpse and then disembowel his victim and ravage the warm internal body parts.

The fact that Chikatilo was an average-looking school teacher allowed him to blend in with the crowds at the busy venues where he selected his victims and, even though he was questioned nine times about the murders, twice near the scene of a murder (once he was carrying a knife in his bag), incredibly, police let him go.

Chikatilo was eventually caught and, at his trial, people fainted in horror as he told in graphic details how he boiled and ate the sawn-off nipples and testicles of his victims. He was executed with a single bullet to the back of the head in 1994. Chikatilo is the subject of the movie *Citizen X*.

The best-known real-life cannibal of modern times is Jeffrey Dahmer, which isn't surprising. Dahmer was a monster beyond the wildest imagination. A handsome young man, who wouldn't have had a problem in the world acquiring any amount of normal sexual partners, Dahmer was a necrophiliac, serial killer and cannibal whose perversions were incomprehensible.

His Milwaukee, USA, apartment was an execution chamber, bordello, abattoir and exclusive café with only human remains on the menu. The beverage of the day was always human blood.

From 1988 to 1991, Dahmer, a 28-year-old chocolate-factory worker, slaughtered 17 young men, raped and mutilated their corpses and then cut them up and ate their body parts. When police arrested him after a young man escaped and led them to Dahmer's apartment, they were overwhelmed by the putrid smell that hit them when they opened the door.

Inside they found three bodies dissolving in acid vats in his bedroom, a man's head in the fridge along with three other severed heads and seven skulls, hands, heads and fingers stored in the freezer. Scattered about the apartment were decapitated penises and used condoms.

Dahmer admitted to having sex with the bodies of the dead men as well as their decapitated heads and mutilated torsos. He pointed out to police that he always wore a condom when having sex with his dead partners or their body parts. Better to be safe than sorry, he said. Jeffrey Dahmer was sent to prison for 1070 years, where he was murdered several years later by another inmate.

More recently is the bizarre case of 42-year-old German computer technician Armin Meiwes who, in 2001, advertised on the internet for someone to volunteer to be killed and eaten by him. He received more than 400 replies.

All of Meiwes' prospective meals contacted him through the Gay Cannibals internet chatroom where he went under the alias of Franky from Rotenburg. Most of the applicants were rejected for a variety of reasons, which included obesity, poor health, being too old or appearing unfriendly. One man, who worked as a cook, fled after being strung up on a butcher's hook and having his body marked out for various edible parts for carving.

Meiwes finally settled on 43-year-old engineer Bernd-Juergen Brandes. For a trial run the pair cut off Brandes' penis, fried it up in a pan with some onions and ate it. Still intent on being killed and eaten, Brandes allowed Meiwes to stab him to death after a prolonged session of sex and sadomasochism.

Meiwes video-recorded killing Brandes to prove that it wasn't murder. He deep-froze and fed on the 20 kilograms of choice cuts he had taken from his victim. Meiwes was arrested after he advertised for another victim on the internet.

Since cannibalism is not illegal in Germany, in 2003 Meiwes was charged with Brandes' murder driven by sexual urges. In his defence Meiwes told the court that his victim wanted to be killed and consumed and that he was searching for a substitute brother he wanted inside him.

In explaining the effectiveness of his method, Meiwes told the court that he found himself speaking better English after eating parts of Brandes' body, reflecting the superior language skills of his victim.

In sentencing Meiwes to eight years in jail the judge said that the defendant had not committed murder in the legal sense but showed 'a behaviour that is condemned in our society – namely the killing and butchering of a human being. They were two deeply psychologically disturbed people who both wanted something from each other.'

The nature of Katherine Knight's crime has deservedly earned her a place on this rollcall of depravity.

Katherine Mary Knight was born in New South Wales on 24 October 1955. At 16 she joined her father, twin sister and brother boning out carcasses in the local abattoirs at Aberdeen, in the Hunter region, where the family had lived since 1969. She kept her beloved boning knives above her bed. In 1973 she fell in love with truck driver David Kellett, 22. Rumour had Katherine attempting to strangle David on their wedding night when he wouldn't make love to her often enough. Kellett later worked at the abattoir with Knight. She would watch him dispatch pigs with a stun gun.

Their first child, Melissa Ann, was born in 1976. Soon after, Kellett left Knight for another woman. He was unable to cope with his wife's possessiveness and violent behaviour. Knight became depressed, and placed two-month-old Melissa on the train tracks. Fortunately, the infant was rescued. Knight later threatened several people at random with an axe. She was diagnosed with postnatal depression and admitted to hospital for treatment.

On 9 August 1976, she was released into the care of her mother-in-law. Katherine and David were soon back living together in Queensland, where David drove trucks and Katherine took a job boning in Ipswich. But Knight still flew into regular violent rages, often assaulting her husband. On 6 March 1980, they had another daughter, Natasha Maree. Then, in 1984, David returned from work one day to find that Katherine had moved out, taking the children. She was back at the Aberdeen abattoir, using her maiden name again.

A year later, Knight's back gave out. She gave up work. The government found her a Housing Commission house, still in Aberdeen. In 1986 the 30-year-old met and clicked with 38-year-old Dave Saunders. Things went well for a few months. Saunders kept his apartment at Scone and moved in with Knight and her daughters. But soon Knight was incorrectly accusing him of infidelity. Their fights turned violent. In May 1987 Knight bashed Saunders unconscious with a frying pan after slitting his two-month-old dog's throat.

In June 1988 Knight gave birth to a girl they named Sarah. Saunders put a deposit on a house in Aberdeen, which Knight paid off when the compensation money for her back injury came through in 1989. She decorated the place with dead animals. The walls were covered in cow hides, water buffalo and steer horns, cow and sheep skulls and deers' antlers. The extensive video collection dealt mainly with horror and death.

Soon there was more trouble. Knight battered Saunders over the head with an iron and allegedly stabbed him with scissors. He left her. Months later, returning home to see his daughter, he found out that Knight had taken out an apprehended violence order against him.

Before long Knight was in a new relationship and pregnant again. The father, John Chillingworth, 43, worked at the Aberdeen meatworks. The baby, a boy named Eric, was born in 1991. But the relationship only lasted three years. It ended when Knight dumped Chillingworth for John Price, an Aberdeen local she was having an affair with. Price had three children, and his marriage had broken up in 1988. His wife had taken the youngest, a two-year-old girl, and Price ended up with their other two children, a teenage boy and girl. He owned a three-bedroom house in Aberdeen and he met Knight at a pub in 1993. He ignored rumours about the way she treated her men.

The relationship started well, but it didn't take long to follow the usual path: accusations of infidelity, plus fights and separations. In late 1995 Knight moved in with Price. Their drinking escalated and they could often be seen at each other's throats in public. After a series of assaults, which included Knight stabbing him in the chest, Price took out an apprehended violence order against her on 29 February 2000. But there was no stopping Knight. That same night, Price was in bed when she entered the house at 11pm. She watched TV for a few minutes and had a shower before joining him in bed, where they had sex.

The next morning blood was found outside the house. Local police were called and entered the house. They wished they hadn't. Inside they found Price's skin 'hanging from a hook' and his 'decapitated remains on the loungeroom floor'. Knight was snoring loudly in bed. It was evident that she had murdered Price. His head was found cooking in a pot on the stove along with a selection of vegetables. Slices from his buttocks had been pan fried and were served up on plates with vegetables, ready for John Price's children's dinners when they arrived home. Fortunately for the kids, they stayed out for the night.

An autopsy revealed that Price was already dead when he was skinned. A knife had been inserted under his collarbone and sliced horizontally across the top of his body, from shoulder to shoulder. It was a straight, clean cut, anatomically precise. Then the knife was turned and cut down the chest, over the stomach to the pubic hairline, and made into a T with another straight line. Tracing the knife tip around his pubic area and careful not to cut his penis or genitals, Knight had cut down the front of Price's thighs, over the knees and to his feet.

She had then moved up the body, held his arms up and cut down the back of each one and across the top of his head. She peeled Price's skin off, including his head, hair and face, all the way down the length of the body to the feet, exposing his intestines. The entire skin – complete with stab holes, and including hair, face, ears, nose, mouth and genitals – was in one piece. It was then hung from a hook in the doorway; the feet dragged on the ground.

According to the forensic pathologist who performed the autopsy, the task would have taken about 40 minutes. It was discovered that after the killing, Knight had withdrawn $1000 from Price's bank account. It was never accounted for.

Knight denied having any recollection of what happened after she arrived at the house and had sex with Price. A week later, on 6 March 2000, she was charged with murder. At her trial in October 2001, she pleaded guilty to murder. According to court-appointed psychiatrists, she was sane when she committed the crimes. On 8 November, Katherine Mary Knight became the only woman in the New South Wales prison system to be sentenced to life imprisonment without the possibility of parole.

But the question remains: did Kath Knight eat parts of John Price after she cooked his head in a pot and fried up slices from his backside? It seems as though some of the pieces of John Price remain unaccounted for. She steadfastly claims that all she recalls of that night is that they had good sex and both climaxed. Then she remembers that Price got out of bed to go 'for a pee' and she watched him come back into the bedroom. After that she presumes that she fell asleep and that was that.

The general consensus of opinion (and in this case everyone seems to have one) is that there is little doubt that she ate part of John Price and found what she did so abhorrent that she chooses to block it out of her mind or conveniently *won't* remember.

In Mulawa Women's Correctional Centre Katherine Knight works as a cleaner in the governor's office. Although she is a very good cook, it is highly unlikely she will ever get a job in the kitchen.

27 THE POISONER OF FROG HOLLOW

Despite unsubstantiated rumours that she was related to the famous bushranger Ben Hall, there was no reason to believe that when baby Louisa Hall was born in 1849 she would grow up to be the last woman to be hanged to death in New South Wales.

Louisa's parents Henry and Catherine Hall worked at a country property called Belltrees in the lush Hunter Valley, a little more than 300 kilometres northeast of Sydney. A curly-haired little darling whose eyes sparkled with the freshness that comes from a childhood spent in a rural area, the young girl was a favourite among the locals of the village where she grew up with her hard-working mother and father.

But Louisa matured physically at an early age and it wasn't long before she started to attract wandering gazes from the males in the area. It was something the buxom girl would come to play on.

Louisa was 16 years old when she took on her first job, working as a housemaid in Merriwa, not far from where she had grown up. Her flirtatiousness meant that she was already popular with the opposite sex, and she is said to have had several boyfriends. It wasn't long, though, before her jolly nature and fast-developing body stirred something in Charles Andrews, a hard-working, widowed butcher who, at the age of 36, was 20 years older than the popular housemaid.

Even though they seemed to have little in common – Louisa was high spirited, the life of the party, while Charles was a calm man with a sober outlook on life – Louisa's mother convinced the young girl that the earnest butcher would make her a good husband. Even though Louisa found her suitor boring, the couple were married on 28 August 1865. It wasn't difficult to see that the union would end in trouble.

The newlyweds soon moved south to Sydney, setting up home in the inner-city suburb of Waterloo, where Charles had grown up. Indeed, his father had owned a shop next to the Cauliflower Hotel which, still operating, was the first pub in the South Sydney area. It was in Waterloo that Louisa and Charles had the first of what would be seven children, a little boy named Herbert.

After a while, the couple moved further south, taking up residence in a semi-detached cottage in Lower Botany, near Botany Bay. The spot where they settled was known as Frog Hollow, and visitors could only reach it by crossing a narrow bridge that stood over a swamp.

With their growing family, Louisa – still wild at heart – rapidly grew bored with what she saw as a mundane and lonely life of motherhood and household chores. She took her feelings out on her husband and, whenever the opportunity arose, she would head straight for the Pier Hotel on nearby Botany Road. The locals at the pub got to know Louisa well, and though described as 'pleasantly plump', she was considered good looking and rather lively, especially with a few beverages under her belt. As a result, she wasn't short of drinking partners.

While at the Pier Hotel, Louisa would hit the bottle and talk openly about her dissatisfaction with home life and her husband. She also began to play around, taking on sexual partners whenever the mood struck her.

While Louisa was out drinking and being unfaithful, Charles Andrews worked and benignly accepted that his wife had a flighty temperament – though it's unclear whether he knew that she was expressing her sexuality with random men at the local pub.

It wasn't long before Louisa decided that the couple should take in boarders at their cottage as a way of earning extra money. Charles had no other choice than to accept the idea, and in no time at all stories began to spread through the community that Louisa was playing around with their boarders while her husband worked hard to put food on the table.

The increasingly boisterous wife still frequented the Pier Hotel, though, and it was there, in 1886, that she first met Michael Peter Collins, a 22-year-old knockabout from Ballarat in Victoria. Michael was best described as a casual labourer who had recently found a job at a local wool-washing shed. Even though the laid-back, handsome man was 14 years younger than Louisa, she felt an immediate spark, and easily convinced him to move in to the cottage as a boarder in June that year.

The resulting affair was anything but a secret in the area. Indeed, it wasn't hard to find the pair holding hands on public transport or enjoying each other's affections in nearby scrubland. Perhaps if they had been more discreet Charles Andrews would never have found out, but the patient man finally blew his lid nine days before Christmas that year, grabbing Michael by the neck and literally throwing the young man out of his house.

Louisa was shocked to see her normally placid husband make such a stand, and she ran to the local police station to report the situation. The officer on duty, Constable Jeffes, somehow managed to calm Louisa down, and even convinced her to return home and try to smooth things out with her cuckolded spouse.

Louisa did as Jeffes suggested, but her mind was running wild. The more she thought about what had happened, the easier it was to blame Charles for her behaviour. He was older than she was, and he was always working, while she was lumbered with the responsibilities of raising their large family. With her contempt growing by the day, she could see only one way to find the happiness that she believed she deserved – and Charles Andrews was not part of the picture. She had a conversation with the local draper, a man by the name of Bullock, asking if he knew just how long after a person died that life insurance money could be collected. It was only a matter of time before Charles took ill.

A physician named Dr Marshall visited Frog Hollow on Monday, 31 January 1887. At 3pm the next Friday, Charles Andrews was dead. Filling out the death certificate, Dr Marshall wrote down acute gastritis as the cause of death. That very afternoon, Louisa claimed £200 from the offices of the Australian Widows' Fund in the city. Even though her children were alone in the house and hungry, she didn't return home until 9.30pm that evening. In her mind, she was now a free woman.

The local draper Mr Bullock was shocked to say the least when, just a few days after Charles had passed away, Louisa called on him to order some dress material in bright colours. Shouldn't a recent widow wear the more traditional dark and sombre colours while mourning? Louisa explained to the merchant that just because her heart may have been heavy, it didn't mean her clothes had to reflect that. And she proved her point by throwing a wild party at her cottage just three days after the death of her husband. The high-spirited affair lasted all night and, once it was over, Michael Collins returned to the house as a permanent resident. Louisa now had what she thought she wanted all along. But if she thought the sailing was to be smooth from this point she was mistaken.

In between collecting her insurance money, throwing a party and getting on with her life as she saw fit, Louisa forgot to tell her oldest son, Herbert – by now an adult living in Maitland – that his father had died. Herbert only learned the news through the proverbial grapevine. Understandably put out, he went to the cottage at Frog Hollow, only to find Michael Collins ensconced there. He confronted his mother about the situation, and brought up the matter of the insurance money, explaining that she should have at least given him a share of it; he could, he said, have opened a shop, which in turn could have supported the whole family. Louisa seemed to care little.

Nine weeks later, the merry widow married her younger suitor at St Silas Church of England in Waterloo – not far from where her dead first husband had grown up. On the official papers, dated 9 April 1887, Louisa took a decade off her age, writing 28 instead of 38 – only four years older than her new spouse. The happy couple then rounded up Charles and Louisa's children and relocated to a cottage in Johnsons Lane, North Botany.

But Michael, Louisa would soon realise, didn't provide the stability of homelife once offered by the hard-working Charles. Indeed, while he had only previously had jobs on and off, with a free roof over his head and food on the table whenever he needed it, now, thanks to Louisa's insurance payout, he seemingly gave up the search for employment all together. Louisa – no doubt realising that their windfall would not last forever – hounded him to get a job, but Michael resisted. In fact, he became more of a drain on their funds than a help – especially with his penchant for gambling, a habit that Louisa had no time for. Her new husband constantly dipped into their ever-diminishing finances to support the vice.

Even when he did manage to find a job after eight weeks of doing nothing, Michael was fired after just three days. Louisa could not believe it, yet she dipped into her savings and lent him another pound, which he used – as usual – to gamble. This time, however, was different. Luck, it seemed, was on his side and Michael came home with over £4. With such good fortune, Michael managed to convince Louisa to part with the last £20 of their insurance money. Needless to say, it wasn't a smart move. Louisa was already in bed when Michael came home that night, dead broke. The married couple cried together thinking about their hopeless situation.

Having fallen on hard times, Louisa seemed to reminisce about happier, more carefree days. She wanted to return to Frog Hollow, but her old cottage had new residents. They moved, instead, to a place nearby, where Louisa seemed to let Michael continue with his ambitionless ways. Seven months after they were married, they had a child. Michael was proud of his son and seemed to care greatly for the infant boy, so he was extremely sad when the little baby died at the age of five months.

A neighbour would comment that the child had 'swollen lips and tongue' when it passed away, but little was thought of the strange condition.

By now, Louisa was growing weary of her seemingly dead-end existence and second marriage. She started to hit the bottle harder than ever, and it didn't take much to get her back to the Pier Hotel, where she took any opportunity to tell her fellow drinkers what a no-hoper her new husband was. On more than one occasion, she mentioned that she would be better off without him.

Back home, Michael did nothing to change his ways. He spent the majority of his days lying around on their dirty bed, while the children ran amok naked through the filthy house. Having done away with her first husband and most recent baby, it's easy to see why Louisa thought she had an easy solution to her problems.

Still, Michael had no life insurance, and was uncharacteristically employed and earning a decent wage of 36 shillings a week when Louisa put her poisonous plan into effect once again. It's unclear why she chose such a time to do away with Michael, but there has been speculation that she already had another man on the side, or that the large amounts of alcohol she was consuming had driven her mad. Either way, Michael soon began to experience acute abdominal pain, which stopped him from attending his job. Dr Marshall came to check on him, and while the physician was there, Louisa played the role of the loving, attentive wife. It didn't help, though, and following Michael Collins' death – and a two-day booze binge by Louisa – Marshall informed the police of his suspicions.

The authorities wasted no time searching the Frog Hollow cottage. Louisa, as usual, was at the Pier Hotel while they went through her house from top to bottom. In the sink, the police found an unwashed glass. A quick check revealed it to contain traces of arsenic. Given her history, and Dr Marshall's suspicions, it was all the evidence police needed to arrest Louisa Collins, and she was taken into custody on 12 July 1887. The bodies of her first husband Charles Andrews and the baby she had with Michael Collins were exhumed the next day. After being examined at South Sydney Morgue, the results came in that both contained traces of arsenic. Louisa would have to face a court of law to answer for her actions.

When the trial began, the two-time widow tried to convince the jury that Michael had committed suicide, but no one believed that a person who wanted to kill himself would chose such a painful and drawn-out method as arsenic poisoning.

Because of the circumstances, though, Louisa would have to go through four separate trials. But there was little surprise when she was finally found guilty at the last one. On 8 December 1888 Louisa Collins was sentenced to death. The quiet Frog Hollow soon became known by the wider public as Arsenic Flat.

A short time after the trial, a dozen witnesses – five of those being reporters – gathered near the gallows at Sydney's Darlinghurst Gaol. They were there to see the first woman executed there in the prison's by-then 48-year history, as well as the last woman to ever be hung in New South Wales.

Days earlier, Louisa had written a letter to her blind mother, inexplicably praising Michael Collins, calling him 'tall and handsome', and describing him as 'good, loving, attentive, sober and honest'. She also wrote of the love he showed for his own son, adding that it 'was beyond all I could describe.'

When it came time for her to face the executioner, two female guards led Louisa to the noose. She wore a long brown prison dress and behaved as if the walk to her death was an everyday occurrence. The jail's priest followed behind the group as Louisa stepped up on to the platform and stood on the trapdoor. The priest whispered in the three-time murderer's ear and then the lever was pulled to open the trapdoor.

But confusion reigned when a pin got stuck and the hole in the floor didn't open. A quick-thinking warder immediately grabbed a nearby mallet and hit the pin until it gave way and the trapdoor flung open. Louisa Collins was left to hang for 20 minutes to ensure she was dead, which was the regulation of the time. The priest told the assembled reporters that she had shown 'great courage'.

28 THE GLENFIELD SIEGE

If it hadn't been so ridiculous it could have been very, very dangerous. It involved a psychopath, a police commissioner, a jail chaplain, a high-powered rifle, a baby and a young mother appropriately named Muddle. And what a muddle it was. The Glenfield Siege will go down in our history as arguably the greatest criminal muddle of all time.

For ten days in the winter of 1968, throughout freezing conditions and rain, a lone gunman threatened to kill a hostage and her baby, who he held in a Sydney house, while the Australian public tuned in on television as if they were watching a 7 o'clock soapie. Enterprising locals set up food stalls and sold pies, hot dogs and steaming cups of coffee to the huge crowd of media and curious onlookers who gathered to watch the drama unfold. None were disappointed.

Australia's most bizarre siege began on the morning of 2 July 1968, when two detectives called on the home of known criminal Wally Mellish in Sydney's outer western suburbs to have a chat with him about a series of car thefts in the district. Twenty-two-year-old Mellish had only been released from prison a few months earlier and had rented the two-bedroom fibro cottage in Glenfield Road where he now lived with his 19-year-old girlfriend, Beryl Muddle, and her 11-week-old son Leslie. In those days Glenfield Road was little more than a bitumen track.

When the detectives informed Mellish of the reason for their visit he began to rant and rave. He flew into a fit of rage and allegedly fired a rifle into the air. What his intentions were was not determined, but the detectives weren't taking any chances and retreated as fast as they could. The Glenfield Siege had begun.

Not sure what to do, given that there was a woman and a baby inside the house, the police called for reinforcements, but all they could do was watch and wait and hope that the hostages were safe. That is, if they were really hostages at all. With little activity coming from the house it was a stand-off, police fearing for the lives of the woman and her baby should they storm the house. And so, as the media and crowds gathered, the waiting continued.

After a few days Wally Mellish made demands from the window for food or he would shoot Beryl Muddle and the little boy. He made no bones about it: it was now definitely a hostage situation. Police, who had surrounded the house at a safe distance, met his every demand and waited for the right opportunity to arise to storm the house without endangering the woman and her child's lives. It didn't come, and the stalemate continued and the crowds grew bigger.

Families from all over Sydney arrived and some pitched tents in the vacant block of land opposite the siege house. They set up barbecues, cooked steaks and sausages and drank beer while they waited for something to happen. The local shops did a roaring trade and the pub never had it so good.

In the meantime, Wally Mellish's demands were becoming more regular and outrageous. After yelling out that he was ready to kill Beryl and the little boy and then turn the rifle on himself, if he couldn't negotiate the situation with a high-ranking police officer, the Police Commissioner, Mr Norman Allan, decided it was time to take positive action and find out exactly what it was that Mellish wanted in exchange for his hostages. And Mr Allan would personally take on the role of negotiator. The newspapers declared it a joke.

Mr Allan rang Wally Mellish on at least ten occasions and, through their cosy little chats, determined that things could be resolved in a hurry if the police commissioner would arrange for Wally and Beryl to be married in the house forthwith, with the commissioner acting as Wally's best man and Detective Superintendent Don Fergusson acting as witness to make the happy occasion legal.

An astonished public, informed up to the minute by the media as to what was going on, cheered uproariously as the Long Bay Jail chaplain, Reverend Clyde Paton, arrived and entered the house to perform the nuptials. Having done that, the now family man Wally reneged on the deal to give himself up and ushered the commissioner, the witness and the chaplain out the door at gunpoint and the siege continued where it had left off.

In a scathing editorial the *Daily Telegraph* reported: 'It is difficult to imagine a more complete and hopeless shemozzle than the handling of the Siege of Glenfield. The public must feel completely baffled and so must most of the police force. Bravery and headlines are not a substitute for judgement and clear thinking.'

The following day Mellish yelled out that he had the rifle against his wife's head and unless they gave him a machine gun he would blow hers and then the baby's brains out. The ever obliging commissioner explained to Wally that he didn't have a machine gun handy but he would provide him with the next best thing, the deadliest police weapon of the day, an armour-piercing Armalite rifle. Mr Allan personally delivered it to the front door. Not only did the commissioner come under attack from the press; his own men, who were in the firing line should Mellish decide to go out in a hail of bullets, were openly vocal about the decision to give him the rifle.

The verbal and telephone negotiations continued through the night and finally, on the 10th day, weak from lack of sleep and with the promise from the commissioner that he would allow him to attempt to join the army should he surrender, Wally Mellish gave up without so much as a whimper. His wife and stepson were unharmed. It was later revealed that before it was given to Mellish the Armalite rifle had been rendered safe by a weapons expert.

True to his word, Commissioner Allan carried out his promise of helping Mellish join the army. Of course, given the nature of his recent activities, it was ridiculous and the army rejected it out of hand. Instead Wally Mellish went to jail for a long time, his marriage was annulled on the grounds that it wasn't legal and, despite a terrible caning from the press, Police Commissioner Allan, along with Reverend Paton, was decorated for bravery.

29 THE JOKE – THE CRIMES OF SIR TERENCE LEWIS, POLICE COMMISSIONER

It was such a ludicrous circumstance that it was referred to by those in the know throughout the Queensland police force and parliament simply as 'the joke'. A police inspector had been plucked out of the bush and installed as police commissioner at the behest of the Queensland premier, Joh Bjelke-Petersen.

And, once there, the new boss became the puppet for those who allowed corruption to run rampant wherever his superiors saw fit while, at the same time, he lined his own pockets with vast sums of money delivered in brown paper bags. It was, indeed, a joke of mammoth proportions played upon the citizens of Queensland.

The man who would be commissioner, Terry Lewis, was born in Ipswich and went to work at age 13 in Pikes' Menswear Store in Brisbane, selling suits until he joined the police force in 1948. At best it could be said that the tall man with a friendly smile was about as ordinary a bloke as you'd ever meet.

Terry Lewis married a Cloncurry shop assistant named Hazel

Gould and they settled into their suburban Brisbane home to raise their family of five children. Lewis worked his way up in the force and spent 15 years in the Criminal Investigation Branch, until he was promoted at age 35 to run the newly created Juvenile Aid Bureau.

Lewis was showing signs of leadership and, in 1968, was awarded a Churchill Fellowship. He had made up for his poor education by studying in his spare time, gaining a degree in arts and a diploma in public administration. In January 1976, 28 years after joining the force, Terry Lewis was made an inspector and transferred to Charleville, a bush town in Western Queensland, with 35 officers under his command.

Much to the astonishment of his peers and the many officers who were better qualified for the job, by November 1976 Terry Lewis had been installed in Brisbane as assistant commissioner and when the incumbent commissioner, Raymond Whitrod, resigned soon after, he was given the top cop job in Queensland. It was Joh Bjelke-Petersen himself who apparently gave the final nod. It all happened so fast that few had time to protest.

What had transpired personally between the new commissioner and the premier prior to the appointment can only be subject to speculation. But the detractors could read nothing into it other than corruption. And time would prove them 100 per cent correct.

Rumours were rampant that Terry Lewis had been a bag man, meaning that he collected bribes and protection money for the previous commissioner, and that he had been involved in police corruption at the highest level. This was the topic of the new commissioner's first press conference, where he assured the media that starting immediately there would be a clampdown on SP betting and that he would not tolerate any political interference to his post.

With Terry Lewis at the helm, Queensland slipped into its blackest abyss as corruption at every level ran rampant and the man at the top got his kickback from the lot. Crooked politicians, illegal casino bosses, drug traffickers and corrupt police did little to hide their activities. It could be said that in that dark time of the Lewis years it was the criminals who were running Queensland as they pleased, as long as they paid their respects with brown paper bags full of cash.

Voted Father of the Year in 1980, Terry Lewis moved his clan into a mansion in posh Garfield Drive, Paddington, that he had had built at a cost of $500,000 – a staggering amount of money for those days, given that he was still on a public servant's salary.

But that was still not enough for the police commissioner. In 1986, after constant lobbying from his family and supporters, Terry Lewis, the suit salesman from Ipswich, became Sir Terence – the only police commissioner in Australian history to receive a knighthood. Hazel, the Cloncurry shop assistant, became Lady Lewis. Now it all really was beyond a joke.

By July 1987 Queensland's Fitzgerald Royal Commission into corruption was well under way and in the light of certain damning accusations levelled at the premier, Sir Joh – who had by now also received a knighthood – had little choice but to stand his old mate down. Terrified that the commission would find out what everyone else already knew anyway, Sir Terence immediately transferred the deeds to the family mansion into his wife's name in a feeble attempt to distance himself from questions as to where the money came from to build it. It didn't work.

Jack Herbert, Lewis' bag man throughout the years of corruption, turned informer to save his own skin. Herbert told the Commission that Sir Terence was collecting around $120,000 a year in kickbacks from the organised crime that ran Queensland's illegal casinos and brothels.

Jack Herbert's wife, Peggy, told the commission that giving the money to Sir Terence was often a combined effort, and she would meet Lady Hazel and slip a brown paper envelope full of cash into her bag beneath the table while they had coffee and scones in a local restaurant. If it wasn't so evil, it would have been hilarious.

After the commission, Sir Terence was given the bullet. He immediately sold the Lewis Paddington mansion for $600,000, of which $450,000 went straight to solicitors he had employed to free up his superannuation entitlements and long-service leave, valued at an estimated $1.4 million. But it was all to no avail. The taxation department got the lot. But worse was to come.

Charged and convicted on 14 counts of corruption, Sir Terence was sentenced to 14 years in jail. Earning just $4 a day in the slammer, Sir Terence had little to provide for his family so Lady Hazel had to claim the dole, thus becoming the first titled woman in Australia ever to go on welfare. We can only wonder if she used her title on the dole papers.

In 1993 Sir Terence became plain old Terry and Lady Hazel went back to being ordinary old Hazel when he was stripped of his knighthood and all other honours from the Queen that went with it. Released from prison after serving a good portion of his sentence, Terry Lewis, the suit salesman from Ipswich who rose to become police commissioner, now maintains as low a profile as possible and prefers it that way.

He didn't even attend the recent funeral of his old mate Joh Bjelke-Petersen.

30 THE JIMMY GOVERNOR MURDERS

Thomas Keneally's 1972 novel *The Chant of Jimmy Blacksmith* and Fred Schepisi's subsequent 1978 film of the same name were based loosely on one of the worst real-life killing sprees that Australia has ever seen. It is a story of racial intolerance that led to the savage murders of nine people. And what made the killings even more abhorrent was that the victims were women, children or old men. They have gone down in our history as the Jimmy Governor Murders.

In the year 1900, 23-year-old Jimmy Governor, the son of a white father and an Aboriginal mother, left the western New South Wales town of Gulgong with his 16-year-old white wife, Ethel Mary Page, and their baby daughter in the hope that they could leave the memories of their tormented existence behind. Growing up torn between the two races had been a nightmare for Governor but that was now compounded tenfold with his young white wife and mixed-race child. Mixed marriages were harshly frowned upon at the turn of the century. The odd couple were ridiculed everywhere they went.

The little family headed west, where Governor found work putting in fences at the Gilgandra property of free settler and backbone of the community, John Mawbey, and they set up camp in the bush not far from the homestead. But nothing had changed and the marriage was openly frowned upon. The Mawbeys didn't hesitate in voicing their opinions. Soon after Governor began work at the Mawbeys, he was joined by his brother Joe, his friends and their families, including the simple-minded Jacky Underwood. As it was, Governor was finding it hard enough to support his own wife and child, let alone the newcomers.

When Governor confronted his boss and asked for extra supplies to feed his extended family, John Mawbey refused. That night, this time with his brother Joe and the simpleton Underwood in tow, Governor again confronted his boss at the old homestead where Mr Mawbey was staying, having left his family at their new homestead a few miles away.

Again Mr Mawbey wouldn't be intimidated and refused extra supplies for the unwanted guests. Enraged at the rejection of food and intent on revenge – yet not willing to take on the foreboding John Mawbey, even though it would have been three against one – Governor and his sidekicks headed off in the direction of the new Mawbey homestead.

The occupants of the homestead were easy pickings for three men armed with nulla nullas and axes and with murder on their minds. Inside were John Mawbey's wife Sarah, the Mawbey daughters Grace, 16, and Hilda, 11, the boys Percy, 14, Sydney 12, Bertie, 9, Cecil, 6, Garnett, 3 and their cousin out from Sydney, 13-year-old George. Also inside the homestead were Mrs Mawbey's sister, 18-year-old Elsie Clarke, and the family's teacher, Helen Kerz.

The younger children were already in bed when the enraged Governor pounded on the door and demanded to be let in. Mrs Mawbey and the school teacher Miss Kerz confronted him at the front door and a shouting match took place before the women slammed the door in his face. The three men smashed the door down and took to the women and children indiscriminately, until they were exhausted and could catch and kill no more. By the time they left Mrs Mawbey, her daughters Grace and Hilda, her son Percy and the schoolteacher Helen Kerz lay dead. Elsie Clarke was severely injured and just barely alive. Somehow, the others had managed to escape.

As the word spread that there were murderous savages on the loose, the Gilgandra and surrounding districts went into lock-down and the hunt for the Governor brothers and Underwood gathered momentum. Jimmy Governor's wife Ethel was quickly picked up at the Mawbey property and was cleared of any part in the terrible crimes committed by her husband and his friends.

The gang's next victim was a 70-year-old farmer on his property at Gulgong, who had argued with Governor some time earlier over payment for a job that Governor had done for him. The three men confronted the older man and axed him to death.

Soon after the Governor brothers unloaded Jacky Underwood, who was unable to keep up the pace as they kept ahead of the blacktrackers and police. Underwood was quickly picked up, tried and found guilty for his part in the killings.

The Governor brothers turned up next at the tiny township of Poggi, east of Gulgong, where they decided to call on the homestead of a Michael O'Brien, who Jimmy had had unsatisfactory dealings with years earlier. But Mr O'Brien wasn't home. Instead in the house was his heavily pregnant wife Elizabeth, their 15-month-old son, and the family midwife, Catherine Bennett.

As Miss Bennett opened the door she was shot point-blank by Jimmy Governor with a rifle he had stolen from his previous victim. As Mrs O'Brien did her best to protect her baby son, she and the infant were chopped to death with a tomahawk. Miraculously, Catherine Bennett lived to identify Jimmy Governor in court.

Their next victim, 70-year-old Kieran Fitzpatrick, was another farmer who Jimmy had had a run in with years earlier. When they arrived at Mr Fitzpatrick's homestead in nearby Wollar they shot him in the shoulder and as he lay on the ground unable to move they hacked him to death with an axe. Soon after Jimmy raped the 15-year-old daughter of a nearby farmer.

With the biggest force of men on horseback ever assembled

outside of war – more than 2000 – looking for them, and with a reward of £2000 for their capture dead or alive, the Governor brothers decided to go their separate ways. On the evening of 13 October 1900, Jimmy Governor was trapped by two search parties on the banks of the Forbes River. They opened fire and wounded the fugitive, but he managed to escape after limping off into the undergrowth. He was eventually arrested two weeks later on 27 October near the coastal town of Wingham. Four days later his brother Joe was shot dead by troopers near Singleton.

After a two-day trial at Sydney's Darlinghurst Criminal Court it took the jury just ten minutes to find Jimmy Governor guilty of nine counts of murder. He was sentenced to death and hanged in Darlinghurst Jail on 18 January 1901. The dim-witted Jacky Underwood had been hanged in Dubbo Jail four days earlier.

31 WOMEN SERIAL KILLERS

On average there is a murder committed in Australia every day. And on average women commit one-third of them. With this in mind it shouldn't come as a surprise to find that of the thirty cases of serial murder in Australia's history, almost a third (nine) of them involve a woman either killing on her own or murdering in tandem with a man.

The reason that this fact is so unusual is because while women who kill are commonplace, women serial killers throughout the world, especially those who murder alone, are rare in comparison to men and considerably less than Australia's average of one in three. There seems to be no logical explanation why Australia's average is so much higher.

'Female serial killers are not as common in numbers as the men because the extreme violence that usually surrounds a homicide is much more common in males,' explains Dr Rod Milton, leading Sydney forensic psychiatrist who worked on such cases as the Granny Killer murders, in which serial killer

John Wayne Glover violently murdered six elderly woman on Sydney's lower north shore in the late 1980s.

'Women are much less violent than men and of the few that do commit serial murder, their crimes are usually more of a passive nature such as quietly poisoning their victims or suffocating babies or elderly women in hospitals where they are least likely to be caught,' Dr Milton says.

'Most women serial killers, for whatever reason they are killing, go about their business in a quieter, subdued, yet deadlier manner than their male counterparts. The classic example would be the 1944 movie *Arsenic and Old Lace*, where two old dears befriended tramps off the streets, fed them, gave them a drink and then poisoned them and buried their bodies under the house,' Dr Milton says.

'Mind you, they were caught, but I think there's a lot more female serial killers out there than are given credit for,' he added.

Statistics show that the USA has 76 per cent of the world's serial killers, of which only approximately 15 per cent of the cases involved a female either acting alone or in partnership with a male who was almost always a lover, but very rarely a husband.

Take away the women who acted as an accomplice and you find that solo women serial killers are a very rare breed indeed, possibly as low as five per cent. And husband-and-wife serial killer teams are the rarest of them all at around two per cent.

True to form, it was the American media, where serial killer hype was first born following the coining of the term by FBI agent and serial-killer profiler Robert Ressler in the mid 1970s, that claimed Aileen Carol Wuornos, a hard-drinking, ex-convict prostitute, as the world's first female serial killer. She murdered seven men on separate occasions by shooting them in the torso with a small-calibre handgun after they picked her up as she hitchhiked throughout Florida in 1990. But in the true sense of serial multicide, where the killer takes three or more lives over a period of time, irrespective of the method of murder, Aileen Carol Wuornos is on the end of a horrific, if not very long list of women serial killers, whose crimes date back to before the turn of the century. And a lot of them are from Australia. In that

Wuornos left a trail of victims linked by bullets from the same gun and not by poison – which 45 per cent of female serial killers prefer when despatching adults – it could be said that she was the first female serial killer of *adult males*. She was executed by lethal injection on 9 October 2002. South African actress Charlize Theron won a Best Actress Academy Award for portraying Wuornos in the 2003 movie *Monster*. It's worth a look.

It was the 1965 case of the Moors murderer, Myra Hindley, and not the Wuornos homicides, which brought women serial killers to the fore, though back in the '60s killers of Hindley's ilk were known as 'mass' or 'spree' murderers, which was defined in later years under the broader term of 'multicide'.

Hindley, an attractive 24-year-old blonde office worker and her 28-year-old factory worker lover, sexual sadist Ian Brady, committed atrocities that defy comprehension. Even more so because they were against children.

On 6 October 1965, police were taken to a house by a man who had witnessed Brady and Hindley murder 17-year-old Edward Evans with fourteen blows to the skull from an axe. Inside the house in Hattersley, near Manchester, England, police found Evans' body and two left-luggage tickets that corresponded with two suitcases left at Manchester Central railway station.

What police found in the suitcases would brand Hindley as arguably the most callous female serial killer of all time. As well as an assortment of sex and torture books, whips, coshes and other items used for perverted activities, there was a collection of photos and two tape recordings.

Some of the photos were pornographic poses of 10-year-old Leslie Anne Downey, who had gone missing on Boxing Day in 1964. Other photos were of Hindley posing next to what would turn out to be the shallow grave of 12-year-old John Kilbride, who had been missing since November 1963, and was murdered and buried on bleak Saddleworth Moor by Hindley and Brady. These photos enabled police to eventually locate not only the boy's grave but little Lesley's as well.

But it was the tapes that reduced hardened police to tears as they listened to the recording of Leslie Ann Downey frantically screaming: *'Don't – please, God help me ...'* as she was sexually assaulted, tortured and eventually strangled by Hindley and Brady.

Both were sentenced to three terms of life imprisonment without the possibility of parole. In 1986 Hindley confessed to the murders of two other children, 12-year-old Keith Bennett and 16-year-old Pauline Reade and, almost a quarter of a century later in July 1987, Pauline Reade's body was found on the moors where Keith Bennett's body still lies despite massive police searches to find it.

Myra Hindley, 60, died in custody of a heart attack in November 2002. Ian Brady, now 64, is in a prison hospital for the criminally insane.

Australia's equivalent to Myra Hindley, in that she committed serial murder with a male partner, is Western Australian housewife Catherine Birnie, who, as a 34-year-old mother of six, helped her common-law husband, labourer David Birnie, 34, abduct, rape, murder and dispose of the bodies of four women aged between 15 and 31 over a six-week period in Perth in late 1986.

At David Birnie's instigation Catherine Birnie strangled one of the women herself and spat on the grave of another after she had led police to their burial grounds. But it was Catherine Birnie who instigated the escape of a fifth would-be victim, who fled semi-naked through an open window and alerted police.

Which begs the question: Would either of these women have committed serial murder alone if they hadn't have been enticed into it by their partners?

'Extremely unlikely,' says Dr Rod Milton. 'In these matters the women play only the secondary part, no matter the bravado they put on, and there is no way that they would have acted alone. I studied the case of husband and wife serial killers Fred and Rose West while I was in England and there is no way that she was capable of murder without him. And I believe that is applicable in most cases of serial killer couples.'

Australia's first recorded female serial killer was petite Melbourne housewife Martha Needle, who murdered her husband, three daughters and her lover's brother between 1885 and 1894 with deadly doses of 'Rough on Rats' brand rat poison in cups of tea. Martha's motive was pure greed and every time one of her brood passed on unsuspiciously from a 'wasting disease', friends, neighbours and relatives couldn't believe her unfortunate circumstances.

After hubby and the kids had gone to God and the grief-stricken 29-year-old Martha had collected a total of £466 in insurance claims, a fortune in those days, she took up with Adelaide saddler Otto Juncken, much to the disapproval of Otto's brother Louis, whom she plied with enough arsenic in his tea to kill ten men. Louis' other brother Herman became suspicious of his death and, on one of his visits to Martha's house, he too became violently ill after drinking tea and was rushed to the doctor where traces of arsenic were found in his vomit. The exhumed bodies of Louis, Henry Needle and her three daughters revealed traces of arsenic and Martha Needle went to the gallows in Melbourne on 22 October 1894.

Another infamous Australian serial poisoner was dear old Caroline 'Aunt Carrie' Grills, a kindly lady in her 60s who was described as 'a person who people looked to in a time of trouble'.

In 1947 Mrs Grills murdered her despised stepmother, Christine Mickelson, by lacing her tea with the slow-acting metallic poison thallium and, in doing so, inherited her house. Then other elderly friends of the Grills family started dying mysteriously. First was 80-year-old Angeline Thomas, followed by 60-year-old John Lundberg, who died after a short illness in 1948 during which his hair fell out. Elderly Mary Anne Mickelson was next to come down with the mysterious symptoms and die. Soon after, the late John Lundberg's widow and daughter began to lose their hair and feel lethargic.

The only thing that they all had in common was that they were all nursed by Caroline Grills, who delighted in giving them constant cups of tea. They decided to keep an eye on her and when she was seen dropping something into one of her patient's cups of tea, the cups were swapped and a forensic examination revealed thallium.

Bodies were exhumed and showed traces of thallium. Other

friends of the Grills family had died mysteriously, but their bodies had been cremated. Had they not, the death toll could have been higher than four plus two attempted murders.

Aunt Carrie was sentenced to death by hanging, which was commuted to life imprisonment, due to her age, and she died in prison in 1960 where she was known as 'Aunt Thally'.

Martha Rendell is arguably the most sadistic female serial killer in Australia's history. In 1906 Rendell lived with carpenter Thomas Morris and his five children, on whom she administered regular thrashings. Soon after Rendell moved in it became apparent that the once healthy and active children had become thin and sickly-looking, and easy prey to colds and other common ailments.

When the local doctor prescribed throat swabs for the children's colds and sore throats Martha Rendell administered the treatment. Within months the two Thomas daughters were dead from what was diagnosed as the deadly bacterial disease diphtheria. A year later 14-year-old Arthur died in agony after having his throat regularly swabbed by his de-facto stepmother.

Young George Thomas was the next to fall ill, but he fled the house rather than tolerate the excruciatingly painful throat swabs. Neighbours alerted police and told them of the agony the children had gone through prior to dying. Their bodies were exhumed and a post-mortem revealed that their throats had been washed with hydrochloric acid after Rendell had first laced their drinks with acid and swabbed their throats with more of the same.

On 6 October 1909 Martha Rendell became the last woman to be hanged in Western Australia.

Frances Knorr made 'baby minding' a profitable business. Not from tending the infants, but from murdering them. In Melbourne in the 1890s it was frowned upon to be a single mother and it was common practice to put the unwanted child in the care of 'child-minders' on a full-time basis and pay a monthly fee. It didn't take Frances Knorr long to realise that it was much more profitable if she simply collected the child-minding fees each month and didn't have to feed or tend to the infants. The obvious answer was murder.

In July 1893, the new tenant of a house in Melbourne's Brunswick was digging in the backyard when he unearthed the remains of one girl and two baby boys. An autopsy revealed that one had been strangled and the other two had been suffocated.

The previous resident, Frances Knorr, now living in Sydney, was arrested and extradited to Melbourne, charged with the murders, tried and sentenced to death by hanging, much to the delight of the huge crowds that gathered outside the courthouse during her trial. She was to become the first woman hanged in Victoria in 30 years.

However, as the hanging day approached, the hangman, Thomas Jones, not altogether at ease with the prospect of hanging a woman, took to the bottle and two days before the hanging date took his own life by cutting his throat. A replacement was quickly found and on the morning of 15 January 1894, the despised baby killer Frances Knorr hummed hymns as she dropped to her death in Pentridge Prison.

Given the period of time that Frances Knorr was in the child-minding business, and the amount of women who clandestinely came forward and told police that they had given her their babies, it is believed that she could have murdered as many as 13 of the unfortunate infants.

In 1892 the bodies of 12 infants were found buried in the backyard of a house in the Sydney suburb of Chippendale. The previous tenants, Sarah and John Makin and their four daughters, were quickly rounded up and all were charged with the murders of the babies. It turned out that the Makins were also 'baby farmers' who had chosen to murder the bubs in their care, yet still go on accepting money from their wretched mothers. The Makin children escaped retribution, but John Makin was hanged and his evil missus did 19 years in jail before disappearing into oblivion.

In Perth, Western Australia, from 1900 to 1906, another child minder, middle-aged Alice Mitchell, was responsible for the deaths of at least 37 babies who were left in her care for the fee of five shillings a week.

When a mother of one of the dead babies complained to

police, they visited Mitchell's child-minding centre to find soiled napkins were heaped in a huge bundle in the corner, flies massed on the sores on the children's eyes and maggots crawled over filthy, soiled bedsheets. Those toddlers who could walk or crawl were allowed into the fowl yard where they were left to immerse themselves in the mud and droppings.

Police also discovered that in the six years from 1900, 37 infants had died in homes managed by her – and they were only the ones on record. Police could only assume that there were many more unrecorded children who had either died of starvation, dehydration or disease, or had been murdered by Alice Mitchell.

Extraordinarily, Alice Mitchell escaped the charge of wilful murder and was sentenced to five years' imprisonment with hard labour for manslaughter.

Every parent's nightmare was Helen Patricia Moore who, in Sydney between May 1979 and early 1980, suffocated a 16-month-old and a two-year-old girl and a seven-year-old boy, and attempted to murder two other infant boys, aged one and two, by suffocating them while they were in her care as a babysitter. Helen Moore was just 17 at the time of the killings.

Moore was caught when she was asked about scratches on her hands and her victim's face after the seven-year-old had supposedly fallen down the stairs and died. She willingly confessed to her crimes. Helen Patricia Moore was sentenced to life imprisonment and was released in 1993, after serving her minimum term of almost 14 years in prison. She was placed on parole until 2005 and one of the conditions of her release was that she was forbidden to be in the company of any child under the age of 16 without supervision.

Helen Moore complicated matters somewhat when, in late March 1995, aged 33, she gave birth to a daughter, Lauren. Moore said that she had no intention of having anything further to do with the father of the baby, who she claimed was one of her first lovers.

Confronted with what to do in such an unprecedented circumstance, the Parole Board eventually decided that both mother and baby must be kept under 24-hour supervision in their home and that the baby must never be left alone with the mother at any time during the parole period. In 1995 the supervision ended when the parole period expired. Helen Moore and her daughter, by then aged 10, then began a new life together somewhere in Australia.

The last recorded case of serial murder by a female in Australia is that of Kathleen Folbigg who, like Helen Moore, murdered children. But unlike Helen Moore, the children were Kathleen Folbigg's own.

Born Kathleen Megan Marlborough, she was just 18 months old in 1969 when her father fatally stabbed her mother 24 times in the street outside their suburban Sydney home. Kathleen was placed in an orphanage and fostered out at the age of three to a family who lived in Newcastle.

Kathleen left school in 1982, when she was just 15. With limited education, she moved from one minimum-wage job to another before marrying 25-year-old steel worker Craig Folbigg at the age of 20. Their first child, a son named Caleb, was born in February 1989. The child was dead just 20 days later. The official cause of death was listed as Sudden Infant Death Syndrome (SIDS).

Kathleen gave birth to another son, Patrick, in June 1990. At 3.30am on 19 October 1990, Craig woke to the sound of his wife screaming. Rushing in to the infant's room to find his wife standing over Patrick's cot, Craig noticed that the small child was still breathing, albeit faintly. The distressed father administered CPR until an ambulance arrived. According to a police statement, 'Patrick regained consciousness, but was [later] found to now have epilepsy and be blind.'

The infant lived another four months. On the morning of 13 February 1991 young Patrick was taken to hospital, but was dead on arrival. According to an autopsy, an epileptic fit resulted in death by an 'acute asphyxiating event'.

The Folbigg's next child, a daughter, Sarah, was born in October 1992. Sarah was healthy and happy for the first 11 months of her life. Then Kathleen said she got up in the middle of the night to go to the toilet and discovered her daughter in the bed, deceased. The official cause of death was once again put down to SIDS, although the chairman of the world SIDS organisation, who conducted the post-mortem, noticed small abrasions on Sarah's chin, as well as 'something unusual' about her throat.

Kathleen and Craig moved to Singleton in the Hunter Valley and two years later their fourth child, Laura, was born in August 1997. On 1 March 1999 Kathleen called an ambulance after Laura allegedly stopped breathing. The medical team arrived but it was too late. An autopsy found that the child was too old to have died from SIDS. The cause of death was recorded as 'undetermined'. A police investigation was ordered. Detective Sergeant Bernie Ryan was assigned to lead the case. When he learnt that Laura was the fourth Folbigg child to die in similar circumstances, alarm bells rang.

By this time Kathleen had left Craig. When Craig found Kathleen's diaries in the house the case took a major turn. Many of the entries were of major concern. The pages were filled with Kathleen's doubts about her skills as a mother and concerns about her inability to breastfeed, despite repeated attempts with all four children. More worrying were the stories of how stress 'made her do terrible things', and that she felt 'flashes of rage, resentment and hatred' towards her children.

Once authorities saw the diaries they decided they did indeed have a murder case on their hands. Still, it wouldn't be an easy case to prove. Detective Ryan took two years getting an argument together that he believed would provide a conviction. On 19 April 2001 Kathleen Megan Folbigg was arrested and charged with murdering her four children.

At the two-month trial at Sydney's Darlinghurst Supreme Court, the circumstantial evidence was plentiful and damning. The prosecution portrayed Kathleen as a woman 'preoccupied with her own life and looks, more interested in going to the gym and nightclubs than in looking after her own children', and asserted that Kathleen murdered her four infant children by smothering them because she couldn't deal with her parental responsibilities.

It took the jury just under eight hours to find Kathleen Megan Folbigg guilty of murdering three of her four children and the manslaughter of the other. She was taken to Mulawa Women's Detention Centre and placed in protective isolation away from the other prisoners, who would kill her in a heartbeat. A lot of them were mothers. In August 2002 Kathleen Folbigg returned to court and was sentenced to 40 years in prison with a nonparole period of 30 years.

On 17 February 2005, in the New South Wales Court of Criminal Appeal, Justice Brian Sully reduced Kathleen Folbigg's maximum sentence by ten years and her nonparole period by five years. Her minimum sentence became 25 years and she will be due for parole in 2028.

32 THE SHOOTING OF ARTHUR CALDWELL

If someone hadn't tried to kill him, it would be fair comment to say that the name of Arthur Caldwell wouldn't be all that familiar with a lot of our younger readers. But someone did try to kill Mr Caldwell, who was at the time the leader of the federal Opposition. And it was the first time in our history that such an outrage had taken place. The closest similar incident could hardly be described as political, being the attempted assassination of Queen Victoria's second son, Prince Alfred, at a picnic at Sydney's Clontarf Beach in 1868.

And so, almost 100 years later on the chilly evening of Tuesday, 21 June 1966, a crowd of 800 of the Labor faithful squeezed into the Mosman Town Hall on Sydney's north shore and rose as one to applaud Mr Caldwell as he ambled down the aisle, stopping to shake hands and kiss the ladies as is the age-old tradition of such rallies.

And they weren't disappointed. Arthur Caldwell was a much-loved leader and a wonderful orator who, at 70, had risen from the working-class environment of Melbourne's industrial suburbs to become one of the most honest and respected men ever in the Labor movement. Mr Caldwell had been the Minister for Immigration from 1945 to 1949 and was the mastermind behind Australia's key postwar immigration policy.

Now, as the leader of the federal Labor Opposition, and with the despised Liberal Prime Minister Bob Menzies out of the way due to his retirement five months earlier, Arthur Caldwell could see an opportunity to seize his ambitions at the next election and become Australian prime minister of a Labor government. And the tough old campaigner was doing it the only way he knew how – by going to the people and shaking their hands and kissing them on the cheeks and talking to them as he was doing that night in Mosman. And they loved him for it.

Earlier that day a man with equal ambition, but far less work ethic, was planning on killing someone of importance so he would be remembered throughout history. He was not a terrorist or fanatical Liberal supporter. In fact, he knew little of politics and even less of the man who was on the front pages of the papers and seemed very important, and who was giving a public talk that evening.

In fact, nineteen-year-old Peter Kocan, an inconspicuous, fair-haired, bespectacled loner, didn't really care who he killed that night – as long as it got him on the front pages. He wanted to become just as famous as the person he had murdered. In his twisted mind, Kocan thought that then, after he was famous, people would look at his poetry and prose in a different light. It would be fair comment to say that Peter Kocan was a couple of pies short of a party pack.

During that day Peter Kocan cleaned his .22 rifle. He had cut down the butt and sawn off the barrel, so it wasn't much bigger than a handgun and would fit comfortably into his belt and wouldn't be seen. Soon he would be as famous as Lee Harvey Oswald, the man who killed President Kennedy in Dallas. He could hardly wait.

In his long overcoat to keep out the evening chill, Peter Kocan looked just like any other spectator as he waited out the front of the Mosman Town Hall for the speech to finish and for Mr Caldwell to come out to his car and be driven away. Security wasn't a problem – there simply wasn't any. No security guards or police and no minders anywhere in sight.

Peter Kocan hoped he would recognise his target as, having never actually seen Mr Caldwell in person, he was only familiar with his face from the newspapers and the posters in the local shop windows advertising the rally. But it was a face not easily forgotten. Craggy and weather-beaten from his years in the political trenches and with a huge nose and lantern jaw, Arthur Caldwell wouldn't be mistaken. His antagonists had likened him to a parrot and given him the nickname of Cockie.

The prolonged applause and cheering told Kocan that the time was near. After much hand-shaking and embracing as he made his way down the aisle, Arthur Caldwell eventually emerged at the front door accompanied by Senator Doug McLelland. Mr Caldwell paused several times and it was obvious by his elation that he could see himself as the first Labor prime minister in 17 years. But not if Peter Kocan had anything to do with it.

As Mr Caldwell brushed by so close that he could have touched him, Peter Kocan reached under his coat for the gun but in an instant the Labor leader was completely surrounded by supporters and a shot was impossible. As Mr Caldwell was ushered into the front seat of his waiting car and closed the door, the opportunity to murder him presented itself. Peter Kocan aimed at Mr Caldwell's head through the glass and fired a shot at point-blank range.

'Oh. I've been shot,' Mr Caldwell cried as blood sprayed all over what was left of the shattered window and he slumped into his chauffeur's lap. But it would take more than a bullet to kill Labor's old warhorse. Miraculously, the low-velocity projectile fired through the thick glass had missed the vital parts and lodged itself in the famous chin that had been the source of much mirth for cartoonists for donkey's years. Now the chin would be even more popular.

Peter Kocan dropped his gun and fled but was run down and captured a short distance away. Mr Caldwell was admitted to the North Shore Hospital and treated for superficial wounds to the face. The people of Australia woke the following morning to the news of the attempted assassination of the leader of the federal Labor Opposition. They chanted as one: 'Who on earth would want to kill Arthur Caldwell?'

Peter Kocan was deemed by psychiatrists to be mentally disturbed but not insane and at his trial he was sentenced to life imprisonment – unlike his fellow assassin of 98 years earlier, Henry James O'Farrell, who was tried and hanged within two weeks of attempting to murder Prince Alfred. Mr Caldwell was present at Kocan's trial and made it clear that he bore no malice, and consoled Peter Kocan's broken-hearted mother outside the court.

During the ten years he spent in the Morriset maximum security mental facility and in prison, Peter Kocan expressed deep remorse for what he had done and wrote a book of poetry and two novels, all of which were published. Arthur Caldwell narrowly missed winning the 1969 federal election and died in Melbourne in 1973.

33 GETTING AWAY WITH MURDER

In 1966, a remorseless 19-year-old Earl Heatley admitted to police that he had murdered 22-year-old Robert Francis Dunn because Dunn was hurling abuse at him and had thrown a bottle at his car. In retaliation, Heatley went home and picked up his rifle, came back to the car park in Granville, Sydney, and shot and killed Dunn. Heatley was sentenced to life imprisonment and, after serving 15 years, was released in 1981.

Thirteen years later it was alleged that Heatley killed two men, one his own brother, in the bungled robbery of a factory that contained no money or valuables. After an aborted first trial, Heatley, now a grey-haired, middle-aged man, was sent to jail for the rest of his life.

It was alleged in court at his second trial that Earl Heatley and his brother, Paul, went to an Asquith warehouse on the outskirts of Sydney in October 1994 with the intention of robbing the premises of legal, but very hard to acquire, chemicals required in the making of amphetamines. The court heard that Earl Heatley was supposedly armed with a pistol and wore a mask.

The prosecution said that the Heatley brothers marched the factory cleaner, Mr Thomas Alan Bithell, into another part of the factory to confront the factory owner, Mr Des Thompson. Thompson, having seen what was going on, was on the phone, apparently to the police.

The court was told that Paul Heatley charged into Mr Thompson's office, punched him in the face and tried to rip the phone out of the wall. Paul Heatley panicked and called for his brother to run away, telling him that the police were on their way.

The court heard that as Paul Heatley started to run away he was tackled by 67-year-old Mr Thompson who, even though he was 20 years older than Heatley, managed to get the better of him and hold him.

It was then alleged that Paul Heatley called to his brother Earl to 'Shoot him, shoot him, shoot him'. Earl Heatley then supposedly opened fire on the pair, sending four bullets into Mr Thompson's head and body. One of the bullets passed through Mr Thompson's body and fatally wounded Paul Heatley.

The prosecution claimed that Earl Heatley then put four more bullets into the mortally wounded Mr Thompson's head as he lay on the ground dying. Earl Heatley supposedly told police later that he did it because Mr Thompson was 'lying there crying like a dog, so I put four bullets in his head'.

Paul Heatley staggered to the outside of the factory, where he fell to the ground and died. During the shooting, the cleaner, Mr Bithell, was wounded in the arm by a bullet that entered his forearm and disintegrated as it shattered the bone.

Earl Heatley was arrested and charged with two counts of murder and one of malicious wounding. He pleaded not guilty on all counts but the alleged evidence against him was overwhelming.

At his trial before Justice McInerney in the New South Wales Supreme Court in February 1998, Earl Heatley offered no evidence that could help his case. He also refused to give the names of the drug manufacturers for whom he and his brother were supposedly stealing the ingredients. In return the court showed him no mercy.

Earl Heatley was sentenced to die in jail for the murder of Des Thompson and became the fourteenth person in New South Wales to be sentenced to spend the rest of his life behind bars under the 1989 truth-in-sentencing legislation. He was also sentenced to 35 years for killing his brother and maliciously wounding Mr Bithell.

He was subsequently granted a retrial on the grounds that the testimony of a witness was unreliable, but this trial was aborted, and two subsequent retrials resulted in hung juries. The Director of Public Prosecutions, Mr Nicholas Cowdrey QC, said there would be no retrial as there was no reasonable prospect of a conviction. Earl Heatley was free to go.

After maintaining his innocence for nine years in jail, during which time he blamed everybody from corrupt police and lying witnesses – including one who thought he was Phar Lap – Earl Heatley was released from prison in April 2004.

'I've always maintained that I'm not guilty of the charges which were finally dropped yesterday and I'm telling you now I didn't do it,' Earl Heatley said at a press conference. With that he picked up his jacket and headed for the door. 'Well, I'm off,' were his parting words.

34 I TOLD YOU I WAS SICK

Under normal circumstances Christopher Skase would have been a folk hero, given that he took the knock for hundreds of millions of dollars on banks and finance companies on his way to bankruptcy. After all, it is the Australian way to loath the huge institutions that prosper through the Aussie battler's wallet.

But Christopher Skase also took the knock on the good and decent Australians – the builders, florists, car-hire operators, restaurateurs and tradespeople – who gave him credit until the end and never got a brass razoo. That is not the Australian way, especially when you have the funds to pay, as Skase did. For this he will be hated into eternity.

Christopher Skase was born in Melbourne in 1948, the son of a well-known radio broadcaster, Charles Skase. Not an especially bright student, he left Caulfield Grammar in his teens to work as a gopher for two years at a firm of Melbourne stockbrokers. From there he worked as a financial reporter at the Melbourne *Sun* and then the *Australian Financial Review*.

In 1974, aged 26 and armed with limited funds, but with the basic knowledge of how the stock market worked and how to manipulate the press, Skase formed Team Securities and showed an immediate flair for making money. One of the public companies he invested heavily in was the country radio and television operator Quintex.

In 1977 Skase parted with Team Securities with a healthy profit and he devoted all of his time to Quintex. In 1979 he married Melbourne ex-model and socialite Jean Nanette Dixon, who went by the name of Pixie, and they moved to Brisbane. In 1982 Skase was appointed executive chairman of the Quintex board and took a major interest in Queensland television. In 1983 he was appointed chairman of United Telecasters. In 1984 Skase became chairman of the Mirage Resorts Trust and spent $800 million on building Mirage resorts at Port Douglas and Surfers Paradise.

But while Christopher Skase's business career was racing along like a bushfire fanned by gale-force winds, it was not the seemingly daily acquisitions that got the headlines, but rather his and Pixie's lifestyle. They flew around the world in their own Lear jet and were entertained by presidents, princes and kings. In turn they reciprocated by flying their international A-list guests to Australia and entertaining them in their $4 million Brisbane house or at one of their Mirage resorts.

They threw $250,000 Christmas parties, where the French champagne flowed and the Beluga caviar came by the bucket load. Skase set up an AFL football team – the Brisbane Bears – ran rural TV stations all around the country, owned a $1 million holiday house in Port Douglas and an $11 million house in Hollywood, a luxury yacht, an interest in Hardy's chain of jewellery shops, which his wife treated as her own personal Aladdin's cave, garages full of the world's finest cars, and had orchids flown in fresh from Singapore every day. It was opulence the likes of which the east coast of Australia had never seen before. It was costing the Skases millions of dollars a week just to live. It was all too good to be true. And it wasn't.

In 1987 Skase paid $780 million for the Seven network. It

Who Murdered Sallie-Anne?: Although she was from a decent family, Sallie-Anne Huckstepp became a drug addict, gangster's moll and police informer. No one was surprised when she wound up murdered in a Sydney park. Although the case is still open, investigators have little doubt who killed her.

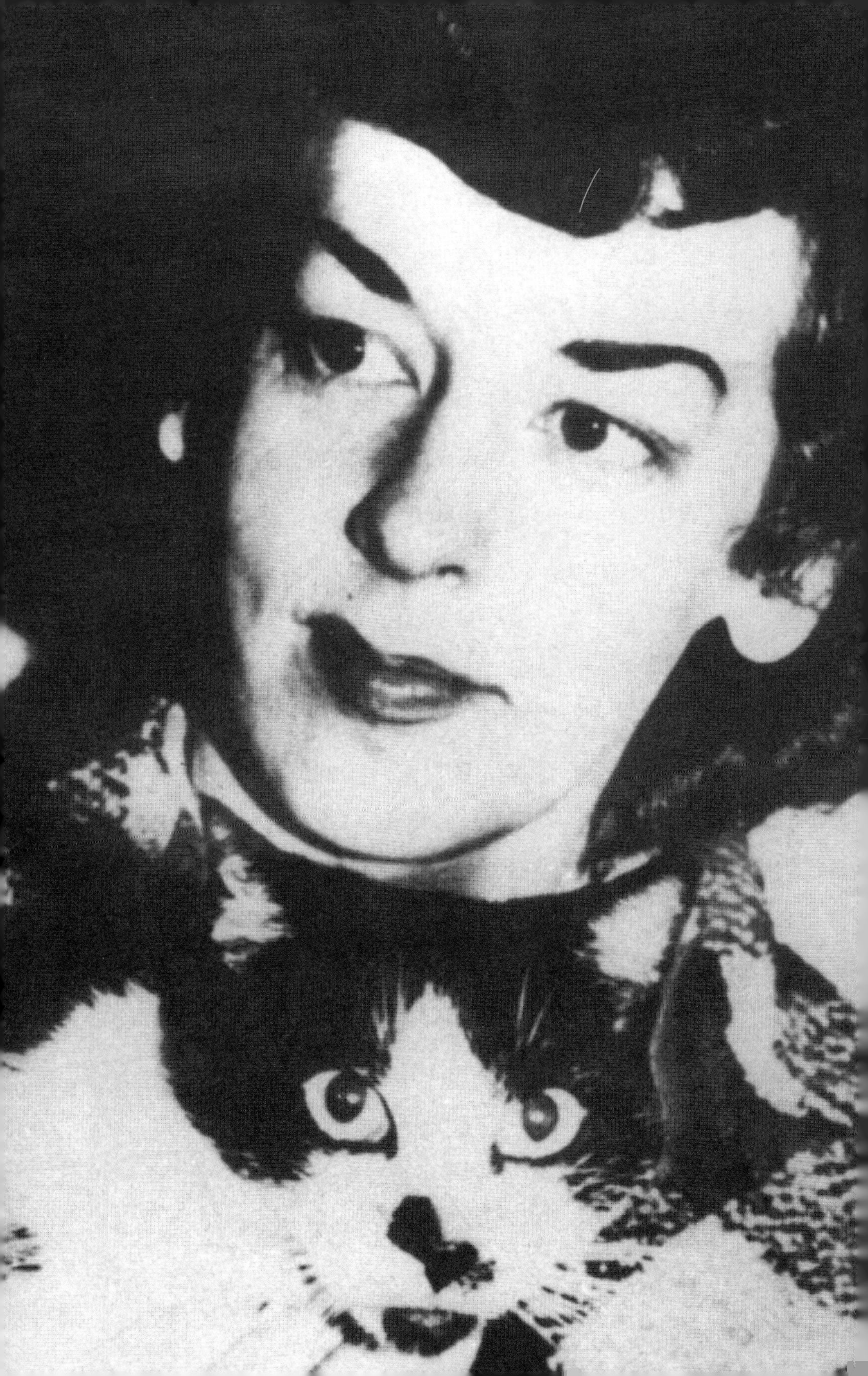

'Darling, you do the renovating and just give me the bills': Former Coles Myer chairman Brian Quinn pictured after his release from prison in October 1999. He served 2? years for fraudulently using his employer's profits in the building of his mansion. Ever the retailer, while in central Victoria's Loddon Prison Quinn ran the canteen more efficiently and profitably than ever before.
Newspix/Trevor Pinder

OPPOSITE **The Wicked Witch of Kings Cross:** Rosaleen Norton was one of the great characters of Sydney's notorious Kings Cross throughout the 1950s, '60s and '70s. Roie was a sight to behold as she swanned through the Cross in her witch's outfit with her entourage of bizarre worshippers in tow. Today her alleged crimes would be laughed out of court.

Azaria – How Could They Have Got It So Wrong?: Lindy Chamberlain and baby Azaria. Just another typical young mother with her family on a holiday to Ayres Rock. Until, that is, she screamed, 'My God, the dingo's got my baby.' These words are now the catchcry of one of the most shameful police investigations and miscarriages of justice in Australia's history. *Newspix*

The Postcard Bandit: Brendan 'Postcard Bandit' Abbott on the run with an unsuspecting Japanese tourist, who didn't have the faintest idea that his new drinking mate was Australia's most wanted man. Rather than a folk hero, Abbott was a lowlife who traumatised the decent folk who were unfortunate enough to be forced to look into the barrel of his shotgun while he was threatening to blow off their head.

'Jockey' Smith – Cop Hater: James Edward 'Jockey' Smith was a horrible little man who always wanted to ride horses for a living but instead spent most of his life trying to kill police officers. Fortunately, the bungling Jockey missed every time. In the end he died in a hail of bullets. Ironically, they were from a police officer's gun.

The Strathfield Massacre: The face of a mass murderer. For no apparent reason, one weekend afternoon Wade Frankum opened fire on shoppers in a packed shopping centre before turning the gun on himself. When the paramedics arrived there were eight dead and many others wounded. Yet Frankum was deemed to be sane at the time of the killings.

BELOW **Bodiless Murder Convictions:** Depraved sexual deviant Daryl Francis Suckling already had 138 convictions for various offences dating back to the age of 11 when he was sent to prison for the rest of his life for the murder of a woman whose body has never been found. Suckling is one of several cases in Australia where there has been a conviction without a victim being located.

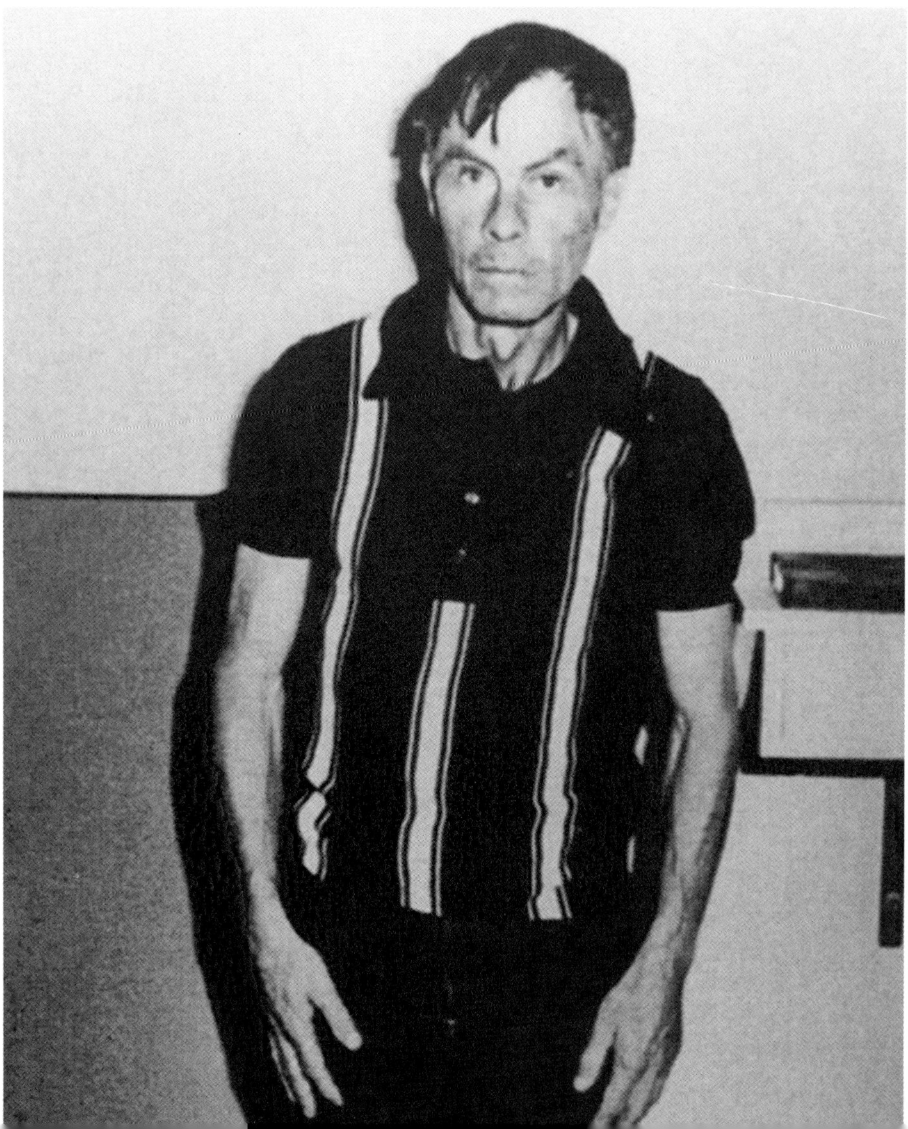

'Last Resort' Laurie Connell: Perth entrepreneur Laurie Connell (right) with another crook Alan Bond (see chapter 43) and entertainer Jackie Love at the opening of Bond's Observation City Hotel in 1987. 'Last Resort' Laurie couldn't believe his luck when, with the assistance of his old mate Western Australian Premier Brian Bourke (who also wound up in the slammer), he opened a bank and suddenly had $500 million of investors' money to play with. Naturally, Laurie spent the lot living like there were no tomorrows. *Newspix*

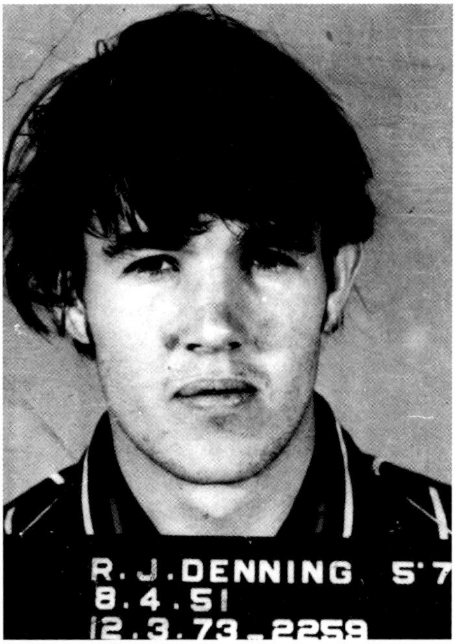

The Outlaw Folk Hero: Career criminal Raymond John Denning made a practice of escaping from jail and telling the press just how bad it was on the inside. For his efforts Denning became somewhat of a hero in some people's eyes and gained the reputation of a likeable scoundrel. Truth be known, Denning was a murderer who would stop at nothing to get what he wanted. *Newspix*

Rex 'Buckets' Jackson and the Prisoner Early-Release Scheme: A big jolly minister for corrective services who was everybody's mate, Buckets saw to it that if the crims on the inside behaved themselves they got an extra early leave pass. If they gave the minister an envelope full of cash they got an even earlier one. Trouble was, Buckets got pinched and wound up in the clink himself.

The Charismatic Crooked Cop: Disgraced former detective sergeant Roger Rogerson takes his first step to freedom from Berrima Prison, New South Wales in December 1995. He would do another year in 2005. Upon his second release Rogerson rejoined the successful pub act comprising himself, Mark 'Chopper' Read and ex-Aussie rules bad boy Mark 'Jacko' Jackson. It inspired the joke: What's got four teeth and seven thongs? The front row at a Chopper, Dodger and Jacko gig. *Newspix*

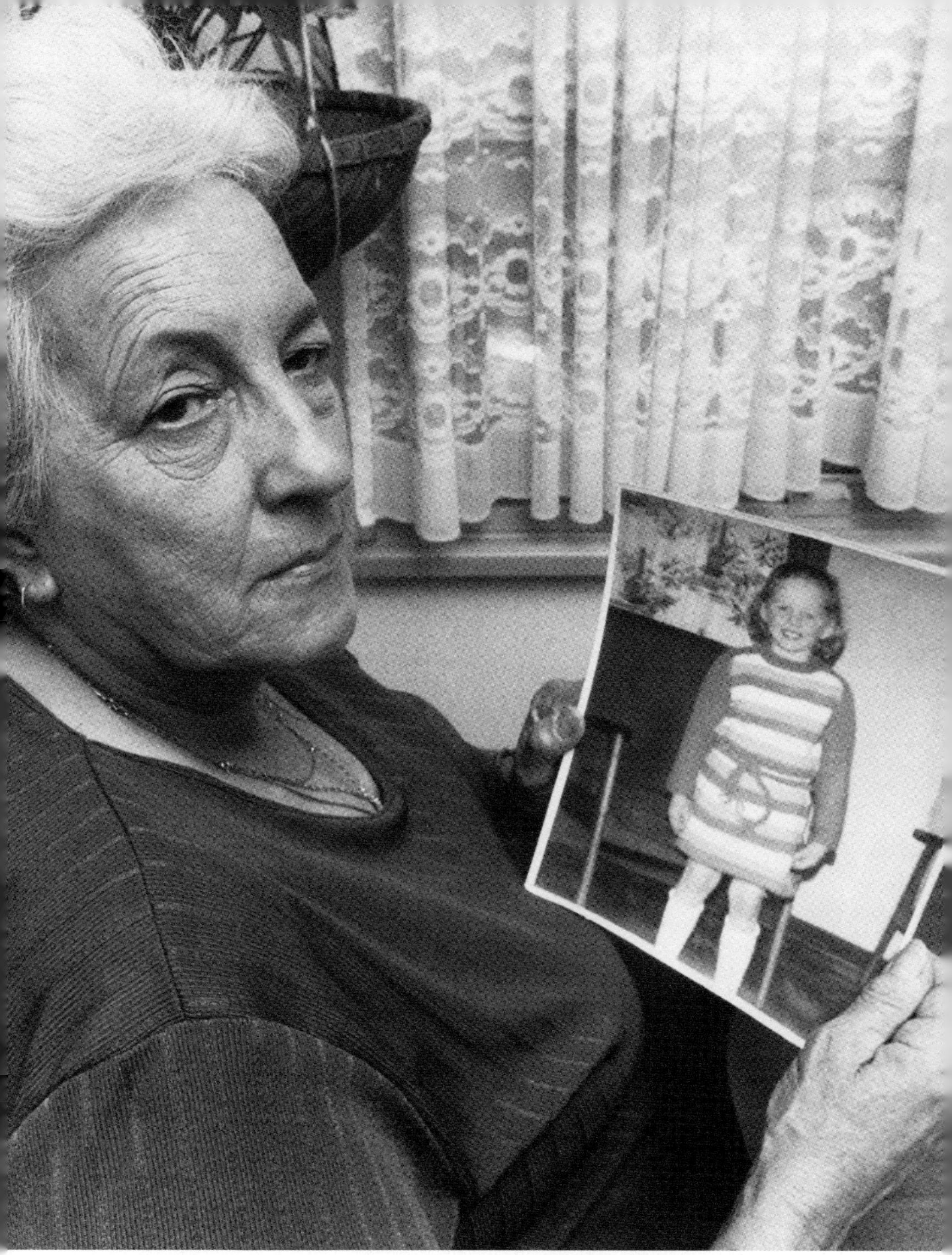

Murder Beyond Belief: Gwen Hanns with a photo of her daughter Nicole, who was savagely stabbed to death by John Lewthwaite in 1972. It was Lewthwaite's intention to rape and murder Nicole's nine-year-old brother, but when he found Nicole in the house he murdered her instead. Amid public uproar Lewthwaite was released from prison in 1999.

The Joke – The Crimes of Sir Terence Lewis, Police Commissioner: From humble beginnings as a Brisbane menswear salesman to police inspector in rural Charleville to Joh Bjelke-Petersen–sponsored Queensland police commissioner and a knighthood, Sir Terence Lewis had it all. Except the ability to control his greed. Sir Terry copped kickbacks from crooked politicians, illegal casino bosses, drug traffickers and corrupt police. He wound up in the slammer and it is believed that Lady Lewis is the only titled lady in Australia to have ever claimed the dole.

BELOW **The Shooting of Arthur Caldwell:** The much-loved leader of the Labor Opposition was the unlikely target of Australia's first political assassination attempt. Yet as Arthur Caldwell left a successful rally a gunman emerged from the crowd and opened fire.

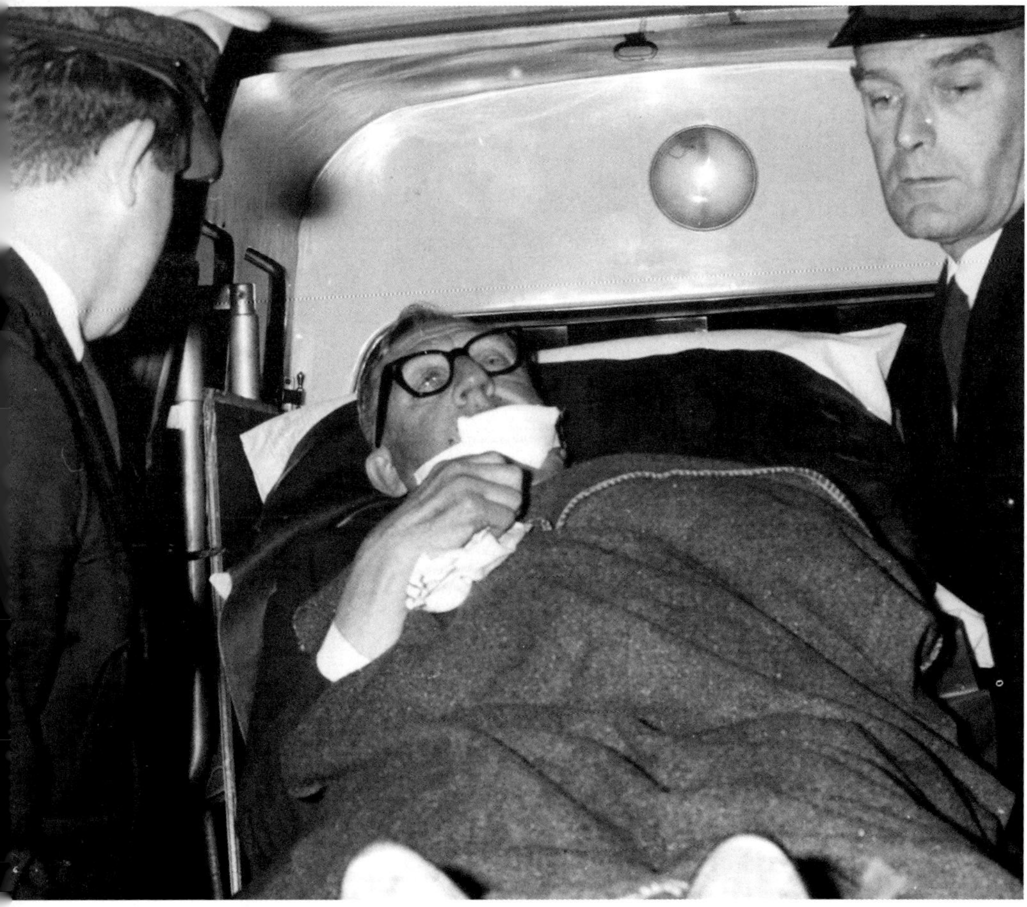

Getting Away with Murder: Earl Heatley served 15 years for murder and, a decade after his release, was sentenced to jail for the rest of his life for killing two men in a bungled robbery. A retrial was aborted and two subsequent retrials resulted in hung juries. Having served almost 10 years in jail, Earl Heatley was freed in April 2004, after it was determined there was no reasonable prospect of a conviction. *Newspix/Nathan Edwards*

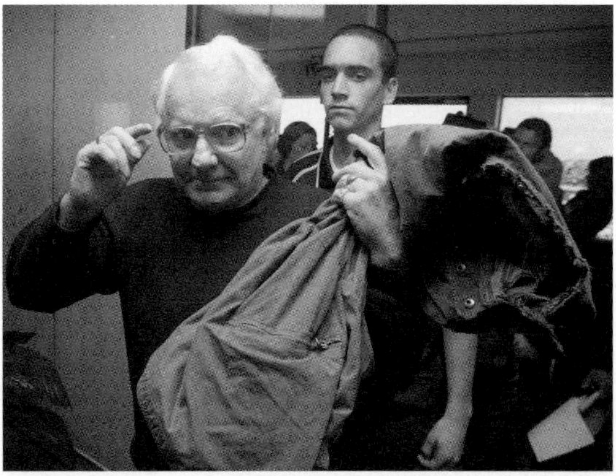

The End of Katingal: Warder Stephen Tandy takes a philosophical look at Australia's most notorious jail as the bulldozers move in to rip it down. In 1975, Tandy was taken hostage at gunpoint by Russell 'Mad Dog' Cox in an escape attempt from nearby Long Bay Jail. Cox was captured and sent to Katingal where he became the only prisoner ever to escape. He was on the run for 11 years. *Fairfax/Wade Laube*

FOLLOWING PAGE **I Told You I Was Sick:** On 16 November 1999 fugitive Australian businessman Christopher Skase – shown here in a wheelchair in court – was released from custody after a Spanish court overturned an extradition order which was granted earlier that year. Back in Australia Skase would have faced charges relating to the 1989 collapse of his Quintex media and resort empire. Sceptics claimed that his ill-health was just another ploy to avoid extradition. He proved them all wrong by dying. *Newspix*

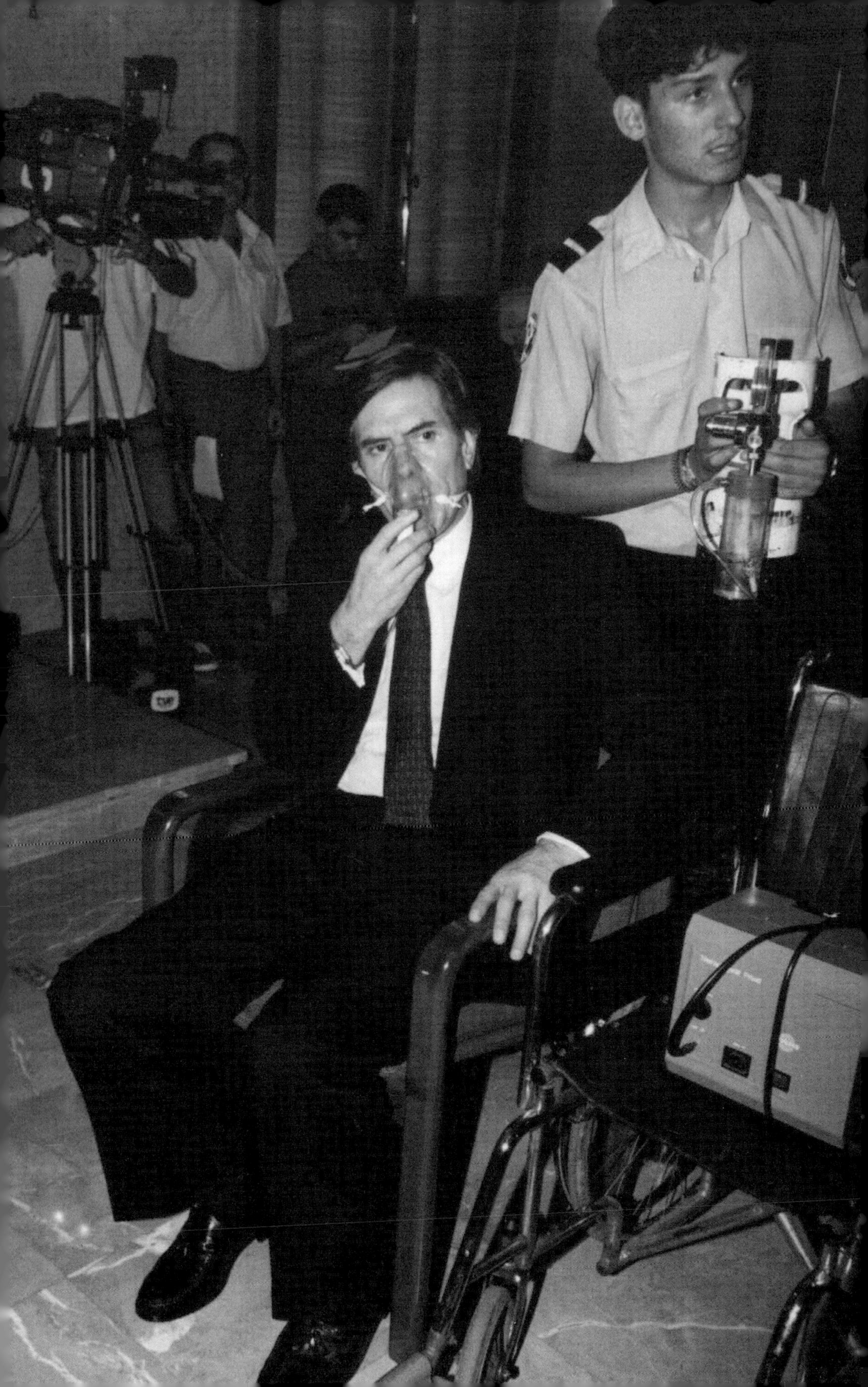

The Legend of Hollywood George: Australia's prince of punters, Hollywood George Edser, was warned off racecourses worldwide in 1961 as an 'undesirable person' after he became involved in a race-fixing scandal. But that didn't stop him from having a punt. Hollywood had men on the course to bet for him and he could be found on a ladder looking over the racecourse fence with his binoculars as the horses went around.

BELOW **Going Out in Style:** If you're a gangster past your 'use-by' date and you're going to be seen off, then the Melbourne Magistrate's Court is as good a place as any to have it happen and leave a lasting memory. Raymond Patrick Bennett had a price on his head and was quite happy to be in custody on a robbery charge where the assassins couldn't get at him. Wrong. Bennett was executed in what you would have thought would be about the safest place in town.

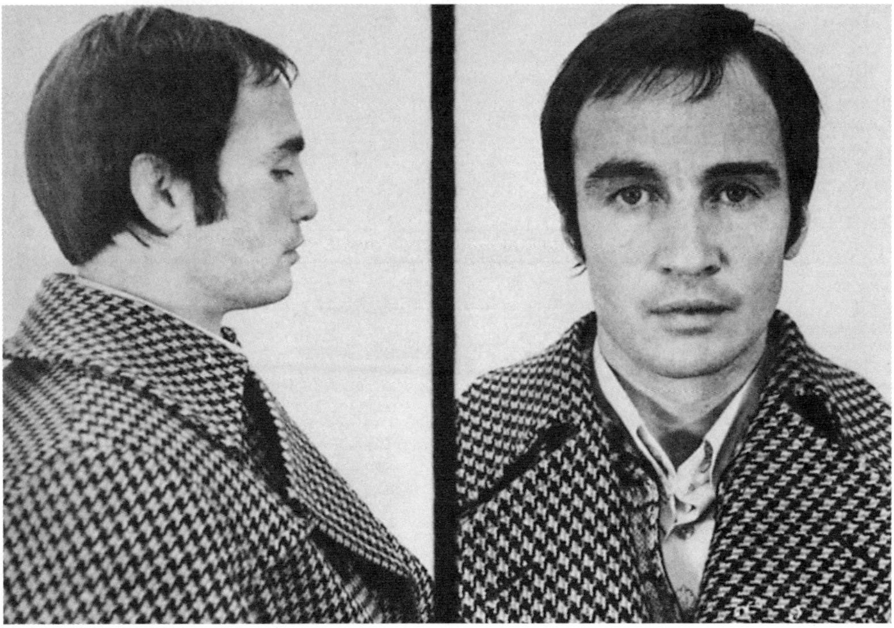

The Port Arthur Massacre: An overview of Port Arthur in April 2006. In the foreground are the remains of the Broad Arrow Cafe where 20 of the 35 victims were killed. In the background is the Port Arthur Penitentiary, which until 1877 housed Tasmania's most hardened convicts.
AAP Image/Robyn Grace

George Freeman – King of the SP Bookies: From dirt-poor beginnings George David Freeman rose to become the biggest starting-price bookmaker in Sydney, with illegal establishments in almost every suburb. And while it was said that he wasn't the Mr Big of organised crime in Sydney, he was reputedly one of the Mr Big Enough's.

The Infamous Dr Reginald Stuart-Jones: The wild man of medicine, Dr Stuart-Jones made his real money from his abortion clinics and spent it as fast as it rolled into his surgeries. An entrepreneur of illegal establishments, he gambled and drank his money away, and was lucky to survive an attempt on his life when three men tried to shoot him and throw him over a cliff. Certainly not what the doctor ordered.

The Murder of Ebony Simpson: Child killer Peter Raymond Garforth is among the most hated men in Australia and will spend the rest of his life in protective custody. Garforth raped and murdered schoolgirl Ebony Simpson at Bargo in the New South Wales Southern Highlands. The death of Ebony Simpson played a key role in the formation of the Homicide Victims Support Group, which cares for the families and loved ones of murder victims.

The Sins of the Father: The Waters boxing family. Patriarch Cec with his boys (L-R) Dean, Troy and Guy. Cec manically drove his boys the same way he drove his marriage. When his wife ran off with the hired help, Cec co-opted those around him to commit murder. *Newspix*

The Peter Huxley Scandal: Throughout the 1960s a dapper mystery man was setting the racecourses alight with huge bets. Sometimes he won, but most times he lost and settled with bank cheques on the Monday night. One Monday he didn't turn up and the bookies were left owed a bundle. The mystery punter was soon on the front pages of the papers for embezzling the bank he ran. *Newspix*

BELOW **Celluloid Serial Killers:** The most recognisable serial killer of them all – Dr Hannibal 'the Cannibal' Lecter. *The Silence of the Lambs* made serial killers a household term, and they became the most popular reading and watching genre of the '90s. But serial killers had been committing their hideous crimes for many years before Dr Lecter – as far back as 1943, when it all began with *Arsenic and Old Lace*. *AP Photo/Ken Regan*

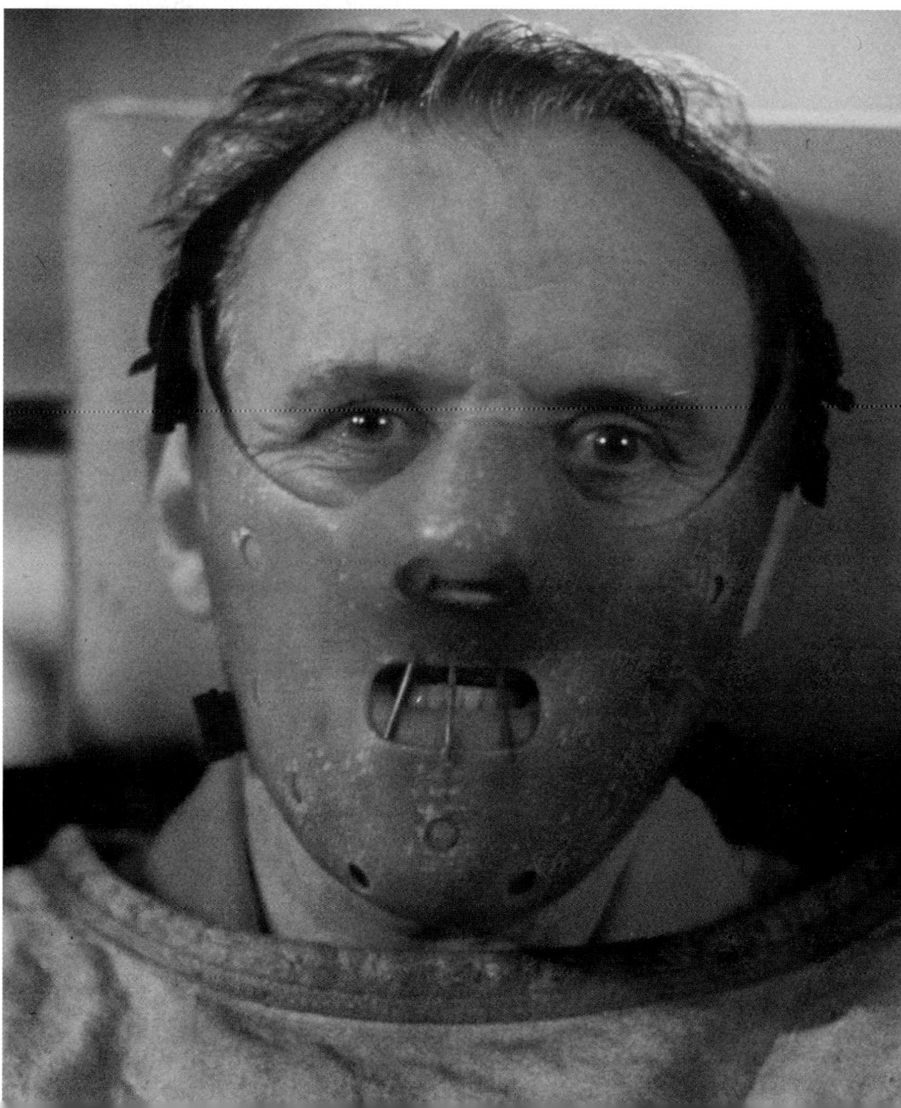

would be one of the rocks that he would perish on, given that he borrowed most of the money to buy it. Then he went even further and bit off more than even he could chew. He tried to acquire the American MGM studios for $1.5 billion, and planned to use the cash flow to prop up his entire empire, which was earning far less than it was costing. But the best he could come up with to substantiate his offer was a $50 million down payment on the deal and Rupert Murdoch snuck under his guard and bought the studio. Skase was out in the cold.

Then, in October 1988, the stock market crashed and Christopher Skase's empire came tumbling down around him. As they say in the Aussie vernacular, he went from the penthouse to the outhouse.

But Skase had a safety net in case of such problems. While billing everything to his companies, he had been paying himself tens of millions in management fees. He maintained a reasonable lifestyle right up to his inevitable bankruptcy. In the meantime, none of his creditors got paid and many local businesses owned by hard-working Australians who trusted him either went to the wall or had to mortgage their houses to stay afloat.

In June 1991 Christopher Skase was declared bankrupt with corporate debts of $1.5 billion and personal debts of $170 million, but Chris and Pixie were taking a well-timed holiday on the Spanish island of Majorca at the time. All he left behind for the liquidators was about $1100 in cash, about $200 in his bank account and some office equipment. In his absence he was charged with 32 jailable offences relating to the collapse of Quintex. He was Australia's most hated man.

Christopher and Pixie Skase and members of their family set themselves up in a $6 million mansion in Majorca, but explained that it was just rented and they were living a very basic lifestyle. The Australian press would have none of it; they hounded them every time they set foot outside its high walls. But, try as they may, the Australian government could not get Skase back to Australia to stand trial and face the people he had so callously ignored. There seemed little doubt that Skase had greased a few palms with his creditors' money to stay put.

When Skase – a heavy smoker all of his life – fell seriously ill with chronic respiratory problems that stopped him from flying and allegedly demanded a lung transplant, it was little wonder that his pursuers thought that this was just another ruse to avoid extradition back to Australia. But Christopher Skase proved them all wrong. In August 2001, aged just 52, he died in Majorca of respiratory failure with his family by his bedside.

Such was the low regard in which Christopher Skase was held by the press back home in Australia that, one of the many unsympathetic headlines simply read: 'I told you I was sick.'

35 THE MASSACRE AT HOPE FOREST

With seven children ranging in age from four to 19, the Bartholomew family lived a modest existence at their somewhat decrepit farmhouse at Hope Forest, south of Adelaide, in the early 1970s. A labourer employed by a firm specialising in earth moving, 40-year-old Clifford Cecil Bartholomew was forced to keep a close eye on his family's meagre finances, and his wife Heather helped out in the local dairy when she could in order to bring in a few extra dollars to help them get by. Though the region was quiet, the Bartholomews preferred it to the relative hustle and bustle of Adelaide, and they made the most of what they had.

It was early in 1971 that the family took in a boarder, a Vietnam veteran in his early 20s who went by the name of Max. A short time later, over the Easter holiday break, Heather Bartholomew announced that she would journey to Sydney in order to visit her younger sister Winnis Keane. Keane was a resident at the married quarters at Holdsworthy army base outside of Sydney, New South Wales. Because the younger sibling's husband was currently away on training, and Keane herself worked during the day, Max went along to keep Heather company. The situation had the added benefit that the veteran could be reunited with some of his old friends from the army.

Clifford Bartholomew stayed at home to care for the children while his wife and the boarder set off on Easter Monday on a coach bus for the long trip to Sydney. Even though the plan was only to be away for three weeks, Heather phoned Clifford a few times from Sydney, as well as penning correspondence to the children. But a short time before the mother and Max were due to make the trip home again, Heather phoned Clifford to say the pair would be delayed for a week as a result of a problem with their return-coach booking.

Wanting to surprise his stranded wife, Clifford spent his recently acquired income tax refund on purchasing a Holden ute, which he drove all the way to Sydney, meeting Heather and Max at the coach station to a decidedly chilly response. Heather protested about the run-down state of the early-model vehicle he had bought to chariot them home, and she seemed to sit close to the Vietnam veteran as the threesome made the arduous trip back to Hope Forest.

While they clicked over the distance slowly but surely, Heather told Clifford about the entertaining time she had spent with Max in the big city. Not much of a drinker, the mother told the story of getting drunk on rum mixed with Coca-Cola. She got so drunk, she said, that she had to be put to bed. Clifford could not have been comfortable listening to such a tale coming from his own wife's mouth. He wondered if she was telling the whole story.

When they finally made it back home, Clifford took note that Heather greeted their children with far more affection than she had afforded him.

Indeed, her whole attitude towards him had changed, with Clifford even going as far as to note in his diary that their love-making that evening was not as romantic as it had been in the past. In contrast, the mother of seven was a ball of energy and laughter when she was around their boarder, Max, while she seemed barely interested when conversing with Clifford. But when the patriarch of the family questioned his wife about her demeanour and change of attitude towards him, she told him nothing was wrong and that he must just be imagining things. Clifford wasn't placated, but he seemed to let the matter slide.

Meanwhile, things went from bad to worse for the large family, with ongoing heavy rain meaning that Clifford was stood down from his job until things cleared up in the summer. As his long-service payment started to dry up while the rains continued to pour down, Clifford grew despondent. He knew the money his firm had sorted him out with could not last forever. He also sensed that his wife was growing continuously closer to their younger boarder. Clifford even confided to his diary that he was sure the pair were engaging in sexual relations.

In an effort to ease the pressure on their family life, Clifford announced that he would take a break by himself at Port Lincoln for a couple of weeks. Heather told him to take as long as he wanted. Shortly before he went off alone he walked into his house to hear the unmistakable sound of his wife's laughter. Heading into the loungeroom, he found Max on the floor with Heather sitting over him giggling. The best excuse May could muster up was that he was only 'tickling her'. Clifford was infuriated but decided to take a laid-back approach to the situation. He called Max outside and told the boarder to 'cut it out'.

Eager to regain his wife's affection, the cuckolded Clifford spent more of his long-service payment on buying her a fancy watch. He also made an effort to be more helpful in the household duties, going as far as serving her breakfast in bed. Nothing, however, seemed to stir Heather beyond indifference to her husband.

Clifford's time in Port Lincoln only served to make him more melancholy. He knew in his heart that he wanted his wife back, with things the way they were between them when they were first married, but he was becoming increasingly convinced her affections now lay with the younger army veteran and boarder. Clifford wrote a letter to his wife revealing his feelings and continuing devotion for her. The reply was short, emotionless and to the point, with Heather signing off, 'Regards ...'

Things were now on a fast downward spiral for Clifford. Returning to Hope Forest, an intense argument saw him threaten to kill himself and his children with a gun. Heather told Clifford she didn't care what he did. She then decided to return to visit her sister in Sydney. Despite being desperately low on funds, Clifford gave his wife the money she needed to catch a plane northeast alone. But it wasn't long before he intercepted a letter sent from Heather to Max. Clifford read the contents and his heart broke – the letter was full of affection from his wife to his boarder. Clifford was crushed.

Not knowing what else to do, he spoke to Max about the letter. The boarder realised matters were coming to a head, so he packed his suitcase and left the Bartholomew residence as fast as he could. Clifford, meanwhile, drove up to Sydney, stopping only for petrol when necessary. He wanted to find out from Heather once and for all what was going on between her and Max. When he arrived at the army base where she was staying with her sister, Heather was fast to explain that the whole letter was just a joke conjured up by the sisters while drinking. For whatever reason, Clifford seemed to accept the flimsy excuse, but the drive back to Hope Forest was even more icy than the previous one. The married couple barely spoke through the whole trip.

Once back at home, and with their boarder seemingly out of the picture, the difficulties between Clifford and Heather became more obvious, with Clifford openly asking if Heather had been unfaithful to him with Max. Heather was staunch in her denial, and before long her sister Winnis arrived to live with the couple. Having separated from her army husband, Winnis now had a new boyfriend in tow, as well as her two-year-old son. Clifford would go on to write in his diary of the pain it caused him to watch Winnis and her younger lover act playfully towards each other, gently touching each other with fondness in public when his own wife would not let him lay so much as a finger upon her.

The situation bubbled until that August when a fierce argument between the married couple saw Clifford vacate the family home and move into his stepmother's house in the town of Meadows, around 15 kilometres away from Hope Forest. The parting was cold, with Heather offering respect to the father of her children, but adding that she had lost all physical affection for him. Clifford was gutted, but at least Heather invited him to spend Father's Day with the family.

Early the next month, on 5 September 1971, Clifford arrived back at the house in his battered ute. He had come prepared, with lollies and soft-drink treats for the children, as well as a .22 calibre rifle, a gift for his eldest son, 19-year-old Neville.

In addition to the sweets and firearm, Clifford had brought along a bottle of rum for Heather and her sister to share, as well as beer for himself. But when he arrived only Neville was at the Hope Forest home – the women had taken the other children to visit friends. The situation angered Clifford, who saw it as yet another slight against him by a wife who clearly no longer loved him. But that was not the last blow for Clifford that Father's Day. Neville soon admitted that Heather was moving to Adelaide with all the children. She intended to work as a waitress and live with Max. Clifford could not believe his ears and waves of anger rushed through his body.

He was still stewing when Heather, her sister and the children finally arrived back home. Only his youngest daughter, four-year-old Sarah-Jane, showed any affection for him, running into his arms for a hug. Clifford was incensed. After dinner he settled down to watch TV with Neville to drink the beer he had brought. He then visited his wife in her bedroom, where he begged her to reconsider the move. Heather told him it was all over. They would never get back together. Clifford could visit his children in the state's capital, she added, but he was under no circumstances to 'interfere' in her 'private life'.

Clifford was crushed. Shell-shocked, he made the drive back to Meadows but could not fall asleep that evening. His anger at the mother of his children grew. Even worse was the thought that he was being replaced by the man he had taken in as a boarder. Clifford decided he couldn't stand for these actions. At 12.30am, Clifford decided he would kill his wife. In the ute he still had the rifle he had bought for Neville. It would be the perfect weapon, he reckoned.

A half hour-later he arrived at Hope Forest, where he loaded up the gun and located a rubber mallet and gloves in the shed. Sneaking into his old marital bedroom, he found Heather asleep with two of his children. Sarah-Jane was snoozing in a nearby cot. Clifford shone a torch in his wife's face, then brought the rubber mallet swinging down upon her head as she woke up screaming for her sister Winnis to help her. Clifford struck her once again. He would later write in his diary about things reaching a 'dead quiet'. He suddenly found himself alone in the kitchen, wondering what he was doing with a rifle in his hands. He poured a cup of coffee and took some painkillers before returning to check on his wife and children. The man had murdered his entire family.

He phoned his stepmother explaining that he intended to kill himself. When the police arrived at the tragic scene, they found Clifford alone and drunk in the kitchen. He had shot his seven children and wife to death, as well as Winnis Keane and her young son Daniel. He would later write in his diary that he 'couldn't stop himself' and that his 'mind was in a state of madness' when he embarked on his killing spree.

Clifford Bartholomew pleaded guilty to all charges when he appeared in Adelaide's Supreme Court in front of Justice Roma Mitchell, who sentenced him to death. That sentence was later commuted to hard labour for life, and Clifford was released on parole on 10 December 1979. The decision caused much public consternation but Clifford still insisted that he had only intended on harming his wife. He had been considered a model prisoner during his time as an inmate.

36 THE END OF KATINGAL

In November 2005, it was announced that the most notorious jail in the history of New South Wales – the concrete bunker within the grounds of Long Bay Jail known as Katingal – was to be demolished, despite being heritage-listed as part of the Long Bay complex. Katingal, which is an Aboriginal world meaning 'separation from social control', was used between 1975 and 1978 to house the state's most dangerous inmates. Katingal was as loathed as it was notorious. There were no tears when the bulldozers arrived in March 2006.

Katingal had been purpose-built to hold the worst of the worst, and its roll call at any given time included the most evil killers, rapists, armed robbers and escapologists within the New South Wales prison system. Until then these 'intractables', as they were known, had been sent to the hell hole of Grafton Prison in northern New South Wales, where little had changed since convict times.

The 1978 Royal Commission into Prisons in New South Wales provided an insight into the cruelty that took place in

Grafton Prison, which had operated for 33 years until it had been closed down two years earlier. Mr Justice Nagle described some of the brutality at the 'unit for intractables'.

'Inmates arrived at Grafton customarily attired in overalls and slippers, their arms strapped to their sides by a security belt to which their wrists were handcuffed,' Justice Nagle said. 'In some instances, the beatings began even before the security belt and handcuffs were removed. The beatings were usually administered by three or four officers wielding rubber batons. The inmate was taken into a yard, ordered to strip, searched, and then the biff began. The word "biff" by no means describes the brutal beating which ensued.

'If most of the inmates are to be believed, the officers had no compunction about beating them around their backs and heads; nor were they averse to kicking them when they were on the ground. They invariably abused them while they were hitting them, calling them obscene and abusive names. Sometimes they threatened to kill them.'

A former prison officer, Mr J.J. Pettit, described the beatings to the commission. 'Sometimes three, four or five of them would assault the inmate with their batons to a condition of semi-consciousness,' he said. 'On occasions the inmate urinated, obviously and uncontrollably out of fear, and his nervous system ceased to function normally.'

And so Katingal – the grey, windowless, three-storey concrete monolith within Long Bay Jail that would house up to 40 of the state's most dangerous criminals at a time, was built to replace Grafton. Escape was deemed impossible through the one-metre-thick walls and the lights were left on 24 hours a day so a prisoner was never out of sight of a guard.

Katingal soon became infamous as the home to beasts such as Kevin Crump and Allan Baker who, in 1973, raped and murdered housewife Mrs Virginia Morse after they abducted her from her farmhouse. And Archibald Beatty McCafferty, the 'Kill Seven' killer, who serial-murdered at the behest of his dead infant son who told his father from the grave that if he murdered seven innocent citizens he would rise from the dead. Another resident was the police informer Raymond John Denning, who had killed a prison guard on one of his numerous escape attempts and was in the bowels of Katingal to save him from both the other prisoners and guards keen to seek revenge for their lost mate.

But, without a doubt, Katingal's star resident, though not for very long, was the notorious bank robber, Russell 'Mad Dog' Cox. In 1974 Russell Cox was arrested in Sydney for armed robbery and car theft and sentenced to 14 years in jail. In August 1975 he attempted to break out of the Metropolitan Reception Prison at Long Bay by taking prison warder Stephen Tandy hostage at gunpoint. He was sentenced to life imprisonment for the attempted murder of the warder and the judge threw in 15 years' hard labour for good measure.

Deemed an 'incorrigible', Cox was sent to the only known place in New South Wales that could contain him – Katingal – and locked in solitary confinement. In November 1977, after noting Katingal's weak spots and the moves of the guards down to the split second, while left alone in his tiny exercise yard for his one hour a day, the super-fit and extremely intelligent Cox removed a bar he had been hacksawing away at for months with a tiny blade and was over the roof and then the wall without so much as a hand laid on him, let alone a shot fired. He fled in a waiting car and was on the run until he was recaptured in a shootout with police almost 11 years later.

When the news spread of Cox's escape the prisoners erupted in the knowledge that one of their own had done the impossible and escaped from what the government had claimed was a mixture of Alcatraz and Devil's Island rolled into one. There were celebrations in the old, and the new jail, that night.

Cox's escape didn't help matters and in 1978, after just three years, and following the recommendations of the Royal Commission into Prisons, Katingal was also closed. Mr Justice Nagle described Katingal as being designed for 'the containment of dangerous violent criminals which arose directly out of general dissatisfaction with Grafton, which had just been closed.' He said that Katingal very quickly began to suffer from the same problems as Grafton and for the same reasons – the classification of inmates as 'the worst one per cent', which allowed the abuse of authority that led to unacceptable conditions. It was described as inhumane and a breeding ground for corruption and brutality. Justice Nagle recommended it be closed forthwith. Katingal's inmates were spread out among the maximum security facilities in jails throughout New South Wales.

At the commission, the Hon. Dr Meredith Burgmann described Katingal as 'the high-tech unit at Long Bay Jail which is so high tech that it now cannot be converted to any other purpose. Indeed, it is built so strongly and is such a terrible obscenity of concrete and iron bars that it would cost a great deal to even demolish it,' she said.

Dr Burgmann's prediction proved correct. It took a costly three months to raze Katingal to the ground with the most modern equipment available. As of June 2006, it was being reconstructed as a central store which will no doubt have its ghosts, no matter how modern and brightly lit it is.

37 | 'I WANT MY MUMMY'

On 29 June 1991, six-year-old Sheree Beasley disappeared from the Victorian seaside town of Rosebud. In September 1991 her body was found forced into a stormwater drain 15 kilometres away. A seemingly respectable 56-year-old man was charged with Sheree's abduction, sexual assault and murder, and with concealment of her body.

Travelling salesman Robert Arthur Selby Lowe was a husband, father and church elder with a sinister double life. Unbeknownst to his wife and children, he had a long list of convictions for public exposure and indecency. At his trial in October 1994, Justice Phillip Cummins wept openly as he heard evidence. 'I want my mummy,' Sheree reportedly screamed. Lowe ignored the pleas as she choked to death while he forced her to perform oral sex on him.

A number of witnesses had seen Sheree that afternoon. A boy her age saw a man place her in a small blue car. A woman remembered the little girl crying inside a small blue car. The vehicle was identified as a late-model Toyota Corolla hatchback. Hundreds of people owned such a car. Police had to contact each one.

During this exhausting exercise, they found Robert Arthur Selby Lowe, who told them he was nowhere near Rosebud when Sheree went missing. He had been at home with his wife and two teenage boys. Police grew suspicious when Lowe refused to give them his home phone number. They checked his record. Alarm bells rang.

In 1984, Lowe had been placed on a 12-month bond after being found guilty of exposing himself and making sexually suggestive remarks to a group of schoolgirls. Four years later, he was arrested after teenagers reported a man accosting them, exposing himself and masturbating. Police were unable to prove Lowe was the flasher in question. He was released.

In 1990, he was charged with obscene behaviour after approaching schoolgirls at Melbourne's Flinders Street railway station. The girls were carrying balloons. Lowe told them the balloons looked like 'big dicks'. Exposing himself, Lowe propositioned them. The girls ran to a police officer. Lowe was fined $700.

Since his 1984 conviction, Lowe had been seeing psychotherapist Margaret Hobbs, who prepared a pre-sentence report. She wrote: 'I am of the opinion that [Lowe] truly believes that he is indulging in harmless behaviour ... It does unfortunately need the intervention of the courts to instil in him the illegality of his actions.'

Still, Lowe appeared a solid member of society. His wife, Lorraine, was a religious woman. He seemed to share her devotion to the church. Married in 1972, the family was a model of middle-class morality. Every Sunday, they attended the local Baptist Church. Lowe was a Sunday school teacher with a group of children in his care. During holidays the family went to their flat at Rosebud, on Port Phillip Bay.

But Lowe had felony convictions in three countries, and had been sent to prison twice in New Zealand for sex offences. He then emigrated to Australia, where his police file became heavy with convictions for indecent assaults on young men and women. In Australia, he regularly exposed himself to boys and girls, often masturbating in front of them and making sexual advances.

Lowe was born in 1937 in England. In 1956, he was convicted of stealing a car and injuring a police officer while trying to avoid capture. The 19-year-old was spared prison. Three years later, his family emigrated to New Zealand, settling in Wellington. Shortly after, Lowe was charged with indecent assault on a young male. In 1961, he moved to Auckland and received his first sentence for sex offences. He was convicted of wilful and obscene exposure again in 1964 and sent back to prison. Shortly after his release, he was convicted for theft.

Lowe had become a source of shame to his family, who were prominent in the local business community. With their encouragement, he started a new life in Melbourne. His family was relieved to hear he intended to wed. He also appeared to have become a devout Christian.

But Lowe was exposing himself to young boys and girls almost daily.

The investigation into Sheree Beasley's disappearance continued. Knowing Lowe drove a car like the one reported, police stepped up their inquiries. They became aware of an ongoing investigation into a man who exposed himself to young boys at a suburban swimming pool in March 1991. The man fled when approached by several adults. The adults saw the offender get into a blue car. They noted the registration number. It was Lowe's.

He became the prime suspect in Sheree's abduction after police received a tip from a woman claiming she knew a man with a history of sex offences. The man had a flat in Rosebud and drove a blue Toyota Corolla hatchback. His name was Robert Arthur Selby Lowe. Police later identified the caller as Dr Margaret Hobbs.

Surveillance officers followed Lowe's every move, observing him loitering around swimming pools and parks. They saw him approach prostitutes. They witnessed him masturbating in public toilets. It was time to move in. They obtained a warrant to search Lowe's home in August 1991, but found nothing to link him with Sheree Beasley's abduction. He denied any involvement.

Finally, Lowe was taken into custody and questioned about the day Sheree disappeared. He stuck to his story – he had been at home with his wife and children. With his alibi intact and no physical evidence, police had to release their prime suspect. Surveillance continued.

Meanwhile, Lorraine Lowe had become aware that her husband of 19 years was a convicted criminal with a long record for sex offences. She ordered him to leave the family home. Lowe's alibi was falling apart. His wife now recalled where he had been on 29 June 1991 – by himself at the Rosebud flat. Her two sons gave statements saying they hadn't seen their father until about 5pm that day.

Then, on 24 September 1991, Sheree's body was found in the paddocks of Red Hill, a suburb on the Mornington Peninsula. An autopsy revealed that she had died of asphyxiation.

Around this time, Lowe returned to Margaret Hobbs for further treatment. It seems he trusted her. She tried to persuade him to talk about the crime. He was unaware that she had decided to help the police. Every time she met Lowe, Hobbs recorded the conversations. Slowly, she gained various admissions. His trust in her grew so much that he drove her to the scene of the abduction and the stormwater drain to show how he had concealed the body.

Twenty-one months after Sheree's abduction, Lowe was charged with her murder and remanded in custody at Pentridge Prison's K Division. Police believed they had a strong case. But there was a chance that the evidence obtained by Margaret Hobbs would be deemed inadmissible. Then K Division inmate Peter Allan Reid came forward. He said Lowe had told him about the abduction and murder. The convicted murderer had decided he too would help the police.

Lowe apparently felt at ease with Reid, presumably believing Reid wouldn't divulge the substance of their conversations. But the criminal code of silence does not extend to child murderers.

Reid provided a statement that helped convict Lowe. He said Lowe had approached him not long after arriving in K Division. He said: 'He seemed to want to talk about why he was there.'

Lowe told Reid how he had abducted and killed Sheree Beasley. He had told his wife and children he was going to the Rosebud flat to fix some tiles. According to Reid, 'He said he just used the tile-fixing story as an excuse ... he had been watching the little girl for some time.'

He continued: 'I asked him how many times he had seen her in the past and he said numerous times.' Reid claimed that Lowe told him details about how he had abducted Sheree: 'He left his place about 2pm. He drove up to an area about 7 kilometres away, where he saw the little girl riding a pushbike ... He said he got out of his car and waved to the little girl to pull over.'

Sheree Beasley did not want to get into the car. Lowe threw her into the front seat. 'He said that he told the little girl that her mummy had said for him to take her home as her mummy was ill,' Reid recalled. 'He said the little girl became suspicious of him, and added that he opened the car door and forced her into the front of his car.'

Allegedly, Lowe also told him how Sheree died. Reid explained: 'He said he then put a seatbelt around her and drove about 15 kilometres to an inland country area and forced her to do the "dirty acts". He said that from terrifying fear and the act she was forced to do, she choked to death.'

According to Reid, Lowe seemed to delight in recalling his crimes. 'Lowe told me he decided to take the girl's helmet off when she was choking,' Reid stated. He added that Lowe also 'told me that before the little girl choked, she screamed, "Take me home to mummy."'

Lowe needed to dispose of the body and evidence. According to Reid, he burnt his semen-stained clothing and put Sheree's clothing in a dumpster. He left her bike on the roadside.

He provided Reid with maps and sketches of the scene of the abduction and of where he had travelled to dispose of Sheree's body. In some cases, he even signed the maps. Reid turned everything over to the police and provided a statement describing his conversations with Lowe. It was all they needed.

On 27 October 1994, at his trial, Lowe must have known he was sunk when Reid's evidence was produced. Lowe's defence relied on his assertion that the Crown case was a case of mistaken identity. The jury took five hours to reach its verdict: Lowe was found guilty on all counts.

Two days later, he was brought up for sentencing. Mr Justice Cummins said he accepted Peter Reid's evidence that Sheree Beasley died by choking while forced to perform oral sex on Lowe. The judge told the prisoner: 'What you did was every child's fear and every parent's nightmare.' He then sentenced the 57-year-old to life imprisonment without the possibility of parole.

38 THE LEGEND OF HOLLYWOOD GEORGE

Of all of Australia's colourful racing identities, there was none more colourful than Hollywood George Edser. But, like so many colourful characters before and after him, Hollywood wound up in trouble with the law. Certainly not as bad as some, but in strife just the same.

A tall, immaculately groomed and softly spoken man who was held in high regard by all who knew him, George Edser was born in the New South Wales coal-mining town of Maitland in 1919, one of seven children. Rather than go to school he spent his early years hanging around the local racetracks selling race books to earn enough to have a bet. By the age of 16 he was punting for a living.

The legend goes that as a handsome 17-year-old one Saturday afternoon in 1936, he went to the Broadmeadows racetrack at Newcastle, with a bank of £3. Backing winner after winner with the local on-course bookmaker Barney Kable, the young Edser soon built his bank up to a staggering £6000. Kable called out over the crowd, 'I wish you'd go to Hollywood, George, and become an actor and leave me alone.' The young Edser walked off the course with a fortune and a name that would create headlines in the years to come.

As his reputation as a fearless punter around the Sydney racetracks grew, by the time the war was over Hollywood George had become one of the characters that the punters would follow around to see what he was going to back next. He seldom let them down.

In the early 1950s he was on the front pages when he sold everything he owned and raised £22,000, which he bet on the short-priced Prince Mari at Rosehill. It won by a nose. In 1955 he won £30,000 (about $500,000 today) when his own horse The Corsican won at Warwick Farm. Hollywood George celebrated his win by handing out £10 notes to the punters who hadn't had such a good day.

But Hollywood's life wasn't all fun and games. In March 1958 he was in the headlines again when, after he returned from the theatre with his wife to their Elizabeth Bay apartment at 11.30pm, he was shot in the groin by a .22 calibre pistol or sawn-off rifle as he parked his car in the garage.

A cardboard box filled with ashes had been left in front of the garage door, obviously to cause Edser to stop and get out so the gunmen could get a better shot at him. But Edser drove straight over the top of it, parked the car and, as he closed the garage door, the two gunmen opened fire at point-blank range. He was very lucky to escape with his life.

Edser told the *Sydney Morning Herald*, 'Believe me, whoever it was was not fooling around. They meant to murder me and almost succeeded. All I remember are the little squirts of orange flame as the shots were fired.' Edser said he didn't know who had tried to kill him or why. Police believed that it had something to do with a betting transaction that had gone wrong.

There had been whispers that Hollywood George had been involved with race fixing for a long time and, after conducting a lengthy investigation into his betting activities, in June 1961 the Australian Jockey Club Committee barred Edser from owning or having an interest in any racehorse in New South Wales. They also barred him from attending any race meetings as he was deemed an undesirable person. This effectively meant that he could not officially attend any race meeting anywhere in the world.

The AJC also cancelled the licence of leading rails bookie Jack Large and said they would not accept any nominations for starters from a well-known horse owner who was associated with Edser. The committee gave no reasons for its actions.

Edser complained bitterly to the press, telling them that for 20 years he had made a living off the racetracks and all of a sudden he was an undesirable person. 'The AJC couldn't give me one reason why they warned me off,' Edser said. 'But they told me that I had not kept my word not to mix with bookmakers.'

Within eight months Hollywood George was on the front pages again when it was revealed that Jack Large, the bookmaker who was struck off, had in fact been betting with other bookmakers with Edser's money and could now not pay his bad debts. Edser was flat broke. Edser admitted that since he had been barred from the track he had been on a huge credit betting spree and, in an effort to recover his losses, he had lost £70,000 (over $1 million today) on credit in the last three race meetings alone.

Unable to pay his crippling debts, Edser continued to bet in small amounts with the off-course starting price bookmakers, but things were never the same. In March 1966, police raided his Vaucluse home and found the garage stocked with 464 cases of stolen Scotch whisky and spirits valued at around $250,000.

Police told the court that apart from being booked twice previously for consorting with criminals at the Royal Oak Hotel in Double Bay, his record showed four betting convictions dating back to 1936. Police described Edser as 'a commission agent and professional punter'.

Judge Monahan said Edser had not been in jail before and because of Edser's age, which was now 50, he said that he didn't want to send him there. Edser received a two-and-a-half-year suspended sentence and a four-year good behaviour bond.

Given that the maximum sentence for such a crime was 20

years in jail, an outrage followed. Hundreds of letters of protest poured into the *Daily Telegraph*. Ormsby Wilkins on Radio 2UE declared that the sentence was a scandal and the *Sunday Mirror* commented how kind everyone seemed to have been to Edser during the case – even letting him through the back door of the Darlinghurst Quarter Sessions to escape the hoards of waiting photographers.

After years of standing on a soap box peering over the racetrack fence with his binoculars to see the races, Edser was finally readmitted in 1979 after 18 years. In July 1981 he and rails bookmaker Robbie Waterhouse were summoned before the stewards who were interested in the running of a horse named Happy Fella, which had finished third in a race at Canterbury. Edser admitted that he had an association with Waterhouse and occasionally borrowed money from him. Nothing more came of the matter.

Hollywood George Edser, arguably the most colourful racing identity of them all and who really was larger than life, passed away from cancer in 1991.

39 GOING OUT IN STYLE

In the history of gangland killings in Australia it would be fair to say that there have been some that could be straight out of a Hollywood movie. One of the most colourful was in 1927, when Melbourne's most notorious gangster of the time, Squizzy Taylor, and infamous gunman Snowy Cutmore pulled guns on each other and fired at precisely the same time, before both slumped dead to the ground.

Another became the famous newspaper headline 'the fastest hankie in the east' when one night in Sydney in 1967 the feared gunman Raymond 'Ducky' O'Connor entered the Latin Quarter nightclub and sat down with three men at a table. A shot rang out and O'Connor slumped to the floor with a bullet to the head. Two detective sergeants sitting nearby arrived just in time to pronounce O'Connor dead, seemingly by his own hand. The pistol found on the floor was wiped clean of prints and no one was ever charged over the matter.

And whoever wanted Sydney crime boss John Stewart Regan dead made no bones about it. In September 1974, Regan was on his way to an illegal gambling casino when three gunmen emptied their police issue .38 revolvers into him at point-blank range, hitting him in the head, chest and liver eight times. As Regan lay dying in a pool of blood they calmly reloaded and emptied their guns into him again, just to be sure.

The list is endless. But there is one gangland hit that stands out above all others for the audaciousness in its place of execution. A place where a crook past his use-by date would think he was in the safest place on earth. The Melbourne Magistrate's Court.

In the 1970s Raymond Patrick Bennett was a well-known crook about Melbourne and a master criminal planner, who was the brains behind one of Australia's most infamous crimes, the Great Bookie Robbery. Bennett conceived the brazen plan while he was in jail in England, where he had been sent for his crimes as part of a gang of Australian shoplifters who had terrorised retailers throughout Europe for years and was appropriately known as the 'Kangaroo Gang'.

Back in Melbourne in 1976 Bennett recruited six crooks he could trust with his life and, using commando skills he had learned in jail from an English team of villains known as 'the Wembley Gang', he set up an army-style training camp in the bush in rural Victoria, where he and his men went over and over every move of the forthcoming robbery until they were like a wartime unit on a secret mission.

The plan was to rob Melbourne's on-course bookies of millions of dollars in cash on Monday settling day at the Victorian Club in Queen Street. Given that the on-course bookies either paid or collected from Saturday's losers and winners in cash, there was a lot of money to steal. The operation went off like clockwork. At gunpoint the balaclavad commandos filled more than 100 calico bank bags with untraceable bank notes. The haul was officially recorded at just over $1 million but because a lot of the bets hadn't been declared to avoid on-course betting tax, the real estimate was somewhere more like $2 million. In today's money that would be in the vicinity of $10 million.

But, in the underworld, crooks with that much disposable income don't stay a secret for long, especially when one of the robbers said to one of the victims, well-known boxing trainer Ambrose Palmer, 'You too, Ambrose,' as he was ordering those present to lie down at gunpoint. Palmer immediately recognised the voice behind the mask as a boxer who had once trained regularly at his gym and who was a known Bennett associate. It slipped Palmer's mind to tell the police, but soon enough it was common knowledge in the underworld where to go looking if they wanted some untraceable cash. And lots of it. And what better way to make a quick buck than to rob the robbers. They couldn't go to the police and complain.

One of the packs of vultures that expressed an interest was a particularly unpleasant group of painters and dockers led by the Kane brothers, Ray, Brian and Les. They provided the unofficial security for the bookies on settling day but it seems that on the day of the robbery their usual armed heavies had been called away on a needless errand, making the way clear for Bennett and his commandos to virtually help themselves to the treasure trove. Blind Freddy could have told them that the guards had been got at and it made them look stupid. And the Kane brothers were not men to be made to look stupid.

Fearing that he and his gang would soon be murdered and the money stolen, Bennett decided to act first. One night as Les Kane and his wife returned home they were confronted by Bennett and three other men. Kane was taken into the bathroom and executed as his wife was held down in another room where she could hear the shots. The killers dragged her husband's body away in front of her, put it in the boot of Kane's car and drove off. Neither Les Kane's body or his car were ever found. Bennett and the three men who were allegedly with him were charged with murder but acquitted due to lack of a body and witnesses.

But there was always going to be an even-up for Les Kane's murder. With reprisals going on all around him and no one hiding the fact that he was next, Ray Bennett was glad to be arrested on an outstanding armed-robbery charge and didn't apply for bail, deeming it safer to stay in jail than go back out on the streets where there was a price on his head. He couldn't have been more wrong.

One morning in November 1979 as three armed detectives escorted Bennett from the holding cells through the old Melbourne Magistrate's complex to his committal hearing, a heavily bearded man in a hat and glasses walked towards Bennett, looked him fair in the eye, pulled out a snub-nosed .38 pistol from beneath his coat, said 'Cop this,' and fired three shots into Bennett's chest at point-blank range. One of the detectives made a move towards the assassin, who pointed the gun at him and said, 'Don't make me do it,' before he turned and fled. Ray Bennett staggered down a set of nearby stairs before he collapsed to the floor dead. His final words were, 'I've been shot in the heart.'

In what was obviously no spur-of-the-moment murder, the gunman escaped through the court complex then through a prepared hole in a corrugated-iron fence in a garage behind the building, into a waiting car, and sped off. No one has ever been charged with Ray Bennett's murder.

40 | MURDER NORTH OF SUNDOWN

It was a crowded Vanguard sedan that travelled east through the lonely desert towards Alice Springs on 4 December 1957. But despite the cramped conditions the happy occupants were busy making plans for their arrival at the famous central Australian town. Riding in the car were Hubert Nigel 'Pete' Bowman and his wife Sally, as well as their two children, 15-year-old Wendy and a younger sister named Marian. Making the dusty drive even more cramped were the Bowmans' two dogs (a corgi and a cattle dog), as well as the family's friend Thomas Whelan, a colleague from the radio station 5AD where Pete worked. The group had been relaxing together for a spell at Glen Helen station, a property belonging to Pete's brother that was situated about 200 kilometres to the west of Alice Springs.

When the distant lights of Alice Springs came into their sights at close to 9pm that evening, the crew's plan was already confirmed. Pete would fly on to Adelaide – where they were all from – with his youngest daughter Marian. It was thought the ongoing and difficult car trip would cause too much discomfort to the physically disabled child. Thomas Whelan would remain with Sally, Wendy and the dogs and drive the Vanguard clear through to Adelaide. After motoring into Alice Springs, the exhausted contingent booked themselves into the Stuart Arms Hotel and settled in for the night, a welcome relief after so many hours on the red, bumpy, sand-filled road.

The next morning Tom Whelan and his passengers set off for the next leg of their arduous journey, with Pete and Marian Bowman waving them farewell from out the front of the hotel. The father and daughter then made their way to the airport for their flight back to Adelaide.

The Vanguard was scheduled to get into Adelaide sometime on the evening of the seventh. When they were still yet to arrive on the afternoon of 8 December, an understandably worried Pete started to ring around. The police could only confirm that the Vanguard had last been spotted stopped at Kulgera, some 282 kilometres south of Alice Springs. But that sighting on the Port Augusta Highway was the last place anyone could pin the car down to. Situated 56 kilometres north of Sundown station, the occupants of the Vanguard had pulled into Kulgera to refuel and top up their waterbags. They drove off from there at 4.30pm. That was the last anyone saw of them. Land and air search parties were organised, but to no avail.

It took five days before the Whelan/Bowman party were officially reported as missing. By then, air search parties had been bolstered by the arrival of an RAAF Lincoln bomber. The air force plane was seen by the owner of Kulgera station, Roy Coulthard, making large circles above his property. It transpired that the Lincoln had spotted the Vanguard. The pilot got into a position whereby they could drop a message to another car travelling in the area, asking the drivers of an Austin if they could check the licence-plate number on the car sitting some 145 metres off the Port Augusta/Alice Springs highway. The driver of the Austin signalled back that it was indeed the car the search party was seeking. But what of the occupants?

A land party was put together featuring two indigenous

Australian trackers along with local police officer Constable Commee. They were soon joined by First Class Constable Evans, flown in from Oodnadatta to lead the case. When they got to the Vanguard, the two officers inspected it and were intrigued by what they found. It seemed obvious to them that the interior had been washed down recently, but in the back of the car they found mysterious stains of blood in the seam around the door trim. When they noticed further blood on the floor and back seat, the signs didn't look good for the Whelan/Bowman group.

The search party split into two groups in their search for the missing holiday-makers, with one segment heading north by foot, and the other heading due south. The group heading south had travelled less than a kilometre before they found a sign of life – the remnants of a camp fire set about 20 steps away from the road. A little more than five metres from that sat the remains of yet another fire. They also found spots of blood on the ground near the first fire, as well as spent .22 cartridges and cases. Noticing animal tracks around the camp fire, the trackers assumed the wild creatures that made them would have been attracted to the blood. They followed the tracks about a kilometre and were shocked to find a pile of canvas. With alarm in their hearts, they looked under the canvas only to find blankets. When they peered under the blankets, though, they found the stinking, decaying bodies of Sally and Wendy Bowman, as well as Tom Whelan. The three bodies were all barefoot.

With dusk close at hand, the search party set up their own camp and settled in for the night. Continuing the investigation the next morning, the police saw what looked to be faint drag marks in the dusty sand near the second fire. Following them for almost 50 metres, they were appalled to find the carcasses of the two family dogs dumped at the foot of a tree and hastily covered with random branches and foliage. Looking around, the men spotted tracks indicating a car pulling a caravan on the other side of the barren highway. Next to them were two separate sets of footprints, seeming to belong to a man and a woman.

It wasn't until the next morning that more skilled investigators from the larger cities of Augusta and Adelaide arrived at the crime scene. The trained experts made plaster casts of the area and took photos. The trackers studied the marks in the ground intently. Something was amiss.

When the authorities had first looked under the canvas they found a pair of hessian bags. The bags looked to have been used as a crude pair of moccasins. The theory was that they had been used to make the animal tracks. A scrap of hessian was also found near the tracks of the car and caravan. This provided investigators with a confirmed link between the deceased bodies and the mysterious automobile tracks. It was their first definitive clue. The rest of the case would soon start to fall into place.

The corpses were taken to Adelaide, where Pete Bowman had the unfortunate task of collecting and identifying his dead wife, daughter and friend. Next, a post-mortem investigation took place. The results told a horrific story. All three of the victims had been clubbed with the butt of a rifle. Sally Bowman had then been shot in the head. Tom Whelan was also shot in the head – a bullet was lodged in his brain – as well as twice in the back. He also had multiple skull fractures.

The authorities questioned Pete Bowman, who told them Tom Whelan had been carrying at least £20 on the journey – a fairly substantial sum for the time. The investigating officers wondered if mere robbery was enough to warrant such a violent crime.

The official questioning continued back at Kulgera, where it was revealed several people had taken note of a grey car with red trimming pulling a trailer and heading south sometime after Tom Whelan had driven the Vanguard past. Police around Australia were told to be on the lookout for a Ford Zephyr matching that description.

Before long, though, the authorities were told of another car that had been seen in the area on the same day – a fairly rare black 1938 DeSoto sedan that was heading in the opposite direction to the Vanguard and Zephyr.

Meanwhile, because the Bowman family enjoyed a high public profile in Adelaide, a local newspaper issued a £500 reward for any information that may help lead to an arrest in the shocking case. Pete Bowman's brother upped the reward to £5000, guaranteeing a large amount of public interest.

It was six weeks after the Bowman mother and daughter and Tom Whelan left Alice Springs that the black DeSoto was finally found. Detective Glen Hallahan spotted a car matching the description in Mt Isa, north Queensland, on 21 January 1958. Noticing that the car had South Australian number plates, Hallahan and another detective named Pfingst waited until they saw a man in his 20s wearing shorts walk up to the car and open it. They pounced. His name, he said, was Raymond Carter. He had been in Mt Isa for a couple of weeks. That was enough for the detectives and they took Carter to the local police station.

Under questioning, it was revealed that Carter did indeed have a caravan that he had been towing behind the DeSoto. He explained with trepidation that it was currently situated 'a couple of miles' outside Mt Isa. His wife and young son were with it. The questioning continued before Carter, out of the blue, admitted that he had given the authorities a false name. He was actually Raymond Bailey. His excuse for using a pseudonym, he explained, was 'for taxation reasons'.

With the suspicions of the detectives further raised, Hallahan asked Bailey if he owned any firearms, but the suspect claimed he did not. Next the detectives decided to have a closer look at the black DeSoto. Bailey's heart must have skipped a beat as the men inspected the front seat and noticed that it had been slashed into and sewn up. The men easily opened the rough cotton fastening and inside the seat they found a .32 calibre revolver sitting in a holster. The best excuse Bailey could muster was that a man in Adelaide had given it to him. It was time to locate Bailey's caravan and wife. His lies were starting to fall in around him.

The detectives had little trouble finding Bailey's mobile home, sitting by the side of the road about 3 kilometres out of the township. Surprising Bailey's wife Patricia and their four-year-old son, the police conducted a search and found a receipt from a petrol station at Alice Springs that was dated 7 December 1957. This proved that Bailey and his family had been in the same vicinity as the Bowmans' Vanguard when it went missing. They also found a bunch of bullets.

Raymond Bailey was subjected to three hours of questioning at Mt Isa police station the next morning. According to his answers, he was 25 years old and a carpenter from the New South Wales town of Dubbo. Finding times tough, he had left Dubbo six months earlier, living with Patricia and their son in the caravan and getting by doing random small jobs wherever he could find them. It was an itinerant lifestyle. He added that when he left Dubbo he had owned a Holden ute, but that car was traded for the DeSoto when the family drove through South Australia.

He also admitted that he had seen Tom Whelan with Pete Bowman's wife and daughter while driving up to Alice Springs in early December. According to his story, Bailey saw the group sitting around a camp fire about 50 kilometres south of Kulgera on the evening of 5 December. He went and spoke to them for a short time and then left them to their business, continuing on his trip north. Detective Hallahan didn't buy the seemingly harmless story and left the room to speak to Patricia Bailey. He came back around 30 minutes later and told Bailey flat out that his story didn't gel with his wife's. Bailey seemed to realise that he was heading for trouble and hastily concocted a new story. In this one, he still drove away after chatting to the Bowman/Whelan group, but pulled over about three kilometres later to sleep in their caravan for the night. Sometime during the evening, he said, he awoke to what sounded like gunshots somewhere in the distance. Putting them out of his mind he went back to sleep, but when he awoke the next morning and prepared to leave their impromptu campsite on the side of the highway, he noticed that his rifle was missing from the DeSoto. Being a good Samaritan, he thought the right thing to do would be walk back the three kilometres to where he had seen the others camping for the night, just to check that they were all right.

Once he reached the Vanguard, however, he could not locate the owners. Then he noticed the suspicious canvas under the nearby tree and, after investigating, was shocked to find the party he had enjoyed a brief chat with the night before. They were all dead. Even more shocking, though, was the fact that his own rifle was sitting in the front seat of the Vanguard. As Bailey described it, the rifle's wood handle was split and the weapon was covered in what appeared to be human blood. Detective Hallahan sat in silence while Bailey said he had been so worried he might be blamed for the apparent murders that he drove the Vanguard away before cleaning it up as thoroughly as he could.

The story sounded so improbable that Hallahan asked Bailey if he believed it to actually be true – did an unknown culprit really sneak silently into his car in the middle of the night in the middle of nowhere, then go back a fair distance to shoot a group of people for no reason other than perhaps robbery? Bailey answered their question with his own question: What other explanation was there?

Hallahan asked about the bullets found in the caravan, finding it strange that someone would steal a rifle, but leave ammunition behind. But Bailey – digging himself deeper into his own well of lies – agreed that none of his bullets had been missing.

No doubt realising that he had pushed an already unbelievable story too far, Bailey hastily concocted a new one, explaining to the detectives present that he would now tell the truth. This version had the accused admitting that he had shot the deceased, but that it had all been an unfortunate mistake. Bailey said that while resting in his caravan for the night he developed a sudden stomach ache. Grabbing his gun he decided to go for a walk in the night air to see if that helped ease the pain. He had no explanation for the bullets in his pocket, or his decision to walk back to the Whelan/Bowman camp, but as he approached their site one of the family dogs came at him. He fired at the unfortunate animal but apparently missed and hit what turned out to be Tom Whelan. From there, Bailey said, he 'must have had a blackout'.

The next thing the by-now self-confessed murderer remembered was being at the opposite side of the road and noticing a bump covered in tarpaulins and blankets. Looking under it, he found three bodies, including that of the 'young fellow' he had shot accidentally. He then saw his blood-splattered rifle in the front of the Vanguard and surmised that he had killed all the victims. It was a devastating blow.

In shock, he returned to his own caravan, washed himself up and went back to the desolate murder scene early the next morning. Wearing a pair of gloves, he drove the Vanguard some distance into the bush, washed it down as best he could, went back to his own DeSoto and continued on his way to Alice Springs with his family, ditching his Huntsman rifle somewhere along the way.

The authorities knew they still didn't have the full story, but at least they had the murderer in custody. That afternoon, two detectives were flown up from Adelaide to take charge of the increasingly strange investigation. With detectives Moran and Hopkins now leading matters it was only a few hours – and a meeting with his wife – later that Bailey had yet another version of the fateful events. In this one, he remembered shooting Tom Whelan, then seeing Sally Bowman run towards him. He hit the woman in the head with the rifle butt, knocking her to the ground before loading a bullet into the firearm and shooting her. After that, Bailey reloaded and put a bullet into teenage Wendy Bowman, who was trying in vain to get to her feet.

Bailey then admitted to covering the bodies in the canvas and walking back to his caravan to clean up. He returned to the murder scene near the break of day. Noticing the Bowman dogs tied up nearby, he claimed that he attempted to let them loose, but was bitten. Bailey retaliated by shooting both of the innocent animals in the head.

After that, he told how he tied the hessian bags over his feet to cover his tracks before checking that the bodies were still covered. He explained that he felt so bad about the killings that he didn't want scavenging birds to violate the cadavers. Still, he seemed to have no problem with searching Tom Whelan's inert body and stealing his wallet.

From there, Bailey drove the Vanguard to his own campsite, washed it down, and explained to his wife that the people they had seen back down the road had been killed and he was worried that they may get the blame. Despite the scenario sounding highly unlikely, Patricia Bailey seemed to accept the story.

The trial of Raymond Bailey began in Adelaide on 12 May 1958. Besides a man who claimed to have sold the Huntsman rifle eventually used in the murders to Bailey for £7 a year earlier (a fee that was never received), the majority of witnesses called were there to verify that they had seen the black DeSoto in the timeframe leading up to or after the murders, either pulling the caravan along the road or camped at Kulgera.

Ballistics experts confirmed that a Huntsman rifle was used in the killings, but the defence then tried to prove that Bailey's statements were taken under duress. They were unsuccessful. It was now time for Bailey to try to talk his way out of trouble one more time, coming up with yet another version of events. In this one he again admitted to pulling up and speaking to the Whelan/Bowman group by the side of the road, but said that was the last time he saw them. He sidestepped the inference that he had robbed Tom Whelan by explaining that he had plenty of money of his own at the time. As this was going on, Bailey heard the distant sound of his wife crying down a hallway. This triggered the first emotions he'd shown since police picked him up, with the accused starting to weep quietly. But the gentle outpouring had no effect on Tom Whelan's mother, who leapt to her feet and shouted out that Bailey was a 'murderer!'

Once he regained his composure, Bailey indicated that his confession had only come about after detectives threatened to pester his wife. He claimed he only signed his statement so the authorities would leave Patricia Bailey alone. But his stories were to no avail and Raymond Bailey was quickly found guilty of the murders and sentenced to death by hanging.

Before he went to the gallows, though, Bailey had one more version of the tragic events to tell the authorities. This time, the story went that it was in fact another man who had murdered the Bowman/Whelan group and the dogs. Bailey had merely stumbled upon the scene and then killed the real culprit in self-defence. Not only that, he buried the man and would show police the remains.

As a result, a search party of around 40 men combed the

Sundown area for a day, digging up anywhere Bailey indicated he may have concealed the real killer. All that time, Bailey remained in the back of a police car, smoking cigarettes while handcuffed. The search was, of course, unsuccessful. Raymond Bailey was hung by the neck until he was dead in Adelaide Gaol on 24 June 1958.

41 THE PORT ARTHUR MASSACRE

Ask anyone where they were on 28 April 1996, and chances are they won't have a clue. Mention the name Martin Bryant or Port Arthur and their faces will frown with recognition. They will recall how they first heard about a terrible crime that had just taken place when a lone gunman slaughtered scores of people at one of Tasmania's top tourist locations. It was one of those terrible moments in history – like the planes flying into the Twin Towers or John Lennon being assassinated – when you never forget where you were when you first heard about it.

Martin Bryant's crimes have been described as the worst firearm massacre ever committed by an individual anywhere in the world outside of war. But, if you can believe it, that is exactly what Bryant wants to hear. Maybe that wasn't his intention when he set out on that terrible day, but that is what he has achieved. He would revel in the notoriety that it has brought him. If he could, that is.

But authorities have seen to it that opportunities to dine out on his killing spree are nonexistent. Where Bryant lives these days at Tasmania's Risdon Prison, every application to interview or photograph him is rejected, depriving him of the publicity that he so desperately craves. Insiders say that this torment has driven him to numerous suicide attempts, any of which being successful would have caused a cheer so loud that they would have heard it in Melbourne. But that is not to be the case as he is guarded around the clock to avoid him getting off that easily. You see, every day alive is another day in a living hell to the Port Arthur mass murderer.

From time to time over the 10 years and more that Bryant has been locked away in Risdon, Tasmania's only maximum-security prison situated about 10 kilometres from Hobart and which houses about 200 of Tasmania's worst offenders, he has been in good company.

Bryant's co-inhabitants have included such charmers as Richard Dickinson, who kicked his mother to death because she complained that he was playing the stereo too loudly; Aaron Jeffrey, who was picked up by police while goading a couple of gorillas into a fight in the Melbourne Zoo after he killed his father in Tasmania and fled to the mainland; and the infamous Dr Rory Jack Thompson, the eminent oceanographer who chopped his wife into manageable parts and flushed her down the toilet. Thompson committed suicide in Risdon in 1999.

Perhaps Risdon's most infamous inmate, Mark 'Chopper' Read, author, humorist, stand-up comedian and self-confessed multiple murderer, was released in February 1998. Only Tasmania's worst offenders are sent to Risdon. And, for what Martin Bryant did, that is where he will die.

The few journalists who have been allowed inside the prison walls to view Bryant's living conditions have not been allowed to carry cameras or tape recorders within view of him because he automatically assumes that they are there to interview him and he gets excited and jumps up and down like a little boy.

Reports indicate that Bryant is infatuated with his own image and on his arrival at Risdon he inquired regularly as to how he was being depicted by the media and how history would remember him. He will be remembered as the most cold-blooded killer in Australia's history.

Shortly after 1pm on Sunday, 28 April 1996, Martin Bryant entered the Broad Arrow Café at Port Arthur, the old convict settlement on Tasmania's southern peninsula. Bryant was carrying a large tennis bag. After he had eaten a hasty meal he took a semi-automatic rifle from the bag and opened fire on the lunchtime diners, picking them off one at a time, rather than taking pot luck by simply spraying the dining room with bullets.

Bryant left the carnage in the café and walked out into the grounds, killing at random as he went. He approached a car, shot the female driver and ordered a male passenger out at gunpoint. He forced the man into the boot of a BMW and took off, leaving thirty-two dead men, women and children behind him.

From Port Arthur Bryant drove 2.5 kilometres to the Seascape guest house where he killed the husband-and-wife owners and the man he had put in the boot of the car. After an all-night siege with police, in which many shots were fired, Bryant set fire to the guest house and was eventually arrested shortly after 8am as he ran from the building with his clothes on fire.

On 22 November 1996, Tasmania's Chief Justice William Cox sentenced 29-year-old Bryant – who pleaded guilty – to jail for the term of his natural life for 35 counts of murder, 20 counts of attempted murder, three of causing grievous bodily harm, eight of wounding, four of aggravated assault, one of arson and one of unlawfully setting fire to property. The youngest victim was three, the oldest 72.

After Bryant had been sentenced and was taken from the courtroom to spend the rest of his life behind bars, someone in the crowd called out: 'May you rot in hell.' He will.

While we can only wonder what would cause a young man to do such terrible things, it has since been claimed by Bryant's defence psychiatrist that the catalyst for mass murder in the well-below-average intelligence – though not insane – Bryant was the massacre a month earlier of 16 schoolchildren in the Scottish town of Dunblane. Prior to that, Bryant was contemplating suicide – what an awful pity he didn't kill himself instead – but

Dunblane and the early portrayal of the killer, Thomas Hamilton, changed everything and the Port Arthur massacre was the result.

In an exclusive interview in *The Bulletin* magazine to mark the 10th anniversary of the Port Arthur massacre, Martin Bryant's mother Carleen said her son had become an overweight zombie who refused to speak. 'I'm worried about his condition,' she said. 'And I've talked to prison officials and they agree that he's depressed but I don't know whether they are treating him or not.

'My poor Martin,' Carleen Bryant told *The Bulletin*. 'He couldn't have shot down all those people at Port Arthur. He didn't have the brains to do it. The guy who did it had dark, greasy hair and pocked skin. My Martin has lovely soft baby skin.'

It seems as though Martin Bryant has claimed another victim to add to the thousands of lives he has already changed forever.

42 GEORGE FREEMAN – KING OF THE SP BOOKIES

Although he hated it with a passion, it was almost as if the term 'colourful racing identity' was created for George Freeman. There were many characters in the racing world of his era – Hollywood George Edser, Eddy 'the Fireman' Birchley, the Waterhouses, Terry Page, Tommy Smith and Perc Galea, to name but a few – but Freeman was one of the most colourful.

But while Freeman's antics on the racecourse gave him the notorious headlines, it was his business as Australia's largest illegal SP bookmaker off the course that gave him the reputation as being if not Mr Big, then certainly one of the Mr Big Enough's of Sydney's organised crime scene. Having said that, it must also be said that in the last 25 years of his life the most that the New South Wales police could convict George Freeman of was a couple of illegal betting charges which invoked small fines.

Born into a dirt-poor working-class family in the inner-western Sydney suburb of Annandale in 1934, George David Freeman was in trouble from the minute he was old enough to steal. By age 13, Freeman had a string of petty convictions for stealing a tin of biscuits, a car radio, fountain pens, money, and an electric fan, and evading a rail fare. He was in and out of juvenile institutions throughout most of his teenage years.

In 1954, aged 20, Freeman was sentenced to three years' hard labour for breaking, entering and stealing. It was around this time that he began a lifelong friendship with another career criminal named Leonard Arthur McPherson. It was a very valuable friendship, given that Lenny McPherson would eventually become the Mr Big of Sydney's organised crime.

Although still a petty criminal in the early 1960s, with convictions for shoplifting, Freeman jumped into the big league in 1965 when he was introduced to Joe Testa, a suspected member of the Chicago Mafia who was visiting Sydney, allegedly examining the prospects for US Mafia infiltration. In 1968, on a false passport, Freeman went to the US and stayed in Chicago with Testa for six weeks and, at Testa's expense, at the Stardust Hotel in Las Vegas for three days.

By the early 1970s Freeman was allegedly heavily entrenched with the operations of the Chicago Mafia in Australia and had his fingers in many pies, including a chain of illegal off-course SP betting shops, illegal casinos and horse-race fixing rackets. It was alleged that Danny Stein, a card-carrying member of the Mafia, opened a bank account in Sydney in 1972 and gave George Freeman power of attorney. In September 1973, Freeman allegedly closed the account and transferred $56,300 to Stein in the USA.

On 16 July 1972, it was reported in the *Sunday Telegraph* under the headline 'The Night the Mafia Came to Sydney' that George Freeman had attended summit meetings of the heads of Sydney's organised crime at the Double Bay home of one of Sydney's leading organised crime figures. The article named the nine men in attendance, which included Sydney's alleged Mr Big at the time, Frederick Charles 'Paddles' Anderson, and named Freeman and Lennie McPherson as 'first among equals of Sydney's Mr Big Enough's'.

In 1974 in the lead up to the Moffitt Royal Commission into

organised crime in Sydney, Justice Athol Moffitt declared Freeman a person of interest and the Crime Intelligence Unit began tapping his phones. The operation, codenamed Southern Comfort, picked up conversations between Freeman, a registrar at Sydney Hospital, Dr Nick Paltos (who would later go to jail on marijuana-smuggling charges) and high-ranking police officers. But what interested them even more were the conversations between George Freeman and Chief Stipendiary Magistrate Murray Farquhar, in which Freeman gave the highly respected jurist tips on the races, which turned out to be 98 per cent to 99 per cent successful.

Through the taps police confirmed what they already knew: that Freeman controlled illegal gambling in New South Wales and also had interests in illegal gambling casinos and horse-race fixing, and that he had improper relationships with police, including two inspectors and a superintendent. Never at any time throughout the operation was there a hint that George Freeman was involved, or ever had been, in vice rackets such as prostitution or had anything to do with drugs. For all his shortcomings it was recognised throughout his life that George Freeman was a gambler and that was that.

In July 1977, racecourse detective Frank Lynch spotted Freeman, who was deemed an undesirable, at Randwick Racecourse seated in the members' enclosure with Dr Nick Paltos and magistrate Farquhar. Freeman was ejected from the course immediately. The following day a photograph of the trio seen watching the races together in the stands was published on the front page of a Sydney newspaper. The results for magistrate Farquhar were damning.

On 25 April 1979, as George Freeman got out of his car at the gates of his mansion on the waterfront in Sydney's south, a man stepped from the bushes and shot him in the neck and face at point-blank range and fled. Bleeding profusely, Freeman was rushed to hospital and lived. Six weeks later an unidentified gunman shot 56-year-old John Marcus Muller dead with three bullets from a 9mm pistol as Muller arrived home to his Coogee residence just after midnight. Although Muller, who had a record of violence stretching right back to 1940, knew Freeman, who was in Noosa Heads at the time of the killing, police said had they no reason to believe that the deceased had anything to do with the attempt on Freeman's life, despite rampant rumours to the contrary.

In January 1983, police distracted the Rottweiler dogs at Freeman's fortified mansion, where he lived with his wife and three children, by throwing meat over the fence. Having gained entry, they charged him with SP betting and he was subsequently fined $500. In August 1984, Freeman, in company with two associates, was charged with having maliciously wounded a man at the Empress Coffee House in Kings Cross. Freeman accurately predicted that witnesses would not identify him and the case was dismissed in October 1984.

When Australia's most notorious Melbourne hit man Christopher Dale Flannery, aka 'Mr Rentakill', shifted his operations to Sydney in mid-1984, Freeman denied that he had ever employed Flannery as a bodyguard. Flannery disappeared in May 1985 while allegedly on his way to an appointment with Freeman. Freeman's house was searched, but nothing was found.

On 20 March 1990, George Freeman died in Sutherland Hospital from heart failure caused by a severe asthma attack, with his devoted family by his side. He was 56. In one of the biggest funerals for a 'man of respect' that Sydney has ever seen, Norman Erskine sang two of George's favourite songs, 'That's What Friends Are For' and 'I'll Be Loving You'. There wasn't a dry eye in the house.

To a man, and woman, everyone there said that George Freeman was the most honest, honourable, lovable bloke that ever lived. A man who never welched on a bet and would never see a mate – or anyone for that matter – go without. A bloke who was terribly misunderstood.

If we are to use George Freeman as an example, it would seem as though there is honour among thieves after all.

43 ALAN BOND – CROOK OR HERO?

The story goes that on the eve of Alan Bond's crack at the final race in the 1983 America's Cup challenge, which would decide the event, one newspaper had two headlines ready. One said: 'Alan Bond wins America's Cup.' The other was alleged to have said: 'Pommy sign-writer loses America's Cup.'

Truth or urban myth, it could be said that it was a fair indication of the regard in which a suspicious Australia held the man who had risen from rags to spectacular riches: you couldn't help but feel that somewhere along the line something was really rotten. Of course, Bond won the America's Cup and he and his team became heroes. Alan Bond was made Australian of the Year. But it could only temporarily postpone his business woes and the doom that lay ahead.

Alan Bond was an English migrant miner's son who came to Australia as a boy and grew up in Western Australia. Fresh out of school he took up sign-writing and specialised in doing jobs that no one else would take on. One of the monuments he is said to have created was the huge red dingo on the silo at the home of Dingo Flour Mill at Fremantle. Or so the story goes.

A wheeler and dealer of extraordinary talent, in 1960 Bond borrowed $13,000 and turned it into a fortune on a property deal. He reinvested the money and was soon on his way to the mega-millions that he always dreamed he would have.

By the 1980s his Perth-based Bond Corporation either owned, or had a slice of, some of Australia's most prominent companies, including Channel 9 in Sydney, Swan Breweries, Arnott's, Castlemaine Tooheys, West Australian Newspapers, Grace Brothers and Walton's department stores, and Fourex Breweries. His overseas interests included British Satellite Broadcasting, a diamond mine and a phone company in Chile.

But there was always the unanswered question: where was the money coming from to pay for all of this? Was it all real or was it a house of cards that would crash as soon as the first card tumbled?

As it turned out, it was a house of cards, and the man who single-handedly brought about Bond Corporation's undoing was Englishman Roland Walter 'Tiny' Rowland, who owned the Lonrho Corporation, which had interests in more than 700 businesses including newspapers, textiles, transport mining and brewing.

The London-based Lonrho was asset rich and cash poor, so when Alan Bond came along offering his help with cash, he was initially seen as a white knight helping Rowland to maintain his empire and keep him at the helm. But Bond's real intent was to take over Lonrho.

When Bond offered to buy out some of Rowland's equity, in what was alleged to be a move to protect Lonrho from predators, Rowland found out that Bond was also acquiring shares on his own behalf through another company Bond owned. In time Bond would acquire enough shares to gain control of the company and become Rowland's successor. It was a clever plan, but Rowland was smarter.

Rowland ordered an immediate investigation into Alan Bond. His 90-page document proved that Bond was insolvent beyond anyone's wildest imagination. Bond's bankers demanded their money back immediately. But it was too late. Alan Bond's house of cards began crumbling around him.

To add to Alan Bond's woes the stock market crashed in 1987 and Bond Corporation went up in flames, with debts to the tune of $8 billion and assets of just $1.3 billion. The final wash-up left a debt of around $5 billion. No one could explain where the money had gone other than on bad investments, America's Cup challenges and a lifestyle for Alan Bond and his directors that made Arab oil sheikhs look like the working class. In 1992 Bond became Australia's biggest bankrupt. He eventually settled by paying creditors less than half a cent in the dollar. For $9 million he paid off a debt of $1.2 billion.

But that was not all. Alan Bond was charged with a host of corporate and criminal offences. On his daily walks to court, Bond looked like the walking dead, which urged journalists to report that overacting should be added to the raft of charges he faced. Bond was eventually sent to prison for defrauding one of the companies he took over – Bell Resources – of $1.2 billion. That sentence, combined with another one for defrauding his company of $15 million over Monet's painting *La Promenade*, saw him spend a total of less than four years in jail. Alan Bond was released in 2000 after having served just 1298 days – or roughly one day for every million dollars he stole.

But, to this day, Alan Bond lives the life of a jetsetting multimillionaire. And little wonder. He was alleged to have shipped $15 million overseas in the late 1980s when the Bond ship was going belly up. In 1995 his then-wife Eileen, two sons and two daughters were estimated to be worth collectively around $70 million in businesses, real estate and other assets.

And it seems as though Alan Bond isn't without very rich and benevolent friends. A company owned by Swiss businessman Jurg Bollag kindly bought a $12.5 million English mansion and 400-hectacre country estate and handed it over to Bond as soon as the bankruptcy was annulled. The generous Mr Bollag also bought over a million dollars worth of show-jumping horses for Bond's daughter Suzanne, along with $700,000 worth of jewellery. Not to mention the $350,000 Mr Bollag kindly contributed to Alan Bond's legal costs.

While it was said at the time by Bond's supporters that the $1.2 billion swindle of Bell Resources was a victimless crime, try telling that to the shareholders who lost their life savings and nest eggs for their retirement. It sickened them to find out that at least $55 million of the money taken from Bell ended up in Bond's private company disguised as director's fees and bonuses to fund Bond's extravagant lifestyle.

Alan Bond ruined countless ordinary Australian citizens' lives so he could drive Rolls Royces, eat Beluga caviar, drink Dom Perignon and play with his super yachts. Perhaps it would have been best if in 1983 Alan Bond and his team hadn't won the America's Cup. His creditors would had have moved in sooner rather than bankrupt an Australian icon, and the truth would have emerged earlier. Lots of battlers who believed in him wouldn't have gone down on his sinking ship.

44 THE CASE OF THE SMILING ARSONIST

There was a time in Sydney in the 1950s, '60s and '70s when a crime reporter covering a case for a newspaper could be as big a celebrity as the high-profile detectives looking for the villains. And, on more than one occasion, it was the crime reporter who solved a baffling murder case after being approached with information that they passed on to police.

Possibly the most famous of these cases was what became known as the Case of the Walking Corpse when, in 1963, a man walked into the *Daily Mirror* building in Sydney and told crime reporter Joe Morris that he had just seen a dead man, whose funeral he had attended six months earlier, walking down George Street. And not only had he *seen* the walking corpse but he had stopped and had a conversation with the man before he ran off into the crowd.

Police investigations revealed that the man was Allan Edward Brennan, who had been buried in Sydney six months earlier after his unrecognisable, decomposed remains had been found beneath his smallgoods shop. Police assumed that Brennan had been electrocuted and after a quick autopsy he was laid to rest. The man who had recognised him in the street, and a few of his old workmates, attended the funeral and laid a wreath.

The remains of Allan Brennan were exhumed and closer examination revealed that it was instead the body of habitual criminal Patrick Joseph Hackett. It looked as if they had found another victim of a serial killer who operated throughout Sydney. The victims, who were all vagrants, were stabbed up to 60 times and had their genitals removed with the skill of a Macquarie Street surgeon. This fiend had been dubbed the Mutilator by the press.

This led to the capture of the mysterious Allan Brennan – real name William Macdonald – who was, in fact, the Mutilator murderer. He was found guilty of the murders and sent to prison forever where he remains to this day, the longest serving prisoner in Australia. The reporter Joe Morris was given full credit for instigating the capture of the Mutilator.

Another horrific Sydney crime that was solved directly by information given to the police by a reporter became known as the Case of the Smiling Arsonist. The journalist was another *Daily Mirror* legend, Bondi Bill Jenkings. At about 12.30am on Friday, 21 June 1968, a ferocious blaze broke out in a block of flats on Campbell Parade, directly opposite Bondi Beach. Before long the building was completely ablaze and *Daily Mirror* photographer John Gasparotto was on the spot to capture graphic images of police and firemen carrying survivors from the burning building.

But while 30 of the residents escaped the inferno thanks to the brave efforts of rescuers, four others, 36-year-old Sydney barrister Paul Francis Walshe and his wife Jean, 28, and English migrants William Simpson and his 21-year-old bride Cheryl, perished in the fire.

The two couples died from asphyxiation as they slept on the third floor of the five-storey building and inhaled the deadly carbon monoxide fumes. The Simpsons had only been living in the block for a few weeks, having arrived recently from England.

Paul and Jean Walshe had only been married a short time.

They apparently died in each other's arms. The *Daily Mirror* reported that rescuers heard the young bride scream: 'Paul, Paul, I love you,' before she and her husband were enveloped in flames.

Police established that the blaze had emanated from the lift spread quickly through the wooden structure of the lift well and into the apartments.

The deceased hadn't stood a chance and it was a miracle that so many had escaped. What was also of enormous concern to police was that there had recently been a spate of arson attacks in and around Sydney, but this was the first time anyone had been killed. Could this be the same arsonist? If so, they dreaded what could happen next.

The following evening photographer John Gasparotto's images appeared all over the front pages of the *Daily Mirror* and newspapers across the country. They were graphic in the extreme showing survivors being carried from the burning building and the full extent of the blaze. The pictures also captured images of bystanders looking on as the drama unfolded. It was one of these pictures that would be the undoing of the arsonist.

Reporter Bill Jenkings was assigned to cover the case for the *Mirror* and it wasn't long after the fire that he was sitting in a Bondi hotel when two of his clandestine 'contacts' sat at the bar beside him. One pointed to a photo on the front page of the *Mirror* and said, 'That's the bloke you're after.' He then finished his beer and left. Jenkings was astonished. Among the devastation was a young man looking at the camera with a smile on his face.

By showing the photo around to residents of the building, police tracked the young man down to factory in suburban Sydney where he worked as a sales clerk. He was a 25-year-old Scottish migrant named James Alexander Sorenson who had recently moved to the western suburbs of Sydney but had once lived in the Campbell Parade units.

After questioning, Sorenson was charged with the four murders and also charged with maliciously setting fire to a house in

Bondi while the owner was asleep inside.

At his trial in the Central Criminal Court the Crown alleged that Sorenson had been drinking heavily on the night of the fire and at around midnight he had arrived at the fourth floor of the block of units, where he was staying with friends. As he vacated the lift he threw in some burning newspapers and sent the lift to the basement. He then went to bed and waited to see what would happen.

In his defence Sorenson said that he was very, very drunk on the night of the fire, that he was deeply sorry for what had happened and was shocked that anyone was hurt. With that he asked the jury to find him guilty of manslaughter but not murder. But the jury would have none of it and it took them just an hour to find him guilty of four counts of murder.

In summing up before sentencing the prisoner, Mr Justice Maguire said that there was a frightening side to Sorenson's character that had not been revealed to the jury. He then sent James Sorenson to four counts of life imprisonment. That would be enough to wipe the smile off anyone's face. To this day, the man who pointed out the killer to reporter Bill Jenkings has never been identified. But whoever he was, he deserves a medal.

45 THE MELBOURNE POLICE STRIKE

Try and imagine if you can a city without police. Some of you may say that that would be beaut, well at least for a while, because you could go as fast as you liked in your cars after you'd had a few drinks and give that noisy neighbour of yours a clip under the ear without fear of a visit from the cops. But to most of us, the thought is abhorrent. Surely it could never happen. But it has happened. And it happened in Australia. There was a time when the police went on strike. And the results were catastrophic.

The trouble began in November 1923, when uniformed officers in inner-city police stations throughout Melbourne took the unheard of move to take strike action and abandon their posts. The trouble had been brewing for a long time over a bitter battle with police administration over low pay, no meal breaks, long hours and terrible working conditions. It was believed among the rank-and-file police that the powers that be were totally inefficient and they had left police morale at its lowest ebb in our history.

But no matter how they pleaded with their superiors to improve their conditions and meet their other demands, it fell on deaf ears and the attitude from the then Police Commissioner Alexander Nicholson was one of 'if you're not happy, get another job'. To add to the insult, Commissioner Nicholson had recently introduced a scheme involving secret police officers, known as Spooks, who monitored the activities of beat police and any officers caught breaking the rules would be subject to fines or more severe penalties.

The 600-strong inner-city police unanimously opposed the scheme but were constantly denied a hearing. Finally, when two Spooks reported two constables for having a cup of tea during working hours and the constables were fined, uproar spread throughout the force. The officers decided it had gone too far and, in what was believed to be an unprecedented move anywhere in the world, went on strike, leaving the heart of Melbourne at the mercy of gangs of hoodlums and thugs who were awaiting their opportunity to loot, bash and rob without the fear of reprisal. It was a sad and black day in Melbourne's history.

The following evening officers refused to report for duty and, at last realising that he may have gone too far, Commissioner Nicholson was quick in letting them know that the Spooks system would be abandoned forthwith. But it was all too late. In what could only be described as one of the worst political decisions of the century, the Victorian premier, Harry Lawson, intervened and said that only over his dead body would there be a change to the system and the Spooks would stay. And if the officers didn't like it, they could lump it.

They chose to lump it and hundreds of officers abandoned their posts, leaving the city and its surrounding districts without any law and order. The striking officers were sacked immediately by the premier who moved quickly to bring in 'scab' police replacements from the country. Unhappy to be the meat in the sandwich, many of these officers joined their striking brothers and they also were sacked. The now desperate Victorian premier called upon retired police officers to return to duty until the strike was settled and, in a move that only enraged the police force even further, he began recruiting civilian volunteers with no policing experience whatever and swearing them in as 'special police'.

Surprisingly, on the first night of the strike there was no serious trouble to speak of. People partied in the streets but apart from the occasion drunken brawl there was no harm done. But by the following day, when the criminal element finally realised that Melbourne really was theirs for the taking, the crowds turned violent as gangs roamed the streets looting and bashing whoever they pleased. Melees broke out all across town and there was little that the 30 or so stand-in police could do about it. They just had to let them go and hope that no one was killed.

As the evening progressed illegal two-up games broke out on street corners. Come closing time at the pubs, the streets filled up with drunken hooligans who set upon anyone and everyone in sight – including what few police there were, who fled for their lives after being pelted with whatever missiles the mobs could lay their hands on.

Before long the alcohol-fuelled gangs had taken over the city of Melbourne and, for want of something else to do, began fighting each other. As department stores were smashed and clothing and household goods stolen, the mobs set upon the thieves for the spoils. Drunken packs lit fires in the streets and drank from bottles and threw the empties at any policeman foolish enough to be within range. Others rampaged through department stores after they gained access through the broken display windows and stole whatever they could lay their hands on. But as they made away with their ill-gotten gain they were bashed and in turn robbed by other drunken thugs.

The riot went on into the night and no one was safe. Not even the rioters were safe from each other. In the frenzy, a tourist from rural Australia was robbed and then kicked to death in the street. But just when it seemed that there was no end to the violence, more than 1000 special police who had been grouped during the day to restore Melbourne to law and order were unleashed on the mob, and the fighting began all over again. But this time the inexperienced police had the upper hand in that their numbers far outweighed the rioters who were sober enough to put up a decent fight.

Under instructions to restore Melbourne to the respectable citizens at any cost, the special police weighed into the mob with clubs and batons. After four hours of brutality the city of Melbourne resembled a war zone, with bodies lying all about groaning in pain from the wounds inflicted in the fight. By midnight the fighting was over and Melbourne was again a safe place to be. Police spent the rest of the night taking the main offenders to jails and hospitals.

For the police force it was a hollow victory. All of the strikers, which was about half of the inner-city police force, were sacked. Immediately the government set about recruiting a new police force and in doing so offered all of the changes that the police force had gone on strike for in the first place. History doesn't tell us whether or not they honoured their obligations once the new recruits were in place, but one thing is for certain and that is that Australia learned from the 1923 Melbourne police strike and nothing of a remotely similar nature has ever happened since.

46 | THE INFAMOUS DR REGINALD STUART-JONES

Despite his flamboyance and double-barrelled name, Australia's most infamous medico of the time – and perhaps of all time – Dr Reginald Stuart-Jones, came from humble beginnings. Born in London in 1903, he was the son of a Scottish father and a Welsh mother with the family name of Jones. The family emigrated to Australia when Reginald was nine and settled at Woolgoolga, near Coffs Harbour, where his father managed a timber factory.

An excellent student, young Reg Jones won scholarships to Wesley College at Sydney University where he studied medicine and excelled at cricket, football, tennis, athletics and rifle shooting. He graduated in medicine in 1929 and in 1931 sailed back to England as the ship's doctor on the *Raranga*.

In Britain the handsome young doctor was introduced into society where he met and married his first wife Shena, who was the heir to a chain of theatres. And in keeping with his new social status he hyphenated his middle and last names. On his return to Australia he worked as a GP at Canterbury until 1935, when the now Dr Reginald Stuart-Jones set up practice in Sydney's up-market Macquarie Street as a gynaecologist. From the start his practice was a raging success and he soon became the specialist the ladies of Sydney's society chose to see for their more personal examinations.

A born businessman and entrepreneur, at night Stuart-Jones ran the Lido nightclub at Bondi and also opened and ran the successful 400 Club in the historic Paris House in Phillip Street, in the city. He owned a string of racehorses, greyhounds and trotters and, at one stage, was the president of the New South Wales National Coursing Association, the controlling body for greyhound racing. He was seen most weekends at the racing venues betting in large amounts of cash.

When his first wife left him in 1936, Stuart-Jones built a five-bedroom, three-bathroom palace in Bellevue Hill with two grand pianos, a billiard room and a pistol range in the basement. He named it Casa Clavel. The parties were legendary, with a full orchestra entertaining his guests who danced and drank until dawn.

In 1944 he met and very quickly married 23-year-old Mary Ryan but within four months they had separated and he sued her for divorce on the grounds of her adulterous relationship with the well-known Sydney criminal Clifford Thompson. Stuart-Jones had found his wife in Thompson's pyjamas in a room in Leichhardt. Stuart-Jones and his young wife reconciled before the divorce was finalised. But the boyfriend, Thompson, wasn't too happy about it.

Around midnight on 31 October 1944, Stuart-Jones went to the door of Casa Clavel, where he was escorted to a waiting car under the guise that he should look at a fellow who 'wasn't feeling very well'. When he reached the car Dr Stuart-Jones was forced into the back at gunpoint by Clifford Thompson and another criminal, Alexander Jowett, who told him that they were taking him for a ride to Maroubra where he would be executed with a bullet to the heart and thrown off the cliffs into the sea.

With two accomplices sitting in the front seat, the car arrived at Maroubra at about 12.30am and stopped at the top of the cliffs in Marine Parade. The accomplices held Stuart-Jones down while Jowett held a revolver to his chest and pulled the trigger. In a million-to-one chance the bullet missed every vital organ except the doctor's lung and, as he severely gasped for breath, he begged the men who had just tried to kill him to drive him to the nearby Vassilia private hospital in Randwick and dump him on the footpath.

Incredibly, that's exactly what the dumbest hit squad in the world did, and Stuart-Jones was rushed immediately to St Vincent's Hospital where an emergency operation saved his life. The four alleged hit men were quickly rounded up and charged with attempted murder.

Their trial was a disaster for Stuart-Jones. The court heard from the defence that the society doctor was in fact Sydney's leading abortionist, sly-grog trader, wife-basher, dope-pedlar and nightclub business associate of some of Sydney's most notorious criminals. To a packed gallery that oohed and aahed at each new allegation, the defence told the court of the sordid details of the abductor Thompson's love for Stuart-Jones' wife, of Thompson's wife's love for the would-be assassin Jowett and other scandalous allegations of love affairs between Sydney's high-society matrons and underworld figures.

It also came out that Dr Stuart-Jones had been in the sly-grog and cocaine trafficking business with Jowett and a recently deceased gangster named Donald 'the Duck' Day, who had been shot dead in Surry Hills. The court heard that Dr Stuart-Jones used his luxury four-master yacht *Sirocco* to peddle whisky, liquor, prostitutes and narcotics to American soldiers and that his associates in these floating Roman orgies on Sydney Harbour included the cream of Sydney's underworld hit men and standover merchants.

The court heard that Stuart-Jones' Lido nightclub at Bondi was really a front for a huge sly-grog operation, and his 400 Club was more like a Chicago speak-easy during prohibition with a band, table service and booze served around the clock. The betting that the doctor did at the racetracks in large amounts of cash was allegedly from his 'cash-only' abortion clinics all over Sydney.

It was also alleged that Stuart-Jones consorted with the worst gangsters of the times and carried a revolver, which he wasn't afraid to use to fire into the ceilings of crowded bars or restaurants when he was drunk. A well-known Sydney standover man of the day testified for the defence that he was present on one occasion when the doctor beat his new young wife and gave her two black eyes.

But as much as the defence enhanced the tainted reputation of Sydney's most notorious doctor in living memory, it did little for Jowett and Thompson, who were found guilty and sentenced to death by hanging. Their sentences were later commuted to life imprisonment.

But the scandal of the trial was the beginning of the end for the now notorious Dr Stuart-Jones. Soon after the trial his clinic in Macquarie Street was raided and he was charged with performing an abortion and narrowly missed a prison sentence. Unable to explain his income from performing abortions all over Sydney, he had to sell Casa Clavel in order to pay a massive tax bill that had accumulated over the previous seven years.

In 1949 he married for the third time to Adelaide beauty queen Adeline Morick, who was less than half his age. During the 1950s he was involved in doping racehorses and race fixing and was disqualified by the Queensland Turf Club for pulling up one of his horses in a race at Bundamba.

In December 1960 Stuart-Jones received a tax bill for £186,000 for understating his income from his abortion businesses. In June 1961, Dr Reginald Stuart-Jones dropped dead of a heart attack. He was 58 years old but it was said that he had lived three lifetimes.

47 THE MURDER OF EBONY SIMPSON

The tiny rural town of Bargo, in the New South Wales Southern Highlands, has a population of around 3000. On Wednesday, 19 August 1992, nine-year-old Ebony Simpson got off the bus on the corner of Bargo and Arina Roads at 4.05pm, after attending the local primary school. Though she was only a 400-metre walk away, she wouldn't make it home. Andrew Peter Garforth was waiting.

Garforth, a short, thin 29-year-old with dirty shoulder-length hair and pale-blue eyes, was an unemployed labourer who lived at nearby Pheasants Nest. As Ebony walked towards her house, she came across him standing beside his car. The bonnet was up and the boot was open. When Ebony reached the car, Garforth bundled her into the boot and drove to a dam seven kilometres away.

Parked near the water's edge, Garforth removed the terrified young girl from the boot and sat her on the front seat with him. Ebony pleaded to be released. Garforth took her to the edge of the dam, where he bound her feet together and her hands behind her back with speaker wire. He then sexually abused her. Afterwards, Garforth threw the still-bound child into the dam, along with her schoolbag, which he weighed down with rocks. He then walked away, ignoring her pleas for help, and drove home.

The next day, at the instigation of his de facto wife and mother of his two young sons, Garforth joined the search for the missing girl. The only clue police had to go on was the description of a man in his late 20s who was seen working on an early-model light-coloured Mazda near the bus stop where Ebony disappeared. Police described the car as being in poor condition, with smoke stains from the exhaust covering the rear end. The car had been seen in the vicinity of primary and high schools in the district several times in the previous months. It had also been sighted following school buses. The man driving it was described as being 177 centimetres tall, with straight brown shoulder-length hair, of thin build and wearing a long-sleeved black top and black jeans. Garforth was soon picked up by police. Admitting his guilt, he took police divers to where he had left Ebony Simpson to drown. Her body was recovered at 12.45am on 21 August.

Garforth was charged with murder and made a full confession. Authorities were horrified at his lack of remorse.

He appeared in a packed Picton Courthouse on 21 August 1992. As he was led from the police cells next door, an outraged crowd of around 200 yelled abuse. In the dock, Garforth hung his head as the police prosecutor outlined the allegations. Garforth pleaded guilty to murdering Ebony Simpson. At his sentencing, on 9 July 1993, the crowded courtroom erupted as Justice Newman handed down the maximum – life imprisonment – under the New South Wales truth-in-sentencing legislation. Garforth would never be released.

In his summing up, Justice Newman did little to hold back his contempt, saying he believed Garforth's attitude to the crime was best reflected by his 'almost casual' answers in the interviews and that his lack of remorse after arrest was 'a matter of gravity'. The judge said that drowning 'is a terrifying and slow manner of death' and the little girl's 'last moments must have been spent in abject fear'.

Responding to a defence submission that Garforth was entitled to leniency because he had been cooperative with police by taking them to the murder scene and then pleading guilty, Justice Newman said, 'This is a case where the prisoner literally had no defence and no chance of finding one. I consider the sexual assault and the girl's fear as aggravating features in the highest degree.'

Justice Newman took into account the fact that if Garforth lived to the average age of males of the time, he could expect to spend 42 years behind bars. As a child murderer, he could expect his time to be 'more arduous' than most other prisoners'. Justice Newman also said that the case 'does fall squarely into the category of the worst type of case', and that the 'objective features of this dreadful crime' outweighed other considerations.

After the sentencing, Ebony's father, Peter Simpson, applauded the sentence. He told the press:

> I'd like to say I'm happy with the decision. It's taken nearly 11 long months to see justice served and this is the best outcome we could possibly hope for under the present legal system in this state of New South Wales in 1993. The fact remains that Ebony Simpson got the death sentence, the Simpson family got the life sentence and Garforth got bed and breakfast. The murderer's been given the very minimum that he deserves, a life sentence. He has shown no remorse, no shame and no feeling. This man has no soul. He abducted, tortured, sexually abused, murdered and discarded our beautiful Ebony in such a cruel and malicious way. How could anyone be sure he would not murder again? Garforth's selfish, barbaric, murderous act has had such a profound effect on so many people's lives, the ramifications of which may never really be known. Ebony's murder need never be forgotten. Ebony's death was untimely, unnecessary and senseless. It has thrown my

> family, myself into a nightmare existence. This man has done the ultimate robbery. He has robbed our dear Ebony of 70 years of her life.

Shortly after he was charged with murder in August 1992, Garforth was attacked at the Long Bay Remand Centre. In October 1993, he was bashed a second time, in Goulburn Gaol. On 30 March 1994 he appealed to the New South Wales Supreme Court against the severity of his life sentence, claiming the murder of Ebony Simpson was not in the 'worst case' category. On 23 May 1994, the Court of Criminal Appeal ruled that the case against Garforth was so extreme that community interest in retribution and punishment called for the maximum term.

In November 1994, Garforth gave notice that he would again be appealing against his sentence, this time to the High Court. 'How many judges do you need to say someone's guilty?' Ebony's mother, Christine Simpson, asked reporters. 'We've had four judges already saying it and now there will be another three. It makes a nonsense of the truth-in-sentencing legislation. If truth in sentencing was in place when we came out of court in July 1993, that should be the end of it. Garforth says his life sentence should be reduced because he cooperated with police and told them where Ebony's body was. But police said they were going to drag the dam anyway. They would have found her because her lunch box was floating on top. My family is shattered at the news of the appeal.'

On 7 December 1994, Garforth's application for special leave to appeal against his life sentence was rejected by the High Court. All his avenues of appeal are now exhausted – Andrew Peter Garforth will never be released from jail.

48 THE DEEP-SEA CONTRACT

In a lifetime of going to sea in pursuit of big gamefish, author Paul B. Kidd has fished with many famous and notorious people. But the one he loved most of all was the notorious gangster, Theo the Boss. As sinister as he was to the rest of the world, Theo was always good to Paul, and he was his friend. Although he may have changed some of the names and the circumstances are slightly varied, Paul maintains that this is a true story.

I will never forget that day as long as I live. We were fishing off Sydney for sharks on Theo the Boss' 56-foot Hatteras gamefishing boat *Saint Theodore*. But believe me, Theo was no saint. He was a card-carrying member of organised crime and had every Sydney politician and cop in his pocket. Theo the Boss was *the Man*.

And only now that Theo is telling 'em what to do in that illegal casino in the sky can I tell this story.

Through the 1960s and '70s Theo the Boss ran Sydney's biggest illegal casino, the Nugget Club, with a confidence that was without fear of reprimand. Collecting bad debts and rubbing shoulders with racketeers, standover men and hired killers was all in a night's work.

And the Boss had them all terrified. He was a proper gangster, straight out of a 1930s movie. If there was an Edward G. Robinson look-alike competition, Theo the Boss would have run first, third and ninth.

A short, stocky Greek with a patent-leather haircut and pencil-thin moustache, Theo dressed accordingly in double-breasted Raymond Peraggio handmade suits, gaudy silk ties and spit-polished black-and-white or brown-and-white Mellers shoes. He wore a diamond the size of a duck egg on the small finger of his left hand, smoked huge Cuban cigars and drank only the finest scotch whisky.

The Boss was chauffeur-driven around town by his ever-present henchman, Gringo, in a huge black Mark V four-door Lincoln Continental Town Car with pitch-black windows. The 'Mafia staff car', the boys called it.

Gringo carried the biggest gun I have ever seen in my life and if anyone suspicious came within cooee of the Boss he would produce it and, if need be, use it first and ask questions later.

Being offside with the Boss was not a good place to be. But if you were his friend, he was the best bloke in the world and couldn't do enough for you. Money was no object and he would spray his clan with the best of everything. The Boss was a beaut bloke and I crewed for him on *Saint Theodore* and I was his friend.

The Boss' two great passions were swearing and fishing – in that order. And he didn't give a shit who he dropped the magic word in front of. In a twenty-word sentence, most of them would be swearwords, highlighted by variations of his favourite word – fuck. And with the Boss' thick accent and sinister delivery, it was hilarious to hear him unleash a gob-full on someone and reduce them to a gibbering mess. Mind you, none of us ever laughed to his face.

And whenever he could, the Boss would escape the art-deco decor and the hustle and bustle of the Nugget Club and go fishing on his magnificent *Saint Theodore*, which was the apple of his eye.

His pride and joy had every possible extra and the boss' minions kept her like a new pin. We even had to take our deck shoes off before we walked inside the main saloon. To do anything against *Saint Theodore* was to put your life in very grave danger.

'Paul B., you bloody fuckin' bastard. You like fuckin' fishin' on my bloody fuckin' beauty bastard boat?' Theo would always ask me as he sat back in his giant leather lounge chair, chewing on a mammoth Monte Cristo and sucking on a vase of 20-year-old Chivas Regal as we headed out to the fishing grounds many miles off the Sydney coastline at around 7am.

'Absolutely, Theo,' I would always reply. 'Fishing on the best boat in the country with you is always fun. There's certainly never a dull moment.' And it was the truth.

Gringo would always analyse what I had said, his dull brain trying to figure out if I was taking the piss out of the Boss or not so he could tug my coat if need be. He never had to.

Cutting into the nicotine and alcohol at dawn was perfectly normal to Theo. After all, he'd been up all night running his gambling house and counting the money into the small hours of the morning. To Theo and his henchman it was just like going to the pub at five o'clock after a hard day's work. Instead, we were heading out in search of giant gamefish.

Curiously, Theo the Boss didn't do much big gamefishing himself, preferring to handline for snapper, or 'snappers', as he called them. So every second Sunday we would fish for snappers, and every other Sunday we would fish the point-scoring competition for marlin, tuna and sharks for the Sydney Game Fishing Club. And we did extremely well.

Our crew consisted of the legendary Watson's Bay boatman, Jack Farrell, the Boss' son Nicky, Gringo and me. Jack was in his early seventies and had gaffed countless world records for most of the big names in gamefishing. There wasn't much old Jack didn't know about bluewater fishing.

The Boss and Jack got on like a house on fire. They were about the same age and the Boss didn't have to put on any of that gangster bullshit with Jack. They would just sit and talk about fishing over a fine old Scotch. Jack wasn't in the least bit interested in what the Boss did for a quid and seemed totally oblivious to the fact that he was the fishing master for the heaviest mobster in Sydney, probably Australia.

Theo's son Nicky was a terrific bloke in his early thirties who had no interest whatever in following in the family tradition. He was content to run his small law practice, which specialised in real estate conveyancing.

Nicky loved anything to do with boats and fishing, and he drove the boat while Jack and I looked after the gear and rigged the baits. We took it in turns to catch the marlin, sharks and tuna because the Boss didn't care if he caught a gamefish or not.

The Boss often entertained characters that we had only seen photos of and had read about in the papers, and they would huddle and whisper in the saloon of the boat with the door closed while drinking whisky amid an expensive fog of blue cigar smoke.

'Don't you take any notice of what you see or hear in there, young fella,' wise old Jack would whisper to me as we rigged the baits and set the lines. 'Fishermen live a lot longer than gangsters.'

Gringo always came along for the ride and looked out of place at sea with his fedora sloped over his eyes and the huge cannon bulging in his jacket. But it was his job to see that the Boss came to no harm, no matter where he was.

This day we were berleying and drifting the Twelve Mile Reef with big surface bait for sharks. It was mid-August and the seas were as flat as a night carter's hat, with a lazy roll from the south. August is mako shark time and they are the meanest, most unpredictable critters that swim. Makos twist and turn in the gaff ropes and often jump into the boat with their jaws snapping ferociously. Anything that gets in the way gets badly bitten. It is little wonder that makos are referred to as 'blue dynamite with a short fuse'.

We hadn't been drifting long when a mako of about 250lb took some bait right at the back of the boat and I took the strike.

It gave me a good fight for an hour or so, leaping all over the ocean, before Jack finally gaffed it and secured it to the side of the boat.

The next strike was another mako of around 300lb, which Nicky took. After another hard fight of about half an hour, it too was captured, tail-roped and tied off a bollard.

Then another mako swam right up to the back of the boat and tried to eat the berley pot. It was a big bastard and it had its mouth around the stainless-steel chum pot, trying to wrench it from the boat.

Jack ran inside and got the Australian record chart. 'How big do you reckon that fish is, Paul?' he asked, knowing that I had seen more than my share of big makos over the years.

'I reckon 600lb would stop it cold, Jack,' I said, as I admired the great fish's magnificent shades of blue and its superb shape that could have been carved out of onyx. Dreading what was to come, I wondered if guided missiles had been designed with makos in mind.

I knew that shortly I would probably be called upon to kill this beautiful eating machine and I hated doing it. But back in those kill-anything-that-swims days of the '60s and '70s it was my job ... and that was that.

'The Australian record for a mako on a 20lb line is just over 500lb and this bloke is around 550lb,' Jack said as he threaded half a striped tuna onto a huge hook, attached it to a rod and reel fitted with 20lb line and fed the bait down the big mako's crockery-encrusted craw. 'OK, let's get ourselves an Australian record that won't be beaten in a hurry.'

The Boss wasn't into catching sharks and he sat on the flying bridge sipping on a Chivas, puffing away on a cigar and happily watching the activity and chatting with Gringo.

Jack wound up the drag on the reel and sunk the hook, expecting the big fish to take off. But it didn't budge. It just stayed there munching on the berley pot and swimming from one side of the boat to the other.

'Piss off, you bastard,' Jack yelled at the shark, but it didn't. It just hung around the back of the boat offering no resistance at all. So I prodded it with the blunt end of a boat hook. That did the trick and with one almighty swish of its tail, which nearly drenched us, it took off like a burning dog.

Jack leaned on the rod in an effort to fight the fish and after about 200 yards of line had disappeared off the reel it seemed that he was winning. Then the line went slack and Jack wound as fast as he could but he couldn't get fast to the fish again. We thought he had busted the line.

But no. 'The bloody thing's swimming back to the berley pot quicker than I can wind in the line,' Jack yelled in amazement as the mako materialised at the back of the boat, munching on the pot, oblivious to the wire trace hanging out of its gob. It didn't know that it was hooked.

'Get the gaff,' yelled Jack. 'It took enough line off the reel to be considered a legal catch. Gaff it.'

'Bullshit,' I said, 'are you crazy? Those things are mental enough at the gaff when they are exhausted after they've been fought for hours. Do you expect me to gaff one green?'

'Yes. So don't argue with me. Just do as you're told.'

I had no choice. That's the unwritten law of the ocean. The captain kicks the mate, the mate kicks the cabin boy and the cabin boy kicks the cat. Like it or lump it, in the pecking order of things on a boat you do as you're told. Even in fishing. I looked up at the Boss for a second opinion and maybe a bit of sympathy.

'Fuckin' bloody do as he bloody fuckin' says,' Theo the Boss growled, obviously unaware that in a minute I would be killed.

So I did as Jack commanded. I attached the end of the flying gaff rope to a bollard on the deck in the corner of the tuck, leaned over the back of the boat, placed the gaff head below the shark's shoulder underneath the gills and pulled on the gaff pole and rope at the same time. The huge gaff hook went straight in.

None of us were prepared for what happened next. The water erupted as if a depth charge had gone off just below the surface. And, as if gaining momentum to leap into the boat and bite my head off for sticking that mammoth gaff into it, the shark plunged as deep as the length of the 14-foot gaff rope would allow and then shot through the surface, leapt the full length of the rope in midair above our heads and came crashing down onto the transom of the boat, snapping, blurting, grunting and biting at anything within snapping distance. Curiously, at the moment of sheer terror, I can recall its breath. Yuk. It was vile.

Fortunately for us it fell out of the boat and not into the cockpit, but as it fell, it lifted the gaff rope over my head and behind me, pinning me in the corner of the boat between the bollard, with the fish going berserk on the end of the gaff rope. I was copping rope burns all over my legs and back as the fish lunged and jumped trying to throw the gaff.

Theo the Boss was far from impressed with what was happening to his pride and joy and was even less impressed when the huge fish started breaking its teeth on the marlin board and smashing holes in the highly polished fibreglass transom with its tail. Finally he'd had enough.

'Fuckin' bloody hell fuck, look what that fucker bloody fuckin' bastard's doing to fuck my bloody fuckin' beautiful fucker boat. No fuckin' bastard fucker does that and fuckin' gets away with it. Gringo, fuckin' shoot that fuckin' bastard,' he screamed.

Although he didn't know it, the Boss had probably just put out the world's first contract on a shark. And Gringo didn't have to be told twice. He produced the cannon from inside his double-breasted suit jacket and climbed down the flying bridge ladder, waving it in the air. As he hit the deck he aimed and took a shot at the shark as it propelled itself head and shoulders above the back of the boat.

I felt the bullet whistle past my ear as it missed the shark and landed in the water a hundred yards off the back of the boat. By this stage I had somehow managed to get the gaff rope over my head but I was bloodied and bruised from head to foot. Nicky had broken a finger trying to get a tail rope on the shark and now we had a totally pissed-off shark and a gun-totin' lunatic to contend with.

The Boss looked on at the mayhem below him and seemed to be enjoying it all. Just as Gringo was about to rattle off another shot, Jack called a halt to proceedings.

'Theo,' he called. 'You can't gaff a record fish with a .45 handgun. It will be disqualified. If we take that fish in to weigh with bullet holes in it there will be an uproar. Call Gringo off.'

The Boss listened to Jack and told Gringo to put the smoking gun away. Thank Christ for that. But we still had the shark to contend with. From the time I gaffed it to the time we tied it to the side of the boat was 45 minutes. We had been battered from one side of the boat to the other and we had the bruises and broken bones to prove it. Not to mention the near-death experience with a bullet.

The mako weighed 556lb. An Australian record for the time on 20lb breaking strain line.

49 | A TERRIBLE WAY TO DIE

On 10 September 2004, Peter David Taber and Ian Craig Styman were literally fighting for their lives. They had appealed their convictions and life sentences in jail without the possibility of parole for committing one of the cruellest murders in New South Wales' history. The Crown had asked for the toughest possible sentence and, given the facts in the case, the law demanded nothing less. And so it was: life behind bars, never to be released.

But there were questionable circumstances in the robbery that turned into a horrible death, which convinced the Court of Criminal Appeal that there were grounds for an appeal. There was a distinct possibility that the murder may in fact have been an act of manslaughter, which would mean a difference in time served in jail of up to 40 years.

The Court of Appeal had heard the case for their sentences to be overthrown from murder to manslaughter. Now, as they waited to hear their fate, Peter Taber and Ian Craig had time to reflect on what had happened on that terrible night ...

When 71-year-old Joy Golbey Alchin's body was found on the bedroom floor of her ransacked home at Greenwell Point, New South Wales, on 19 January 2001, police estimated that she could have been dead for up to two days. Tied to her bed, Ms Alchin had been gagged with her own soiled underwear. Her hands and feet were trussed with cable ties and duct tape. Her head was covered with a pillowcase that was tied at the neck. She had bruising and cuts to her face and body, and swollen lips. The bruising was consistent with sexual assault.

For almost two months the death remained a mystery. Then, on 19 March, acting on a tip-off, police raided two homes in Brisbane, arresting Shannon Troy Styman, 22, his uncle Ian Craig Styman, 37, Peter David Taber, 27, and Ms Alchin's niece, Leonie Kaye Ravell, 19. Only then was it revealed that on the night of the attack an anonymous caller had rung the 000 emergency line and reported that an elderly lady had been assaulted and tied, still alive, to a bed. The call was regarded as a hoax and ignored. Authorities admitted that if they had taken the call seriously Ms Alchin would probably have been found alive: it took her up to 10 days to die from dehydration and suffocation.

The committal hearing began on 19 February 2002. The court was told that it was common knowledge Ms Alchin kept paper bags full of $100 bills in her house, and that family members often borrowed money from her. It was alleged that Ravell had made it known to the three other accused that there was a lot of money in her aunt's house, and that the men had gone there on her instigation and tortured the old woman until she told them where the cash was.

Committed to stand trial for murder, robbery, deprivation of liberty in aggravated circumstances and sexual assault, Ian Styman and Peter Taber pleaded not guilty when proceedings began on 8 September 2002. Shannon Styman pleaded not guilty to murder and sexual assault, though he pleaded guilty to robbing Ms Alchin and depriving her of her liberty in aggravated circumstances and in company. He refused to name his accomplices.

Joy Alchin was born on 28 November 1930, had three sisters, had been married and divorced and had a daughter. At 50 kilograms and standing 149 centimetres tall, the elderly recluse lived alone in her small fibro house. Around 1987 she began drawing her money out of the bank in $100 notes and hoarding it.

A boarder at Taber's house, Donyelle Louise Turner, 20, told the court that when she had returned home from a trip to Sydney on 16 January 2001, she found several new household appliances that she had never seen in the house before. She became suspicious of her landlord's sudden good fortune and sneaked into his bedroom to look over his new belongings. In the bedroom she found $900 in $100 bills in his de facto wife Leonie Ravell's purse. Given that Taber had recently tried to borrow $2000 from Ms Turner, she wondered where the money had come from.

Ms Turner also recalled that Taber had recently asked Leonie's sister, Melinda Ravell, for a loan of $2000, without success. Taber had then suggested a visit to Leonie's aunt, Joy Alchin. Ms Turner then told the court that in a conversation she heard between Leonie Ravell and Taber before Christmas 2000, Ravell said: 'We can always kill her. It is not like anyone will notice she is missing.'

The court also heard that a man named Alan Stoker sold a car to Ian Styman on the afternoon of the day Joy Alchin was left lying helpless on her bedroom floor. Styman paid $4300 in cash. Around $1000 of the money was in $100 notes.

The court heard that a police search of Taber's South Nowra residence – South Nowra is a short drive from Greenwell Point – produced rolls of duct tape similar to that used in Ms Alchin's assault. In the loungeroom was a bag of similar cable ties. Screwed-up duct tape was found in the backyard and in the back of a ute. DNA found in blood on the duct tape later proved to be a match to Ms Alchin. The residence also contained a free-standing fan, a Sony PlayStation, a sandwich-maker, a TV and a stereo – and the empty cartons they came out of. In the garage, police found surgical gloves and masks.

Sarah Burgess, a checkout operator and workmate of Leonie Ravell, told the court that on 8 January Taber and Ravell went shopping at the Nowra Kmart and approached the checkout with two trolleys full of household appliances, which added up to a total of around $1500. They paid in $100 notes.

Taber told the court he had denied to police (on 24 January 2001) that he had discussed killing Ms Alchin with Leonie Ravell. Taber also said that Joy Alchin was so disliked by her family that her daughter was alleged to have said that if other people hadn't murdered her, she (the daughter) would have done it herself.

The court heard that Taber had told police he worked as a shed builder, and that he was often paid large sums in cash. Quite often he worked for elderly people who paid him in cash. Although his bank account showed very small balances, Taber said that over the previous 15 months he had had his 'hands on 40 or 50 grand, probably a bit more'.

A record of the interview with Ian Styman presented to the court revealed that he was living on unemployment benefits when he spent $5100 on a car and a TV the day after Joy Alchin was robbed. Married with two children, Styman received $407 in social security benefits a fortnight. The court heard he made around $200 to $300 per week as a computer technician when he could find work, and since the beginning of the previous year he had made $8000 installing a computer chip that enabled people to play pirated video games. Styman said he had about $20 in his four bank accounts and nothing in his wife's account.

A friend of Styman told police that late in December he had come across Taber practising tying up Styman, and that he had then driven them to Greenwell Point late at night. They had allegedly tried to break into Ms Alchin's home but she had woken up and they had fled. The following day Ms Alchin had had new security doors fitted.

Taber took the stand and said that on the night of the attack he was at home, and had played a computer game lent to him by Ian Styman until the early hours of the morning. Taber told the court that while he was playing the game Shannon Styman arrived and told him that he (Shannon) had just robbed a drug dealer. Taber later learned from Shannon Styman that he (Styman) had in fact robbed an old woman in her home. Taber told the court that Shannon told him that he got $23,000 from the robbery and then that Shannon gave him (Taber) and Ian $5000 each.

Leonie Ravell then told the court that she did not remember seeing Taber playing computer games. She said she went to bed at about 8pm that night and he did not join her until the following day.

Ian Styman told the court that the first he knew of the crime was when his nephew, Shannon Styman, told him he (Shannon) and his friend Peter Taber had 'done an old lady's place over'.

Ian Styman denied that he and Taber had tied up Ms Alchin and ransacked her house while his nephew kept an eye on her. He said that on the night of the murder he was at home fixing a computer in his garage. He said he was cooking at 3am when he received a call from Taber telling him that Shannon had done something stupid and to meet him (Taber) right away.

Ian Styman's wife Sharyn told the court her husband wasn't home that night and didn't go to bed at the usual time.

Shannon Styman told the court that he, his uncle Ian and Taber had broken into Ms Alchin's house and left about 20 minutes later, as soon as they found the bag of money. He said Ms Alchin didn't let out 'so much as a moan' when she was surprised and grabbed by the three men in the early hours of the morning. He denied that Ms Alchin had been bashed or sexually assaulted.

When asked if it appeared that Ms Alchin had been unconscious throughout the ordeal, he replied that she had moved only slightly, but she was breathing and offered no resistance. Styman said it had taken about one minute to bind Ms Alchin. He said it was his job to stay with her while the others ransacked the house. He said Taber allegedly told her: 'Just tell us where the money is.'

Shannon Styman denied that Ms Alchin could have been unconscious throughout the ordeal because she had been bashed, and claimed he had no idea how Ms Alchin had sustained the injuries to her vaginal and rectal region. Asked why it was necessary for him to stay with Ms Alchin while the others searched the house, Styman said it was so she wouldn't fall off the bed and hurt herself.

He told the court that when he asked Taber and Ian Styman if the old lady was going to be untied before they left, he was satisfied with the answer – that they would ring 000. He said that he had checked that Ms Alchin was breathing before they left the house.

He said Ian Styman had found $23,300 in cash in a bag beside Ms Alchin's bed and the trio returned to Taber's house and divided up the money, with $14,000 going to Taber, $7000 to Ian Styman and he himself getting $2300; he believed $7000 was to go to Leonie Ravell.

The prosecution said that when Ms Alchin was found, she had curled her legs up beneath a table, and that there was evidence she had wriggled around the room and bruised herself while trying to get free. Doctors assumed that as she had been unable to do anything, she would have lapsed into a coma after about 10 days and died.

On 13 December 2002, Peter Taber and Ian Styman were found guilty of murder and aggravated break and enter for the purpose of committing a serious indictable offence. Shannon Styman was found guilty of manslaughter, but not guilty of murder. All three were found not guilty of aggravated sexual intercourse without consent or of sexual intercourse without consent.

On 28 February 2003, Taber and Styman were sentenced to life imprisonment without the possibility of parole. Shannon Styman was sentenced to a minimum of 10 years' jail. Leonie Ravell was released on a two-year good behaviour bond for hindering police. A manslaughter charge against her was dropped after she entered into a plea bargain in exchange for her evidence.

On 10 September 2004 Taber and Styman had their murder convictions overturned. The New South Wales Court of Criminal Appeal quashed both murder convictions and ordered a retrial, allowing the Crown to replace the murder verdicts with manslaughter convictions. It was deemed that they did not intend to kill Joy Alchin and were convinced that their 000 call would see to it that help would arrive and free the old lady.

On 15 December 2005, in the New South Wales Supreme Court, Peter David Taber and Ian Craig Styman were both sentenced to 18 years' imprisonment with a nonparole period of 13 years for the manslaughter of 71-year-old Joy Golbey Alchin at her home Greenwell Point, New South Wales, in January 2001.

50 | MURDER THROUGH THE CLASSIFIEDS

The last time anybody saw navy ship's steward John Bridger alive was when the 26-year-old English immigrant left a photographic studio at 419 George Street, in Sydney's central business district, on a warm autumn day in 1872. The two men with him, however, would soon become infamous, even though the strange murder case would eventually end up shrouded in mystery.

A slightly overweight gentleman with red cheeks and a friendly disposition, Bridger had spent the previous year working for the navy on the HMS *Rosario*, anchored in Farm Cove, when he answered an ad in the *Sydney Morning Herald* on 4 March 1872. The ad – placed in the Professions, Trades section of the well-respected paper – was one of two calling for men to work in a country store, in the roles of clerk and the driver of a horse-drawn wagon. Most likely bored with life on the water, Bridger was quick to reply and was thrilled to be accepted, especially as employment situated on dry land was hard to come by in those tough times.

Bridger spent much of his first day away from the navy and the *Rosario* celebrating his good fortune and impending new life at the Oriental Hotel, in Circular Quay. It was one of several pubs in the area that he frequented, and as a result he knew many of the local drinkers.

The next evening, Bridger arrived at the photographic studio to pick up a portrait of himself that he had earlier commissioned. Photography was still something of a gimmick at the time, and the owner, a man by the name of Chandler, told Bridger that the job wasn't ready yet, and that he should return in a few hours. When he came back that night, Bridger was accompanied by two men. One was a stocky fellow in his mid-30s who was distinguished by a dense, curly beard. The man's name, detectives would later find out, was George Robert Nichols. The other member of the group was a younger male named Alfred Lester. Lester would later be described as having a pasty face and a thin blond moustache.

Also responding to the ads in the *Sydney Morning Herald* was a rather fey man with a fastidious nature by the name of William Percy Walker. At the time, Walker – who had only arrived in Sydney from Victoria three weeks earlier – was living at a boarding house ran by a Mrs Stephenson at 6 Bridge Street. While in Victoria, Walker had worked as a bookkeeper and also acted as an unordained preacher.

After hearing that he was successful in his application for a position at the country store, Walker enlisted the help of Mrs Stephenson's 16-year-old son Frederick to help him take his baggage on the 10-minute ride by horse and buggy to nearby Parramatta Steamer Wharf. When the pair arrived, they were greeted by the pasty-faced man with the wispy moustache, Alfred Lester. Lester was standing in a boat intended to take them to their destination. He explained that the five-metre-long vessel was going to be completely filled up with provisions for their journey, and that the best idea was to stow Walker's gear at a pub, where they would call for it at a later date.

Nichols soon arrived on the scene, and the four males retired to the Commercial Hotel on the corner of Sussex and King streets. As the group took a table and placed Walker's pigskin trunk under it, Nichols ordered beverages. After the one drink and some fairly stilted conversation, the group left the pub, with Walker taking a private moment to bid a fond farewell to young Fred.

Even at the time, though, it seemed strange that Walker removed a sizeable gold watch from his waistcoat and held it to Fred's face before making the boy 'swear' that the older gentleman was in possession of the timepiece. Fred did as he was asked and then went on his way.

It was 12 March 1872, some eight days after the fateful ads had appeared in the paper, that John Bridger's body turned up, floating slowly up the middle of the Parramatta River, with a heavy rock attached to his ankles by a length of rope. The body was first spotted by a man fishing on the river's bank near Kissing Point. The fisherman quickly notified the authorities and Senior Constable Samuels – in charge of keeping the peace in the suburb of Ryde at the time – and the fisherman then faced the somewhat unpleasant job of towing the corpse to Ryde Wharf before dragging it out of the water and loading it onto a cart, which they used to transport the body to the Ryde Hotel. There a preliminary inquest would be held in a room to the rear of the pub.

Two of Sydney's best detectives – Richard Elliott and William Camphin – were called in to examine the bloated body. Inside a jacket pocket they found Bridger's naval discharge papers. Learning the name of the deceased was an important early breakthrough in the case. The detectives also noticed a wound on Bridger's right temple, which they were soon able to ascertain had happened before the body was dumped in the river. They could also surmise that, because the body had the large stone tied to its ankles, and had been floating down the middle of the waterway, it must have been thrown from a boat, most likely by at least two men. But because the culprits had left the identifying papers in Bridger's jacket, they obviously expected the body to sink to the river's bed, helped on its way by the hefty rock. Unfortunately for the murderers, they hadn't taken into account the fact that gases produced in a deceased body would make it rise whether it was weighted down or not.

The detectives traced Bridger's recent history back to the Oriental Hotel, where the locals told them about their friend's apparent good luck finding a job in a country store. The news found its way to the local papers, where it was seen by the Stephensons, who hadn't heard from their former lodger William Walker since he had shown his gold watch to young Fred at King Street Wharf. They wasted no time in informing the authorities of their fears, and the police soon started searching the Parramatta River. Walker's body turned up floating through Five Dock Bay on 19 March. Around his neck was tied a stone that was even larger than the one attached to Bridger's body.

Having learned that both men had answered an ad in the *Sydney Morning Herald*, the paper's office was the next logical place for the authorities to visit. They soon uncovered the booking sheet for the help-wanted placement. The name on it was A.T. Norton. The clerk said that he could recall the man who had placed the ad. He described him as having a curly beard.

The next breakthrough in the case came from the man who ran the photographic studio on George Street. Not only was Chandler able to provide a photo of Bridger when he was alive, he could also give a description of the two men who had been with him that night. Simple detective work then led the police to identifying the men as Nichols and Walker, both of whom had recently been released from Darlinghurst Gaol. Nichols, it transpired, had been serving an 18-month sentence for theft and fraud.

Detective Elliott soon caught up with Nichols at an auction room on Pitt Street, where the former prisoner was trying to offload some of Bridger's belongings. It was unfortunate timing on Nichols' part to say the least, and he was quickly arrested and taken into custody.

With one of their suspects already found, detectives Elliot and Camphin visited his home. Nichols had been living in The Rocks area, with his wife and two children, in a large but dim room at the back of 52 Princes Street. The two policemen questioned the well-liked Mrs Nichols. When they left, they took a portion of her clothes line for examination.

Proving to be not the most careful of criminals, it wasn't long before the authorities also caught up with Alfred Lester, who had been trying to get some money in return for William Walker's watch – the same item the deceased had made a point of showing Fred Stephenson. When Lester took the watch to a Haymarket pawnbroker named Issac Moss, Moss took it out to the back room to show his brother Charlie. The men discussed the situation and told Lester to come back to the shop a short time later. They then called the police and, when Lester returned, Detective Elliot was waiting for him. When Lester was taken into custody, Elliot noticed some initials on his shirt collar. They read 'WPW', which just happened to stand for William Percy Walker.

The very next morning, a Sunday, Elliot and Camphin went to a terrace house at 53 Holt Street, Strawberry Hills. The detectives were met there by the landlady, Mary Blaker, who took them up to a room that had been rented by Nichols and Lester. Blaker explained that the men had told her they had recently arrived in town from the Friendly Isles.

Inside the room, the detectives found three boxes sitting on the floor. It only took a quick look inside one of them to realise they had their murderers – the first thing they looked at was a shirt that had John Bridger's name printed on it. They took the boxes back to the station for further examination. There they found what was known in those days as a neddy – a weighted bludgeon often used by criminals of the time. Nichols was quick to say that anything in the boxes must belong to Lester.

Meanwhile, two separate inquests into the death of William Walker were being run – the original one at the Ryde Hotel, as well as another one at the Observer Hotel on George Street in The Rocks. At Ryde, they found that after Walker answered the ad for the job at the country store, he was interviewed by a man going by the name of Mr James, who was later identified as Nichols. As Mr James, Nichols had said he was the manager of a store in the rural Bathurst area, west of Sydney. The store,

Nichols added, was owned by a man named Norton. After offering the position to Walker, Nichols told him to meet him at King Street Wharf where they would travel on the Norton's family boat up the Parramatta River to the store owner's house.

Things weren't looking good for Nichols and Lester. The inquest next heard from an Isabella Buckley, who ran Buckley's Boat Shed. The woman confirmed that she had hired a boat to Lester on the day Walker went missing. And Fred Stephenson had no trouble recognising the pair. On top of that, the boy recognised several items of clothing found in the boxes from the pair's Holt Street room.

Next the authorities matched the piece of clothes line taken as evidence from Mrs Nichols with the rope that had attached the heavy stone to Walker's body. Equally as damning was the fact the neddy found at Holt Street fit perfectly into the indentation on Walker's skull. For good measure, the authorities compared the handwriting on the job sheet for the ad placed in the *Sydney Morning Herald* with that of the accounts book at the Sydney Meat Preserving Works where Nichols had been employed as a clerk. They also matched perfectly.

With so much evidence against them, the next step was for Nichols and Lester to face a preliminary hearing in court, which they did on 26 March 1872, just 22 days after their help-wanted ad had ran. When they arrived at what was then called the Old Central police courts, opposite Sydney Town Hall, on the site now occupied by the ornate Queen Victoria Building, the pair were greeted by an angry mob baying for blood. They were then taken to appear before magistrate Captain Scott. The two accused couldn't have appeared any more different; Nichols stood up straight, seemingly projecting an air of quiet confidence, while Lester slumped over, looking beaten already. The onslaught of damning evidence didn't help his demeanour.

Witness after witness appeared against the accused, including the photographer Chandler, who once again identified Nichols and Lester as being with Bridger the last time he was seen alive. A barrowman named Driscoll also spoke of being hired to take Bridger's luggage from the Oriental Hotel to Grafton Wharf, where he had been met by Lester. Suspiciously, Lester then told the barrowman to take the baggage on to Royal Standard Hotel. A barmaid from the hotel testified that Nichols and Lester came and took away the baggage themselves the next day. The final destination for Bridger's baggage was a room rented by Lester at a lodging house at 35 Crown Road, Millers Point, a suburb right next to The Rocks.

The actual trial against George Nichols and Alfred Lester started at Darlinghurst's Central Criminal Court on 20 May 1872, where – contrary to popular public opinion – the accused declared they were not guilty of murder. Still, their defence team, including future Australian Prime Minister Edward Barton assisting, did manage to sow a few seeds of doubt, seeds that would grow almost a century later. Because Walker's body was in such a state when it was found, Fred Stephenson was not in a position to identify it with any certainty. Also, the driver of the horse and buggy that took Walker and young Stephenson to the wharf on the day the murdered man disappeared could not confirm that it was actually Nichols who the pair had met up with. Another fairly weak point for the defence came when the barmaid from the Commercial Hotel could not confirm that Lester was with Nichols when he called back for Walker's baggage.

Still, even though much of the evidence against the pair was circumstantial, Judge John Hargraves decided that there was so much of it that it couldn't be ignored. The jury agreed, and Nichols and Lester were both soon found guilty of two counts of murder each. Lester broke out in tears, while Nichols stood up and managed to squeeze out a few quiet words before falling in an unconscious heap on the floor. After he was finally brought around with the help of a nip of brandy, the judge passed the death sentence on both men.

With their days now numbered, Nichols and Lester put their confessions to paper, both admitting that the murders took place upon the hired boat. The victims, they confessed, were given brandy that had been laced with laudanum – an addictive analgesic derived from opium – to knock them out. Despite the confession, though, there were still several unanswered questions.

A large crowd was on hand on the Tuesday morning of 18 June 1872; all were eager to see the murderers swing from the gallows at Darlinghurst Gaol. While only those who had been able to obtain tickets were allowed inside the gates, a number of people waited outside, as Nichols was the first of the pair to be led to the hanging platform. Before he stepped up to the noose, he addressed the assembled gathering, thanking those who had kept him incarcerated, and all involved in the trial. He read a psalm from the Bible and then he was hanged by the neck until he was dead, a process that took an uncomfortable 10 minutes. Alfred Lester followed shortly afterwards.

But that wasn't the end of the story. The undertaker who held the contract for Darlinghurst Gaol, Edward Pople, took note of the widespread public interest in the case and came up with a way to turn a quick dollar. Pople, it turned out, was also involved with the Morning Star Hotel in Waterloo, so instead of taking care of the bodies of Nichols and Lester immediately, he put them on show in the parlour of the pub, where anyone with a spare sixpence could view the cold, infamous corpses. But even though the bodies proved to be a popular attraction, it wasn't long before the authorities issued Pople with a strong reprimand and cancelled his contract with the prison.

The interest in the case eventually died down and the deaths of John Bridger and William Walker would have been consigned to the record books, an open-and-shut case, if it weren't for the efforts of author Leicester Cotton some 90 years later. Cotton stumbled across reports of the murders in a Sydney library, and certain points didn't sit well with the amateur sleuth. The more Cotton looked into the matter, the more things didn't feel right. For a start, he pointed out, Nichols and Lester had little to gain from killing the two victims. Once their initial outlays were taken into account – placing the ad, hiring the boat – they would have been lucky to come away with £10 profit for each victim, and that was only after going to the trouble of pawning all their belongings.

Also troubling Cotton was the fact that the men hung for the murders seemed to do so little to cover their tracks. Besides using a fake name to place the ad in the *Sydney Morning Herald*, Nichols and Lester were easily recognised by any number of people they came in contact with – barmaids, the photographer Chandler, young Fred Stephenson.

Then there was the fact that Bridger and Walker weren't the only men to respond to the ad in the paper. Indeed, Nichols interviewed other applicants in the busy Petty's Hotel on York Street, Sydney.

Cotton would go on to point out other interesting details, such as the fact that when Walker's body was fished from the water, he had no moustache. And his corpse was measured as being 170 centimetres tall. Walker, though, was generally regarded as standing no taller than 162 centimetres.

It seems the mystery of the Parramatta River will remain just that: a mystery.

51 THE REPUTABLE FIRM OF CROWLEY AND BUCKLEY

When police raided what they thought was a small starting-price betting operation just 100 metres from the New South Wales TAB headquarters in Thomas Street, Ultimo, in inner-Sydney, in September 1979, little did they realise that they had tapped into an illegal enterprise that employed hundreds of people and turned over as much as some of the larger public companies on the stock exchange. What they had stumbled onto would lead them to a massive SP operation that was using the latest in computer technology to take and place bets in every major capital city around the country.

When the police smashed the door down they discovered a projector flashing up-to-the minute TAB odds and betting fluctuations onto a huge screen on the wall. A barrage of phones were ringing nonstop and were answered by a small army of women, who took bets in coded names or sent the larger bets through to a man sitting in the middle of the room who was obviously running the show.

Among the weeping phone operators who were rounded up and put into the paddy wagons and taken away were four grandmothers aged from 63 to 74. Some of the ladies said they had been working for the company for decades. They knew little of their employers and all they could tell investigators was that the name of the company that paid their above-award wages – minus tax and with a group certificate supplied at the end of every financial year – was known only by the initials 'CB'. The women told police that a condition of their employment was that they must never tell anyone what their job really was outside of being a 'phone operator'.

It didn't take police long to realise that they had hit the mother lode. It seemed as though Australia's biggest SP betting network had been operating right under their noses for the best part of 40 years, obviously with the help of crooked cops.

Under the pretext of being a respectable company, CB was using the very latest in computer technology, operated about 10,000 accounts and accepted bets up to $20,000 over the phone. It also seemed as though some of their telephones tapped into the TAB just up the road, from which they listened to the latest prices and betting fluctuations.

CB turned out to be the initials of the legitimate business name of the firm of Crowley and Buckley, who had applied for registration as 'commission agents' with the New South Wales Corporate Affairs Commission on 14 September 1971, and gave their head office address as the second floor of 74 Pitt Street, Sydney, in the heart of the CBD. The application said that the firm had begun trading 30 years earlier in September 1941.

The proprietors were listed as Humphrey Michael Crowley of Mosman on Sydney's north shore, and Rita Mary Buckley, wife of the late James Buckley, of nearby Manly. The business name registration had been renewed in 1975 with the same proprietors; in 1977 it had been renewed again, only this time with Crowley listed as the sole proprietor. It had been renewed again in 1980 with the same details. The firm of Crowley and Buckley was a current, registered business. But legitimate? Well, that was another story entirely.

With the bust all over the front pages, the informers came forward at a million miles an hour. It seemed as though C&B – as they were known in the trade – was the biggest SP betting operation in Australia and from humble beginnings was allowed to thrive and grow throughout the Sir Robert Askin Liberal government era in New South Wales in the 1960s and '70s. An SP bookie in opposition to C&B described them as an 'absolutely massive operation' that operated on every TAB meeting – horses, dogs and the trots – and had an annual turnover by the late 1970s of around $100 million a year.

And it wasn't hard to tell why. The initial bust at Ultimo was just the tip of the iceberg. It led to numerous C&B SP joints throughout Sydney, including massive operations at the registered offices in Pitt Street, as well as at premises in Rushcutter Bay and in the Haymarket area, where they catered for the fanatical Chinese gambling population.

During the 1979 crackdown by police who weren't on the C&B payroll, more than 150 people, mainly consisting of middle-aged female phone operators, were arrested and charged with taking bets over the phone and processing the accounts that were all in code – usually either a nickname or someone's initials. It turned out that many members of state parliament, including Premier Askin, had accounts and bet regularly with them.

At C&B headquarters in Pitt Street police found 30 phones; another 40 were in use at the Rushcutter Bay branch. In total they closed down betting houses that collectively had more than 200 phones in operation. Some of the premises were guarded by a small dummy operation in an office in the front of the building, in case of unexpected police raids, while the much larger business went on at the back behind soundproofed steel doors and was accessed only by a secret door.

One woman who worked at a C&B operation in Cowles Road, Mosman, told police that she had got her job through a friend who worked in a telephone exchange. She explained that you had to have an 'in' to work there – that is that you have to be recommended by someone who can be held responsible should you talk too much about what you did for a living. She said that the office was in a very inconspicuous old, white office building full of doctors' surgeries. They had two upstairs offices: one was a dummy with a telephone and a few fake betting slips on the desk. They took turns sitting in this office.

She said that against the wall was a small bookcase with a hidden catch that opened first onto a verandah and then into the air-conditioned real office, which was like a fortress with armour-plated doors on rollers. In the event of the police raiding the smaller office and taking the phone operator away, she would be charged and ultimately fined for operating an SP and be back at work the next day. She would be given a bonus for her heroics.

But for the magnitude of the C&B operation, convictions – apart from all of those arrested at the time of the raids and fined – were nonexistent, though it is believed that the taxation department gave the principals a rough time. Three years after the raids that shut them down, John William Buckley, the son of the original proprietor, the late James Buckley, appeared in court on SP betting charges for operating an SP in the city and was fined $200.

But by 1982 in New South Wales, due to raids led by incorruptible police such as Merv Beck and his squad named Beck's Raiders, large-scale SP betting establishments turning over multimillions of illegal dollars and making huge profits for their operatives became a thing of the past.

52 THE SINS OF THE FATHER

There was a time it seems when the boxing Waters family were always on the TV. Patriarch Cec, in his trademark beanie, with his young wife and his three boxing sons. We saw the Waters at their unusual boxing camp where Cec, the loving father and family man, trained them, while surrounded by countless stray dogs they had saved from the pound, a dozen or so horses they had reprieved from the knackery and a variety of other stray and unwanted animals who had wandered in.

But, beneath the surface lay the horrific story of a sexual deviant who beat his family and had his estranged wife's lover murdered by one of his own sons. Cec Waters was, in fact, a monster and far from the lovable old boxing trainer he made out to be.

Born in 1926, Cec Waters emigrated to Australia from the United Kingdom in 1972 with his wife Christine, who was 22 years his junior, and his four young children, Dean, Guy, Troy and Tracy, all of whom were from the last of his previous three marriages. Christine had been involved with Cec since she was 17, and had been living with him for five years prior to their 1972 marriage. The family settled on a ramshackle farm at Mangrove Mountain on New South Wales' Central Coast and this became their home, training camp and menagerie for their stray pets.

Cec Waters came across as a squeaky-clean fitness guru, vehemently opposed to cigarettes and alcohol, who dedicated his life to health and fitness and raised his brood accordingly. Through order and discipline Cec raised his three boys to fulfil his dream of them becoming boxing champions. From an early age, boxing was all the boys really knew and they came up admirably through the amateur ranks until they gained the status of professionals. While Dean and Guy won numerous titles, it was Troy who stood out to become a serious world contender.

By 1987 Cec realised that he had a highly marketable gimmick as the battling dad with the three boxing sons, and he enlisted pop singer Marty Rhone to help him promote it. The public couldn't get enough. The boxing Waters were the flavour of every month. But beneath all the hoopla there had been bad trouble brewing and it was only a matter of time before it boiled to the surface and erupted.

Earlier that year a petty criminal with a long record, Allen Hall, had turned up at the farm and offered his services as a sparring partner to the now-famous Waters brothers. Hall also proved to be good with the horses and was soon welcomed into the family, which by now included a Damon Ashley Cooper, a former motor mechanic turned training partner for the Waters brothers. Cooper had become like another son to Cec.

By now Christine had lost all sexual interest in Cec and, in rejecting his advances, Cec assumed that she had turned frigid. To solve the problem, and make her interested in him again, Cec suggested that Hall have an affair with his wife. Hall didn't mind in the least but, when Christine and Hall moved out and set up house together at nearby Jilliby in December of that same year, Cec was far from impressed.

Terrified that a divorce would cost him his beloved farm, Cec tried to terrorise his wife into returning. The Jilliby house was mysteriously burned to the ground and soon after Allen Hall received a note in a handwriting very similar to Cec's telling him that he was worthless and that there was more of the same around the corner if he didn't send Christine home forthwith. When Christine hadn't returned by May 1988, Cec took Dean into the Ourimbah State Forest where the pair of them dug grave-shaped holes. When told that the hole he was digging was for Christine, Dean dropped his shovel and walked off in disgust, with his father screaming that he was a coward.

On the night of 29 June 1988, Dean Waters and Damon Cooper hid in bushes outside the Warnervale home where Allen Hall had moved to with Christine. When Hall came out to see why his dogs were barking, Dean shot him with a 12-gauge shotgun and Cooper let fly with a .22 calibre rifle. Allen Hall fell to the ground dead. Dean and Cooper fled, disposed of the firearms and cleaned themselves up to remove any evidence.

In August 1988, Dean was charged with killing Hall, and Cec with being an accessory after the fact. In March 1989 the charges were dismissed due to lack of sufficient evidence. Eight years later on 8 February, 1996, Dean Waters, his life in tatters, decided that he could no longer live with the truth of what happened that night and, having found God with his brother Guy, made a full confession to Gosford police in the company of his solicitor. In the meantime Troy Waters, the most promising of the brothers, had fought for three world titles that he seemed capable of winning. He lost the lot.

Damon Cooper was arrested immediately and charged with murder and in May 1996 was convicted of the lesser charge of manslaughter, a strange verdict given that the killing of Allen Hall was clearly premeditated. The jury believed Cooper's plea that he was under the spell of Cec Waters and had not acted of his own volition. Judge Newman wasn't impressed and handed down a stiff sentence of 18 years with 12-year minimum term, and another three years to be served concurrently for burning down the house at Jilliby.

Dean's confession resulted in him also being charged with

murder and Cec being charged as an accessory. Cec died of a heart attack before he could be brought to trial. Dean pleaded not guilty to murder on the defence that Cec had brutalised him and his siblings so badly and so often throughout their lives that they would do anything he said out of sheer terror of what would happen if they said no. This, apparently, included murder.

The court heard that the Waters children had been humiliated and brutalised since they were infants and subjected to regular beatings with a piece of hosepipe equipped with brass fittings. Dean's sister Tracy told the court that at age 14 she had been taken to Kings Cross by her father and photographed naked with another woman.

The appalling litany of terror inflicted by their father on the Waters children over the years was not lost on the jury and, despite the fact that Damon Cooper had been sentenced to 18 years' jail for the same crime only months earlier, Dean Waters was found not guilty of murder or manslaughter and set free. Despite numerous appeals, Damon Cooper is currently in Cessnock Prison and will not be eligible for parole until May 2009.

53 HORROR IN THE HAMLET OF CARCOAR

Located in the central tablelands of New South Wales, almost 260 kilometres west of Sydney and around 50 kilometres southwest of the nearest major city, Bathurst, modern visitors to the scenic town of Carcoar often find it hard to believe the quiet streets could have such a dark history of violence and murder.

Sitting about 700 metres above sea level and surrounded by beautiful, rolling green hills, the town is recognised by the National Trust thanks to a number of classic surviving examples of 19th-century architecture. It was in one of these very buildings – the Carcoar branch of the City Bank of Australia, still standing but now housing a craft centre – that horror descended onto the town in the early hours of Sunday, 24 September 1893, when a robbery turned to tragedy – with a most unexpected perpetrator. Sadly, though, this was not the first time life had been lost in the quaint little hamlet.

Renegade convicts and bushrangers were a problem in the town – the third oldest west of the Blue Mountains – as far back as 1840, when a man was shot to death trying to stop the theft of a local racehorse. As a result, martial law was threatened, but things had calmed down by 1850 with the arrival of more police officers and a magistrate. In the years that followed, Carcoar became something of a banking and administrative hub, but there was still lawlessness in the air, and the town was the site of Australia's first daylight bank robbery in 1863, when two of the notorious Ben Hall gang – Johnny Gilbert and John O'Meally – held up the Commercial Bank, which still stands to this day. The men were forced to flee empty-handed, though, when a teller fired a gunshot into the ceiling. That same year, Ben Hall himself held up a local Presbyterian minister, but let the man go unharmed. There was no major crime of note after that until hell broke loose in 1893.

By then, Carcoar could best be described as a modest town, the epicentre of a successful farming district. It claimed six pubs and two banks, including the City Bank, located on a hill on the main street. The branch manager at the time was a man named John Phillips, and on the fateful September night, the shy and nervous but well-liked and respected gent was preparing to leave Carcoar – he had accepted a promotion to lead operations at a much busier branch of the bank in Young. He was due to leave on Monday, 25 September.

His wife, Anne, and two young children, baby Gladys and three-year-old Dorothy, were going to stay behind in their rooms above the bank where they lived, along with their domestic servant Agnes McVicar who slept in the basement, until John Phillips could organise a house for them all to live in Young. While John was away, Anne would be kept company by her sister Susan Stoddart, and Susan's friend Frances 'Fanny' Cavanagh. Both women were in their early 20s and had caught the train up from Sydney, arriving at the closest station to Carcoar, Blayney, at around 10pm on the Saturday night of 23 September. They were met at Blayney by John Phillips and his friend, the Reverend Frank Clark, and transported back to Carcoar.

Tired from their journey, the women had dinner with John

and Anne, and then all four retired for the evening, as did McVicar – though the baby Gladys was unsettled all night and Anne was forced to get out of bed several times to attend to her.

Through her fitful sleep, Anne heard a strange sound some time between two and three in the morning. From her bed, she peered out through the room's open door and was shocked to see a faint dash of candle light moving on the stairs in the hall. Scared, she woke up her husband.

The law of the day dictated that any bank managers who lived on the premises must keep a gun with them. John's loaded pistol was under his pillow. Anne lit a candle and John grabbed his gun – which a court would later be told was not in working condition – before the pair ventured out of their room and down the stairs, where they found their dining room door ajar and light emanating dimly from inside. Looking through the entrance, they were shocked to see a man. The intruder wore a black mask over the lower half of his face, and in his hand he held a menacing hatchet.

Before the pair could do anything, the man turned and hit Anne Phillips in the hand, knocking the candle to the floor. At the same time, though, the woman managed to rip the mask from the intruder's face. Chaos erupted in the dead of night. There was shouting and John Phillips was knocked over by the intruder. His wife cried out for him to hand her the gun so that she could shoot the bandit, but John could only fall to the floor, almost taking his wife with him as he let out a pained groan.

At that point, Anne's maternal instinct kicked in and she ran back up the stairs for her children, crying out 'murder' to alert the others in the house.

As she reached baby Gladys in the bedroom, the intruder was right behind her, the hatchet still in his hand. He hit the woman on the side of the face with the weapon and she fell crashing to the floor.

By now, Susan Stoddart and Fanny Cavanagh had been awoken by the scream and the pair rushed to check on the children. Fanny picked up baby Gladys and started for the front door, but the intruder was upon her in no time. He lashed out viciously with the hatchet, and Fanny Cavanagh died on the spot. His blow also severed two of the infant's fingers.

At this point, Susan Stoddart entered the room and saw her sister, lying groggily on the floor. She told Anne that she should remain there as she was in a bad way, but the intruder had other ideas. He wanted the money from the bank downstairs, and it was already clear that he would stop at nothing to get it. Brandishing the blood-splattered hatchet, the man demanded the keys for the bank's safe, and Anne Phillips made her way unsteadily to her husband's trousers and retrieved them from his pocket. The intruder grabbed them and left the room as Susan Stoddart tried to attend to her sister.

But the man returned within moments, angrily informing the women that they had given him the wrong keys. Trying to remain calm, Anne Phillips informed the intruder that, as her husband was no longer the bank manager for the Carcoar branch, he no longer had the safe keys. The intruder asked who had them, and Anne told him it was a Mr Healy, the new manager. Healy, she said when asked, was staying at one of the town's hotels.

By this time, the housekeeper Agnes McVicar had been awoken by Anne's scream of 'murder' and heard people moving around upstairs. She ran up, only to be confronted by the inert body of Fanny Cavanagh. She noticed blood all over the stairs and her heart started racing in fear for the children. She bolted to the bedroom, where she found the sisters Anne and Susan, as well as a strange man holding a hatchet and a candle. Agnes listened as Anne begged the intruder to leave them all alone, at which point the man turned around and saw Agnes walking into the room. He held the hatchet in the air as if he would bring it crashing down upon her at any time.

Perhaps realising that his plans weren't working out as easily as they should have, the intruder started to back out of the room cautiously, telling the women that he would kill them if they followed him. The women remained silent until the anxiety became too much and Anne ran out to check on her husband. Susan Stoddart followed her down the stairs, only to find her friend

Fanny, laying dead and bloody on the floor with the unconscious baby Gladys. It seemed like the walls were closing in around Susan, and she ran from the house screaming. Agnes followed her to the house next door, where the bank's accountant Joseph Derwin lived.

The hysterical cries of the two women soon roused Derwin from his slumber and the group ran back to the house to investigate. The scene that confronted them was shocking. Anne Phillips was holding her moaning husband's head in her arms while blood dripped out of it. Derwin checked the safe, but found that it was still secure.

Derwin soon sounded an alert and at the break of dawn, the men of the region set out to track down whoever had perpetrated the violent break-in. At this stage, it was believed more than one man had been involved.

The search was looking fruitless until it was reported that the local priest Reverend Clark's horse and bridle had gone missing. Before long, searchers also found a dark suit and blood-covered hat stashed near Cowra, about 40 kilometres west of Carcoar. Soon after that, Reverend Clark's horse made its way into Cowra without anyone on it. The searchers realised they should concentrate their efforts in the immediate vicinity. By this time, John Phillips had died as a result of the hatchet blow to his head.

It was 11 hours after the initial attack that police arrested a man for the murders of both John Phillips and Frances Cavanagh. At 1pm that day, Constable Meagher of the Cowra police force entered the local barber's and laid charges against 25-year-old Herbert 'Bertie' Edwin Glasson, the handsome and popular son of one of the region's richest families.

Glasson was a well-known figure in Cowra and its surrounding areas, so the arrest was a shock to the public. The young man had married his childhood sweetheart – musician Annie May Summerbelle – at the start of the year, and the pair were regulars on the local social circuit whenever they were in town, though they spent most of their time residing at the Hotel Metropole in Sydney. On top of that, Bertie – considered a harmless larrikin at worst – had won a number of prizes as a show jumper, but the general public were not privy to his more criminal exploits. Described as the black sheep of the wealthy family, Bertie had once almost brought shame to the Glassons when he was caught forging cheques worth £1200. The family used their influence to settle the matter before it came out in the media.

Indeed, Bertie had even offered to join the search parties out looking for the Carcoar murderer, declaring any person who would commit such a crime to be a 'bloodthirsty scoundrel'. But his tune had changed by the time Meagher collared him, with Bertie loudly protesting his innocence before crying out, 'I am mad! I don't know where I have been or what I have done.'

His claim was backed up in part by a letter found in his pocket when he was arrested, the contents of which were later published in newspapers in Sydney. The letter, addressed to his wife still back in Sydney and written on the back of a concert program, said that he had found himself that very morning covered in blood in a paddock. Repeating the claim that he was 'going mad', Bertie added that he had no idea what he had done, explaining that he remembered leaving Sydney to go to Orange. He had no recollection of whether he had reached his destination or not. 'I feel so terribly strange now, darling,' he wrote, adding that it was 'better for me to be dead than for you to have a mad husband'. He ended the letter saying that he intended to walk to Cowra and catch a train back to Sydney.

But the next train Bertie caught was to take him as close to Carcoar as it could, where he could face up for his horrific crimes. When the locomotive arrived in Blayney, Bertie was confronted by an angry mob hurling abuse at him. He was in shock, and restrained by handcuffs and leg-irons, and his stunned appearance quickly silenced the crowd. Accompanied by two police officers, Bertie was taken to the local holding cells, where he asked the man in command, Sergeant Boyd, what his restraints were for.

Even though there was only little hope that Anne Phillips would survive her injuries, the widow refused to leave town to seek better medical treatment. Unaware that her husband had passed away – the information had been withheld because of her already fragile state – Anne was taking solace in the fact that her family had survived their ordeal, despite the loss of her youngest daughter's fingers.

It wasn't long before the authorities started piecing together what had happened with the help of witnesses. Bertie, it transpired, had arrived in Blayney on the same train as Susan Stoddart and the murdered Fanny Cavanagh, and then he walked through the night to Carcoar. When he was later put in an eight-man line-up, Susan Stoddart was quick to identify him. With the sister of his victim screaming, 'That is the man,' at him, Bertie merely stared blankly and didn't utter a single word.

On top of that, Anne Phillips had managed to stir from her daze enough to inform authorities that Bertie Glasson was the man who had broken into her home. She had recognised him when she ripped the black mask from his face, and had even spoken to him by name, telling him to leave the family alone.

As the story unravelled it became obvious that, whether actually insane or not, Bertie had money troubles. His bank account was overdrawn to the sum of £50, and Mr Derwin had asked him several times to rectify the situation. When the requests were only met with excuses and promises that the matter would be attended to, John Phillips had to take a strong stand; he served a writ against Bertie Glasson.

On top of that, one of Bertie's business ventures, a butchery in Carcoar, was in trouble. The man who ran it, Tom Turner, had worked without being paid for three months. The bank had ordered the business be sold. It fetched £19, hardly enough to sort out the financial tangle.

When the inquest into the break-in and murders got under way in Carcoar, Bertie was still incarcerated. He was also acting rather strangely, appearing sedate and rational until anyone spoke to him, at which time he would become extremely bothered and behave violently.

The evidence offered up at the inquest didn't seem to help Bertie's case, either. A still-shocked Agnes McVicar testified that she recognised Bertie as the man who had threatened her with the hatchet. Susan Stoddart also confirmed that she was 'positive'

Bertie had been the intruder, though she only gave evidence after asking for all of the attacker's relatives to be removed from the red-brick courthouse first. She then told of the 'bloodstained half-axe' she saw Bertie wielding, adding, 'I know his face. I will never forget it.'

While this was going on, Bertie sat silently and stared blankly ahead. Five days after it began, the inquest finished with the coroner J. Lithgow Cobb calling the crime one of the most 'painful, dreadful and shocking ever recorded'. Bertie was then taken under police escort to Bathurst, where his trial began on 20 October 1893 in front of Justice Innes. The defence maintained that their client was insane.

Anne Phillips, meanwhile, was making a slow but steady recovery – though no one involved felt strong enough to give her an honest answer when she asked how her husband was doing. She would, of course, eventually learn the tragic fate of the man she loved, accepting that there was nothing she could have done about it.

The first witness called by the defence was Bertie's wife, Annie. Looking frail and obviously shocked by the sight of her husband, she said that, yes, she knew her husband was facing financial difficulty, but she had no idea of the extent of the problem. She added that he had been behaving a little oddly leading up to the crime, adding that he hadn't been sleeping well and had complained of pains in his head. Bertie, she testified, had also suffered from severe sunstroke a week before the attack at Carcoar, which caused him to cry and declare, 'I am going mad.'

Later, she told of her husband's departure from their residence at the Hotel Metropole on the Saturday before the murders, explaining that he had told her he was heading to Orange to collect some money owed to him.

Another witness for the defence, an old family friend, told the court that there was a history of insanity on Bertie's mother's side of the family. This claim was supported by a physician from Orange, Dr Kelty, who had treated Mrs Glasson when she had shown symptoms of madness. Kelty had even prescribed sedatives to the mother when she became suddenly aggressive.

In summing up, the defence contended that even if Bertie had committed the violent crimes of which he was accused, he had not been responsible for his actions. The prosecution, however, came back strongly, declaring that Bertie's actions were premeditated from the start. The jury believed the prosecution, and it didn't take long for Justice Innes to pass the death sentence.

Edwin Herbert 'Bertie' Glasson would never publicly accept that he was guilty, maintaining that he was 'unconscious' of any crime. He was hanged on Wednesday, 29 November 1893 at Bathurst Gaol. He was thinking of his wife to the end, admitting, 'To think of her and what she has to suffer is awful.'

Annie May Glasson, however, did not attend her husband's funeral. The only mourner at the lonely service was his brother, John.

54 THE PETER HUXLEY SCANDAL

Throughout the late 1960s in Sydney a dapper gent was setting the Sydney racetracks alight with massive bets that were big even by today's standards. The punter was always immaculately groomed in an expensive suit, collar and tie and polished shoes. Sometimes he won, but most times he lost. When he lost he settled with bank cheques.

The bookies never asked any questions as to the identity of the mystery punter and on the occasion when the racing columnists told of his Saturday betting exploits in the Sunday papers he would vanish, only to resurface a few weeks later. He began betting a thousand at a time but, by the mid to late 1960s, he was winning or losing hundreds of thousands of dollars in a day. The money had to be coming from somewhere.

The rumours circulated, as rumours do on the racetrack, but not a soul knew for sure who the clandestine gambler was. Or if anyone did, they weren't saying anything. And that's the way he liked it. Even when the bookies gave him credit as they competed for his business, they often found themselves in the dubious position of being owed hundreds of thousands of dollars by a man whose name they didn't know. But they had no cause for worry. He always settled in bank cheques.

At the same time, in what seemed another world a million miles away, a brilliant young man was racing up the corporate ladder a lot faster than most of the favourites at Randwick. A 43-year-old father of five, Peter Geoffrey Huxley was past-secretary of the then Rural Bank, of which he had been tipped to become president until he resigned in 1969 and took up the position as managing director with the highly respected Red Hill Station Pty Ltd.

On his climb to the top and the corporate riches that lay in waiting, Peter Huxley had earned a reputation as one of Sydney's most respected bankers and was a regular name on the A list for invitations to social functions.

Huxley sat on the boards of, and was personally involved with fundraising for, numerous charitable organisations such as the Freedom from Hunger Campaign, Unicef Australia and Austcare. They entrusted him to bank their funds where they would earn the best return before they were distributed to their worthy causes throughout the world.

So when the police arrived and took Peter Huxley away on suspicion of embezzling his previous employer and numerous charities of million of dollars and losing it at the racetrack, most of Sydney's elite clutched at their pearls and couldn't believe that it was the same Peter Huxley they had taken into their trust.

It seemed as though the dapper gent at the races and the leading Sydney socialite and 'boy most likely' were one in the same. In Huxley's absence the Rural Bank did an audit and was found to be missing a total of $5,297,919. By today's standards that would be between $90 and $100 million. The police believed that Peter Huxley could help them with their inquiries. As it turned out he could, and the minute he felt the cold hand of retribution on his shoulder he revealed all.

Huxley told police that he had stolen money from the Rural Bank by simply opening an account in the name of the Freedom from Hunger Campaign and using it as his own. He replenished it with his ever-increasing misappropriations from other accounts over which he had financial control, and was drawing or redepositing large sums of cash as he pleased. When needed he would draw a bank cheque against the account, allegedly for some worthy cause, to pay his punting bills.

By the mid-1960s Huxley was betting thousands on each race and knew that he needed a huge win to meet his debts. He told police that the opportunity came when he backed a horse to cover all of his debts and the horse won by an eyebrow. As he was leaving the course, determined that his life of crime was over and he would never be discovered, he was horrified to hear over the loudspeaker that a protest had been lodged against the winner. It was upheld. He went back to the betting and dug his grave deeper.

Huxley told the police that a lot of his major losses were with rails bookmaker Bill Waterhouse, with whom he bet on-course or alternatively rang on Saturday mornings to place a bet. In late 1967 and early 1968 Huxley paid cheques totalling $702,577 into accounts, which were eventually paid over to Waterhouse.

But not all of Huxley's betting binges were disastrous. In one period over 12 days Huxley outlaid a total of $383,000, but lost only $110. Waterhouse told police that initially Huxley had made cash bets with him for some months and that from about May 1967 he allowed Huxley, who he knew nothing about and knew only as 'Peter Hunter', to bet with him on credit.

Waterhouse said that on at least two occasions Huxley owed him around $700,000 but he (Waterhouse) made no inquiries about Huxley. He even made no effort to trace the mystery gambler when Huxley stopped betting with him in 1969 (which was when Huxley left the Rural Bank to join Red Hill) still owing him about $700,000. Waterhouse simply explained that it was quite obvious that Hunter had gone and had disappeared as mysteriously as he had arrived. When Huxley was arrested a year later he claimed that he owed Waterhouse about $600,000. Good luck getting it.

But while these days most people would recommend Huxley for a Victoria Cross for doing to the bank what banks have been doing to us for years, he made one monumental mistake in that in the wash-up he had not returned money to the Freedom from Hunger Campaign account to the tune of $1.8 million. It was deemed that he had embezzled money from the starving people of the world. And the $1.8 million was never accounted for. Not a good look at all.

Huxley pleaded guilty to 129 charges of fraudulent misappropriation, forgery, uttering and other matters relating to the manipulation of funds. Given that there was no proof that the Freedom from Hunger Campaign's $1.8 million had dissipated along with all of the other funds that went to the bookies, Judge Head handed down the heaviest sentence ever for a white-collar crime in New South Wales – 20 years in jail.

In 1971 the AJC refused to renew Bill Waterhouse's license and did not give it back until 1973. Waterhouse was quoted as saying at the time: 'Huxley was my downfall.'

In September 1977, a review of Huxley's case caused huge public debate and in December of that year Huxley unsuccessfully appealed against his 12-year nonparole period. A year later Huxley was released from prison on licence, having served almost nine of his 20-year sentence.

55 CELLULOID SERIAL KILLERS

The History of Serial Killers in the Movies

The history of real-life and fictional serial killers in the movies dates back to as early as 1943, though the villains in those days weren't known as serial killers. They were labelled as psychopaths, psychotics, sex criminals, maniacs or mass killers. They didn't officially get the title of 'serial killers' until the late '80s.

Research indicates that the first serial-killer movie ever made was in 1943, and it only seems right that it was made by the original master of suspense, Alfred Hitchcock. It was called *Shadow of a Doubt* and is about an outwardly respectable relative known as Uncle Charlie, played by Joseph Cotton, who was in fact the Merry Widow Murderer.

Also made in 1943, *Arsenic and Old Lace* is a light-hearted affair about a pair of delightful old dears who murder vagrants and bury their bodies in the cellar. They were labelled as neither psychopaths nor insane, just a couple of public-spirited senior citizens doing their civic duty by hurrying along the inevitable and saving the City of New York the cost of pauper's funerals. Also released in 1943 was *Bluebeard*, starring John Carradine, about the infamous turn-of-the-century strangler of women.

Released in 1947, Charlie Chaplin's *Monsieur Verdoux*, a black 'comedy of murders' about a Parisian Bluebeard who murders his wives for their money, was widely rejected by critics and audiences alike and rapidly faded into obscurity, although these days it is acclaimed as a masterpiece.

Released in 1960, Alfred Hitchcock's *Psycho* was the first genuine modern-day serial-killer movie and at the time, and for many years later, was arguably the *scariest* movie ever made. Just prior to *Psycho*'s release, competitions were held in major cities throughout the world to find couples who were game enough to view the movie, alone, in a pitch-black theatre, at midnight. If they survived dying of fright they won a prize, which from memory was a life-size pin-up of Norman Bates. But, as frightening as it was for the time, and no doubt to the disappointment of the promoters, no one came to grief.

Psycho was followed by three sequels, all of which suggested that poor demented Norman should have been lobotomised and left in the rubber room at the local mental facility rather than be let out and inflicted on an unwitting general public over and over again. Fortunately for Mr Hitchcock, and no doubt to his eternal gratitude, he died before the sequels were made.

Also in 1960 came the disturbing *Peeping Tom*, which was denounced at the time as being too distressing to sit through. It tells the story of a psychopathic killer who photographs his victims as they draw their last breath. Certainly not to everyone's taste, but it was critically acclaimed in the years to come.

In 1968 came *The Boston Strangler*, which was the first movie/documentary of the activities of a serial killer. From 1962 to 1964 Albert De Salvo terrorised Boston, raping and strangling 13 women in their homes, each time leaving his calling card: he strangled his victims with their own stockings, which he tied in the same knot every time. Unfortunately it was a grossly inaccurate portrayal of the facts of the killings – and casting Tony

Curtis as a multiple strangler, when the world was still laughing at his hilarious antics in *Some Like it Hot* and *The Great Race*, must rate as one of the worst cases of miscasting in the history of the movies.

Also in 1968 came the much-acclaimed *No Way To Treat A Lady*, a romantic black comedy with Rod Steiger as the serial-killer strangler and George Segal as the cop on his trail.

It was the chilling *10 Rillington Place*, the true story of the horrors perpetrated by the fiendish serial killer and necrophiliac John Christie in London in the early '50s, that had audiences fainting in the aisles in 1971. In 1972 it was Alfred Hitchcock again who thrilled us with *Frenzy*, the edge-of-the-seat drama about a man wrongly accused of the serial murders of young women in London. This time Alfred got right into serial-killer mode and had the naked bodies turning up with a man's necktie tied tightly around their necks, the signature of the Necktie Murderer. It is believed that Hitchcock got the necktie idea from the Boston Strangler case.

Also in 1972 Clint Eastwood was magnificent as *Dirty Harry*, who was hot on the trail of a serial killer named Scorpio. This was the first in a string of excellent Dirty Harry Callahan serial-killer movies, such as *Magnum Force*, *Sudden Impact*, *The Dead Pool* and the thrilling *Tightrope*, in which Eastwood broke the Harry Callahan mould and played the part of a New Orleans cop in search of a sex murderer. All of these films were action-packed and carried plausible story lines, but all of them stood in the shadow of the original.

It is worth noting here that while the 1974 movie *Badlands* is listed in some movie guides as a serial-killer movie, it isn't. Admittedly the main character, Charlie Starkwell (Martin Sheen), did kill 10 people in Texas and South Dakota in 1959, but they were what is known as 'spree killings' in that after he murdered his girlfriend's father he killed his other victims while he was on the run from the police. That is not serial murder.

In 1980 in *Cruising*, chameleon detective Al Pacino went deep undercover looking for a serial killer who picked up gay men in the most sordid bars imaginable and then sliced them up. It was widely panned by the critics and strongly criticised by the gay community for its sordid content and the depiction of homosexual men as sexual deviants.

It was 1986 that gave us *Manhunter*, the first serial-killer (though they never use the term) movie to give an insight into how the modern FBI builds a psychological profile on these killers and how they track them down with modern technology. *Manhunter* is the screen adaptation of Thomas Harris' international bestseller *Red Dragon* (the forerunner to *The Silence of the Lambs*) and is the macabre tale of a 'psychotic killer' who specialises in slaughtering entire families, and how FBI agents Will Graham and Jack Crawford track him down before he kills again.

But as yet the term 'serial killer' had never been used in a movie. From all of my research I believe that the first time it was ever actually spoken on screen was in 1988 – a few years after FBI agent and world-renowned serial-killer profiler Robert Ressler coined the phrase – in the almost unnoticed yet enthralling serial-killer thriller *Cop*, starring James Wood as a strung-out detective who stumbles across a series of murders that follow a similar pattern.

Also in 1987 two top-quality serial-killer movies were released, *Black Widow* and the spine-tingling Al Pacino thriller *Sea of Love*, though neither referred to their villain as a serial killer. *Black Widow*, featuring Debra Winger and Dennis Hopper, is unique in that the murderer is a woman, a very rare breed indeed in the annals of serial murder, even in the fantasy world of the movies.

Then in 1990 came the dark, depressing and grizzly (yet highly acclaimed) *Henry: Portrait of a Serial Killer*, about the life and times of America's most prolific serial killer Henry Lee Lucas. This was followed in 1991 by *To Catch a Killer*, the TV movie that went to video about Illinois serial killer John Wayne Gacy, who murdered 33 teenage boys and buried their bodies beneath his house. Curiously, Gacy was never referred to as a serial killer in this movie so the name hadn't quite stuck yet.

But it was only a matter of time before the serial killer phenomenon would hit and it is indisputable that it was director Jonathan Demme's 1991 screen adaptation of the Thomas Harris novel *The Silence of the Lambs* that deep-etched the term 'serial killer' into the vernacular forever.

The impact of *The Silence of the Lambs* was extraordinary and Clarice Starling, Hannibal Lecter and the term 'serial killer' became household words overnight. *The Silence of the Lambs* went further than any serial-killer movie had gone before and took up where *Manhunter* left off, using some of the same villainous and heroic characters, though portrayed by different actors.

The serial-killer craze had well and truly arrived and in *The Silence of the Lambs* the now legions of salivating serial-killer movie fans even got to hear the beast himself, Dr Hannibal 'the Cannibal' Lecter, boast of his exploits as he told terrified FBI agent Starling that he once ate a census taker's liver with some fava beans and a nice Chianti. They lapped it up ... so to speak ... to the tune of more than $US270 million worldwide.

After *The Silence of the Lambs* the serial-killer movie floodgates opened and if anything was ever going to challenge it for riveting, edge-of-the-chair, cop-tracking-down-a-serial-killer suspense, it was episode one of the 1991 English TV miniseries *Prime Suspect* (which, along with the rest of the series, went to video in 1996), starring Helen Mirren as the tenacious Jane Tennyson, serial-killer sleuth extraordinaire. Episode six in the series is also a superb serial-killer thriller.

In 1992 came the sleeper *Jennifer 8*, which was mostly missed at the box office. This was a shame because it is a serial-killer classic, with cop Andy Garcia hot on the trail of a killer who specialises in killing blind women. *Jennifer 8* has since created its own cult following and deservedly so.

In 1995 there were more serial-killer movies released than in any other year to date. There was *Citizen X*, which depicts the real-life adventures of a charming bit of work named Andre Chikatilo, who murdered and ate children. *Copycat* is about a serial killer with a difference – one who copies infamous American serial killers from the past such as Son of Sam and Ted Bundy.

1995's *Se7en* is a stand-alone classic of the genre and one of the best serial-killer movies of all time. It's a believable action-packed drama that has you hanging by your fingernails until the very end. The cast is superb; Morgan Freeman, Brad Pitt, Kevin Spacey and Gwyneth Paltrow, and the story is like nothing you've ever seen before with an ending that you really don't want to know about, but you just can't take your eyes away it. *Se7en* blitzed 'em at the box office, taking $US328 million worldwide, putting it just behind *Hannibal* and a long way ahead of *The Silence of the Lambs* in the all-time money stakes.

Oh, yes, serial-killer movies had arrived. The year 1997 saw the release of the screen adaptation of James Patterson's international bestseller *Kiss the Girls,* a roller-coaster-ride thriller that introduces us to cop Alex Cross, whose niece has gone missing, and then there was *Switchback*, which features the screen's very first serial killer of a certain type of human being. You'll have to see it to find out what I am referring to.

Denzel Washington led a star-studded cast in the 1998 *Fallen*, but the longer it went the cornier it got. *Summer of Sam*, a 1999 release, is about the lives of fictional New Yorkers at the time that the nonfictional David Berkowitz, better known as the serial killer Son of Sam, was running around bumping off young couples in cars with a Bulldog 44. Also in 1999 we saw *The Bone Collector*, a classy but grisly tale of a quadriplegic detective's pursuit of a signature serial killer on the loose in New York's underground.

Other serial-killer movies of the late '90s include the forgettable *Diary of a Serial Killer* and *Star Trek: Deep Space Nine*, an outer-space serial-murder mystery that should have stayed in deep space.

The 2000 screen adaptation of Brett Easton Ellis's book *American Psycho* was acclaimed by some reviewers and denounced by others. Some reviewers rated it among the top movies of the year, a serial-killer thriller to rival *The Silence of the Lambs*. But the vast majority of serial-killer movie buffs rejected it as a trashy, sensationalist, wall-to-wall-blood-and-guts piece of tripe that was an insult to the genre. You judge for yourself. But be warned before you spend your money. If you hated the book then the experts say that the movie is worse, if that is possible.

In 2001 the legions of serial-killer buffs flocked to see *Hannibal*, the long-awaited sequel to *The Silence of the Lambs*, and while it wasn't in the same class as the original (and it's likely that no serial-killer movie ever will be), from all accounts few walked away disappointed. Director Jonathon Demme and Jodie Foster were sadly missed, but it still showed them that the good doctor hadn't lost his touch. It brained 'em at the box office, taking over $350 million, the all-time record for a serial-killer movie.

Also in 2001 was *Along Came a Spider*, another screen adaptation from a James Patterson (*The Bone Collector, Kiss the Girls*) novel, and again featuring Morgan Freeman as investigator Alex Cross, which took more than $US100 million at the box office, and yet another yarn about Jack the Ripper, *From Hell*, featuring Johnny Depp as the opium-addicted police inspector who gets a lot of his leads from his narcotic-induced dreams.

In 2002 we saw the remake of the 1986 *Manhunter*, this time under the title of the original book by Thomas Harris, *Red Dragon*. There's no shortage of buffs who reckon that *Manhunter* was the better movie, but that's a brave call given that the 'real' Hannibal Lecter (Anthony Hopkins) is back in *Red Dragon* along with a stellar cast.

In 2003, in the brilliant *Monster*, we saw the performance of a lifetime as South African actress Charlize Theron won a Best Actress Academy Award for portraying Aileen Carol Wuornos, a true-life hard-drinking, ex-convict prostitute who serial-murdered seven men. Wuornos sat on Death Row in Florida until she was executed by lethal injection on 9 October 2002. The movie takes you from go to whoa and the transformation of the beauty queen Theron into the hideous Wuornos is one of cinema's greatest achievements in modern times.

The year 2004 brought us the highly recommended *Twisted* with Samuel L. Jackson, Ashley Judd and Andy Garcia, the forgettable *Taking Lives* with Angelina Jolie, the Ben Kingsley shocker *Suspect Zero* and the Australian-made bone-chiller *Saw*, which cost $A1.2 million to make and took over $US100 million at the box office.

The serial-killer box office success of 2005 was *Saw 2*, which was (if it's possible) grizzlier than the original. The additional blood and guts must have been popular with the punters as it took around $US50 million more (total $US151 million) at the box office than the original. Another 2005 Australian serial-killer thriller was the excellent *Wolf Creek*, based (very) loosely on the outback disappearance of Peter Falconio and the Backpacker Murders. It's good enough to get in the Top 20 list at number 12.

Paul B. Kidd's Top 20 Serial-Killer Movies of All Time

1/ *The Silence of the Lambs* (1991) 118 minutes

A little-known fact about this extraordinary movie is that the horrific activities of the serial killer Buffalo Bill are loosely based on the exploits of a dreadful trio of real-life serial killers named Ed Gein, Ted Bundy and Gary Heidnik.

Ed had a penchant for wearing human skin and he made clothes out of the corpses of females he had either killed or dug up. When the cops eventually caught up with him on his farm in Wisconsin, USA in 1957, they found lampshades made out of human skin, a soup dish made out of a hollowed-out human skull, a belt made of nipples and human-skin slippers.

In *The Silence of the Lambs* serial killer Buffalo Bill lures his victims into his van by asking them to help him lift an item of furniture because his arm is in (fake) plaster. Once in the van the victim is knocked unconscious and whisked away to Bill's dress-making dungeon to become a part of his winter collection. This method of abduction was originally used by American psychopath Ted Bundy on some of his victims when he kidnapped, raped and murdered up to 40 female college students from 1974 to 1977.

In Philadelphia in 1986 Gary Heidnik kidnapped women and kept them chained up in his cellar as sex slaves, eventually murdering some of them and eating their remains. The description of Heidnik's cellar is similar to that of Buffalo Bill's in the movie, though unlike Bill he kept as many as five women in there at a time, beating and torturing them regularly until one escaped and called the cops.

These were just a few of the many fascinating angles that combine to make this by far and away the best serial-killer movie (and one the best movies in general) of all time. And that's not just my opinion. The judges awarded *The Silence of the Lambs* the five top Academy Awards (picture, actor, actress, director and screenplay) for 1991, making it only the third movie in history to achieve such an honour (the other two were *It Happened One Night* in 1934 and *One Flew Over The Cuckoo's Nest* in 1975) and it comes in at number 66 in the American Film Institute's Top 100 Movies of All Time.

Jodie Foster, Anthony Hopkins, Scott Glenn and Ted Levine as Buffalo Bill are unbelievably good in a movie that is flawless in every detail. Hopkins' Hannibal Lecter is mesmerising, particularly when we get our initial glimpse of him in his cell as he meets FBI agent Clarice Starling (Foster) for the first time.

And they thought *Psycho* was scary! *The Silence of the Lambs* makes it look like the *Wizard of Oz* and Hannibal Lecter makes Norman Bates look like Mother Teresa.

2/ *Se7en* (1995) 126 minutes

Se7en's serial killer, known only as John Doe (Kevin Spacey) who specialises in bumping off perpetrators of the seven deadly sins – gluttony, greed, sloth, envy, wrath, pride and lust – wasn't modelled after a real-life murderer simply because no one in real life could be this bizarre. And if ever there was a celluloid serial killer with purpose, John Doe is it.

At the beginning of *Se7en* the teaming of Brad Pitt and Morgan Freeman as the cops looks like it might not work, but it doesn't take long to realise that the dialogue between the young, new cop and the old, retiring cop, particularly in some of the grisliest scenes you're ever likely to see, is a highlight of an excellent thriller that will keep you enthralled until the very end. And don't tell any of your friends the ending!

Gwyneth Paltrow adds a bright ray of sunlight in a movie that is otherwise black, rainy ... and bloody terrifying. If you want to have the daylights frightened out of you, then this is the movie that'll do it.

3/ *Prime Suspect* Episode 1 (1991) 208 minutes & Episode 6 (1994) 100 minutes

This magnificent detective series was made for television and both of these episodes were put onto video in 1996 and later onto DVD. Number six is a sequel to number one, though many years later, and both can be found in mainstream rental shops.

Episode one sees District Chief Inspector Jane Tennyson (Helen Mirren) in a brand-new job in charge of a bunch of blokes and investigating a brand-new case involving the brutal murder of a young woman. It becomes increasingly obvious that if Jane doesn't persist in her line of inquiries, which leads her (and her alone) to believe that the bloke that did this murder has done a few others in different parts of England, the killer will not only get away with one murder, but lots of others as well.

Come with Jane as she battles the blokes who want her replaced with another bloke, the bureaucrats who want to replace her to please the blokes and the booze she quaffs by the vasefull, which seems to be the only thing that can console her after her lover leaves because she's spending too much time tracking down the serial killer.

During nearly three and a half hours of superb film-making you find yourself almost jumping out of the chair to cheer Jane on through all of her dramas. Watch as she triumphantly brings the case to its riveting finale, spits in the eye of bureaucracy and becomes best buddies with the blokes who started out hating her.

This is much, much more than just another serial-killer movie. This is about life, adversity and winning against all odds. That is why it is must-see viewing. In episode six the bloke who has been locked away for the serial murders in episode one has had a book written about him claiming that he is innocent, which seems highly likely when the bodies of young women start turning up with similarities that only the jailed killer and the police (Tennyson in particular) would know about.

Did Jane lock up the wrong villain? If not, is there a copycat killer on the loose and, if so, how did he/she find out the secrets of the previous killings? It's riveting stuff. Jane's love life is still in turmoil, only this time she's involved with a different bloke, and the bureaucrats are still trying to cut down the tall poppy.

This is a serial-killer movie for all the family and not to be missed by any serious serial-killer movie fan.

4/ *10 Rillington Place* (1971) 111 minutes

Be prepared to meet one very scary guy in this true-life classic as necrophiliac serial killer, London's John Christie, arguably the most heinous fiend that ever lived, murders his way to the gallows. Over a 13-year period, until his capture in 1953, John Reginald Halliday Christie murdered seven women, including his wife and the baby daughter of one of his victims. Christie gassed the women, strangled them and then raped their corpses.

The Christie murders case is one of the most famous in the world, not especially for the murders themselves but for the fact that Timothy Evans, the dimwitted lorry-driver husband of a Christie victim, Beryl Evans, and the father of the murdered baby Geraldine, was incorrectly hanged for their murders while the real killer Christie went free.

Richard Attenborough's performance as Christie is mesmerising, as is John Hurt's portrayal of the intellectually challenged Evans. Who will ever forget the spine-chilling scene in court with Evans pointing to Christie, the chief witness against him, and saying, 'It was Christie what done it, Christie done it,' after the judge sentenced him (Evans) to death by hanging.

The setting for *10 Rillington Place* is exactly where it happened, the depressing squalor of London's Notting Hill just after the war, then possibly the worst bit of residential real estate on the planet.

It is factual horror at it ugliest and a truly brilliant piece of cinema.

5/ *Manhunter* (1986) 119 minutes

Say hello to the Tooth Fairy, a really likeable guy whose speciality is murdering and butchering entire families on the full moon. Mum, dad, kids, pets, the lot. What with the teeth and the full moon you could be fooled into thinking this is some sort of a vampire movie, but it certainly isn't – even though the serial killer does have a nibble on his victims (that's how he got his name) with his outrageously large choppers.

But that's not what the plot is all about. Adapted from Thomas Harris' international bestseller *Red Dragon* (the novel before *The Silence of the Lambs*), it's the tale of how FBI serial-killer catcher Will Graham, played by William L. Petersen (he went on to bigger success as Grissom in *CSI*) is brought out of retirement to catch the Tooth Fairy before he kills another entire generation of a family.

Will's claim to fame is that he caught Dr Hannibal Lecter in the first place, and if he could do that he can catch anyone. We get to meet Dr Lecter (Brian Cox) in his cell, which is very disappointing if you've seen Anthony Hopkins' later portrayal of Lecter in *The Silence of the Lambs*. For all its complications, twists and turns *Manhunter* is a classic in the serial-killer genre and the scientific detective work used to track the killer down is awesome. A must for every serial-killer movie buff.

6/ *Red Dragon* (2002) 124 minutes

A lot of enthusiasts maintain that this remake of the 1986 *Manhunter* (adapted from the Thomas Harris novel *Red Dragon*) isn't as good as the original. I'm inclined to agree with them, even though Anthony Hopkins is back as Hannibal Lecter and the rest of the cast is stellar. I think that it's because the original was streets ahead of anything else in the serial-killer genre at the time, and was the first movie that gave us an insight into FBI profiling.

And while it's impossible to go past Anthony Hopkins in the role that he was born to play, I believe that *Manhunter*'s Tom Noonan was a much better Tooth Fairy than Ralph Fiennes, Dennis Farina a far superior Jack Crawford to Harvey Keitel (and Harvey Keitel's one of my all-time favourite actors) and *CSI*'s William L. Peterson played Ed Norton off a break as serial killer profiler Will Graham.

Having said that, I believe that *Red Dragon* is brilliant in that it took the liberty of filling us in on all of the bits we had wondered about over the years, such as how did Will Graham actually catch the cannibal quack? Fantastic stuff.

Both *Manhunter* and *Red Dragon* are superb. Do yourself a favour and watch them back to back – *Manhunter* first – and see what you think.

7/ *Monster* (2003) 111 minutes

True to form, it was the American media, where serial-killer hype was first born, that claimed Aileen Carol Wuornos, a hard-drinking, ex-convict prostitute, as the world's first female serial killer. Of course it wasn't true, even though Wuornos murdered seven men on separate occasions by shooting them in the torso with a small-calibre handgun after they picked her up as she hitchhiked throughout Florida in 1990. There had been many female serial killers before Wuornos, but none who murdered adult males with a handgun. Maybe that's what they meant.

Anyway, it had the desired effect. The punters flocked to it in droves. That and the fact that South African actress Charlize Theron and Wuornos were hard to pick apart in looks and mannerisms. Theron won a Best Actress Academy Award for portraying Wuornos in what has been described 'the performance of the decade'.

8/ *Hannibal* (2001) 121 minutes

The long-awaited sequel to *The Silence of the Lambs* isn't in the same class as the original, but only the world's greatest optimist could possibly have hoped it would be, given that originals Jodie Foster and director Jonathon Demme vetoed the project. But there are lots of other serial-killer treats to make up for it.

Anthony Hopkins is yet again brilliant in the role that he seems to have been born for, that of the evil Hannibal Lecter: scholar, teacher, intellectual and bon vivant of exquisite taste, especially his penchant for certain cuts of meat.

And we get to meet possibly the most grotesque screen villain of them all; billionaire paedophile, disgruntled outpatient and long-time Lecter nemesis Mason Verger, who wants to have a word with the good doctor about the time he filled him full of drugs and encouraged him to shave his own face off with slivers of broken mirror. As a result Mason looks like Cyclops who's had all of the skin from his ass grafted onto his face by a surgeon on a bad acid trip. Actor Gary Oldman passed up a mention in the credits, claiming that no one would have known it was him anyway.

While in lots of folk's eyes only Jodie Foster will ever be Clarice Starling, Julianne Moore makes a fist of it. She is convincing as the boots-and-all FBI agent in pursuit of the dreaded Lecter in an attempt to regain her job with the FBI after being discredited by Verger cohort and FBI agent Paul Krendler, played by Ray Liotta.

Set in America and France, *Hannibal* bowls along at a ripper pace and, while it doesn't stick too closely to the book, especially the ending, it is still an excellent film for the genre. With more twists and turns than a bucket of blood worms, viewers shouldn't be dissatisfied with *Hannibal*, but they must not compare it with the original, which must have been one of the hardest acts to follow in the entire history of the movies. It took over $US350 million worldwide and is the highest-grossing serial-killer movie in history.

9/ *Psycho* (1960) 109 minutes

And in the beginning ... there was Alfred Hitchcock's *Psycho*. Those of you old enough to remember will never forget the impact *Psycho* had on our society. For its time *Psycho* was totally outrageous, over the top, horrifying and ghoulish. After all, it was 1960. Compared with what's out there today it's more like *The Sound of Music*, but even 40 years down the track it still packs a punch and is worth another viewing every few years or so.

Again, it was American serial killer Ed Gein (also mentioned previously in *The Silence of the Lambs* review) who was the role model for Norman Bates. When poor farm boy Ed's mother died in 1944 he kept her corpse in the bedroom, leaving everything exactly as it was the day she died. Then Ed took to digging up women's corpses in a local graveyard and would wear bits of their flesh and play with their sexual organs. When Ed tired of draping the human skin from the corpses over a tailor's dummy in a crude attempt to resurrect his mother and the smell of the rotting bodies drove him from the house, he took up killing fresh people to satisfy his bizarre fetishes.

So, when the *Psycho* publicity blurb said that there had never been anyone like Norman before, they were wrong. There had been Ed Gein, hadn't there? But, as *The Silence of the Lambs* was the benchmark serial-killer movie of the '90s, *Psycho* was the most ground-breaking thriller of the century, even though most of us thought it was total fiction, that folks like Norman Bates could never possibly exist and that it was all a figment of Alfred Hitchcock's imagination. And it would be terribly remiss of me to let any review of *Psycho* go by without a mention of Janet Leigh and the shower scene that frightened the living daylights out of everyone, and that she had to live with for the last 44 years of her life.

Ah yes, how could we forget the very forgettable Bates Motel that the super-highway bypassed with its 12 cabins, 12 vacancies … and 12 showers. Do yourself a favour and rent *Psycho* again (or for the first time) soon. Trust me, it's as scary as ever.

10/ *Dirty Harry* (1972) 102 minutes

Who can ever forget Dirty Harry Callahan looking down the barrel of the biggest handgun in the world and begging the crook at the end of it to 'go ahead, make my day' by making a move. Prior to this Harry had walked out of a deli and gunned down a team of bank robbers as he munched on a hot dog.

This was the world's introduction to cool Harry and to a serial killer named Scorpio, who Harry pursues through the streets of San Francisco with relentless vigour. The character of Scorpio (Andy Robinson) was purportedly modelled on a series of real-life murders in California in 1968 and '69 when a serial killer calling himself Zodiac killed five people and wounded two more over a period of a year. He followed up the killings with letters to San Francisco newspapers giving gruesome details that only the killer could have known, as well as cryptic clues regarding where and when the next killings would be. Each letter was signed by a symbol of the Zodiac: a cross superimposed on a circle.

And so *Dirty Harry*'s Scorpio terrorises the city of San Francisco, demanding money and threatening to kill at random. Many people may not even be aware that *Dirty Harry* is a serial-killer movie because it's so much about the Dirty Harry Callahan character, his mammoth gun and cool dialogue. But a serial-killer movie it definitely is. And a good one at that. Good plot, a really hateful villain and that oh so cool dialogue. And even after all this time it isn't dated.

11/ *Frenzy* (1972) 116 minutes

It was 12 years since Alfred Hitchcock made *Psycho* and he had obviously been waiting for the right idea before he embarked on another psychopathic killer thriller. *Frenzy* was it. And it was something ghastly that happened in those 12 years that was the inspiration for what would eventually become *Frenzy*.

In Boston, USA from 1962 to 1964 a heinous fiend named Albert De Salvo raped and strangled 13 women in their homes. He became known as the Boston Strangler and was the first of a kind: each of his victims, who ranged from young students to elderly women, were left with an identifying 'signature' – after he had strangled his victims with their own stockings or underwear, the Boston Strangler tied the garment in a neat bow beneath the victim's chin.

In the same fashion as the Boston Strangler, the evil killer in *Frenzy* also leaves a calling card after he strangles his victims with a necktie. After a succession of naked bodies of young women are found all over London he becomes known as the 'Necktie Killer'.

An innocent man is accused of the murders and the hunt is on. But it is the Hitchcock brand of black humour that gives *Frenzy* its class. The dialogue at dinner between the ever-so-proper police inspector and his wife is priceless as he explains the day-to-day developments of the grisly Necktie Murders and she dishes him up equally gruesome meals she has learnt in her home-cooking classes. Not to be missed.

12/ *Wolf Creek* (2005) 95 minutes
'Based on a true story', the opening credits tell us. Well, not quite. But this Australian shocker that makes the *Texas Chainsaw Massacre* look like *Mary Poppins* certainly does have *links* with two famous Australian murders cases. The most recent is the disappearance of British tourist Peter Falconio in the Northern Territory in July 2001, and the subsequent conviction of Bradley Murdoch for his murder. The second is the most notorious case of serial murder in Australia's history, the Backpacker Murders, in which Ivan Milat was convicted of murdering seven backpackers between 1989 and 1992 on the outskirts of Sydney.

John Jarratt plays Mick Taylor, the friendly outback loner who befriends two girls and a young bloke who have broken down in the middle of nowhere. Kind Mick offers them a tow, which they take only to find themselves in the graveyard of lots of other luckless young tourists and their vehicles. All of this peripherally relates to the Peter Falconio disappearance and the real-life murderer Murdoch could be likened to the make-believe Mick.

The similarity to the Backpacker Murders comes when Mick refers to one of his victims as 'a head on a stick' after he has severed her spine with a huge Bowie knife. This was the same method used by Ivan Milat on all of his victims to render them helpless, but leave them still alive so he could have his way with them without any interference.

Wolf Creek is a very scary movie. But what is scariest of all is that it is very believable. There could very well be a Mick Taylor, or several for that matter, out there preying on kids on an adventure in their $2000 Holden station wagons and VW Kombis. And I guess it's us Aussies who would have the best understanding of this, given our knowledge of the vastness of the outback, the times between seeing another vehicle and the distances between civilisations.

So it is little wonder it was panned unmercifully by the unknowing US critics, who couldn't get past the blood and guts and soak up the reality. The doyen of them all, Roger Ebert, gave it zero stars and said, '*Wolf Creek* is more like the guy who bites the heads off chickens at the carnival sideshow. No fun for us, no fun for the guy, no fun for the chicken. In the case of this film it's fun for the guy.' Another said, 'It made me want to vomit and cry at the same time.' Yet another: 'It must be giving Australia's Outback tourism industry a bad case of heartburn.'

Still, at a cost of about $A1 million, and with worldwide box office takings of over $US24m, I guess the producers couldn't care less. I thought it was great.

13/ *Cop* (1987) 110 minutes

If nothing else this excellent, yet hardly noticed, thriller is the movie that will go down in history as the first to use the term 'serial killer' in its dialogue. And what a good serial-killer movie it is. James Woods plays the cop who investigates the grisly murder of a woman, only to uncover a can of worms that involves no less than 16 killings dating back donkey's years, a crooked dope-dealing cop and a short affair with an enormously endowed hooker until she ... well, you'll see for yourself why the affair is so short.

It is a very credible movie that moves along at a rapid pace and includes all of the usual traits of a cop-in-pursuit-of-a-serial-killer movie, in that his boss doesn't believe that the murders are connected and tells him to get off the case or he'll be sacked, his home life is a disaster and his detective partner (Charles Durning) keeps covering up for him.

But in the end James gets his man. Definitely worth a look.

14/ *Jennifer 8* (1992) 127 minutes

This excellent serial-killer thriller went virtually unnoticed at the box office but has created a huge cult following on video, and deservedly so. Andy Garcia features as the off-the-wall big-city cop working a serial murder case in a small northern Californian town.

Naturally the local hillbilly cops hate the detective from the big smoke and do everything in their power to stop him producing the killer. But all is not lost for Andy, who falls for the stunning Uma Thurman, a blind student who looks pretty certain to be the serial killer's next victim.

In many ways, *Jennifer 8* is a serial-killer thriller in the vein of many that came before: the cop stumbles onto a killer, no one believes him, he pursues it anyway much to the disgust of the hierarchy and with brilliant detective work and against all odds comes up with the goods.

The fact that Andy and Uma are supported by the likes of John Malkovich and Lance Henriksen in a very strong cast only adds to the movie's class.

15/ *Citizen* X (1995) 105 minutes

Made originally for TV, and now available on video, this true-life charmer is about the life and times of Russian murderer Andre Chikatilo, one of the most prolific serial killers the world has ever known, and a detective's (Stephen Rea) dogged eight-year pursuit against all odds to bring him to justice.

Chikatilo tortured, murdered and raped the corpses of at least 53 people, mainly children. He disembowelled many of them and ate their body parts, before he was captured in 1992, tried and executed by a single bullet to the back of the head.

This is a movie, not a documentary, and the story-line about the detective's continued frustration with Russia's bureaucracy that hampers his bringing Chikatilo to trial is as entertaining as it is factual. The strong supporting cast includes Donald Sutherland and Max von Sydow.

16/ *Sea of Love* (1989) 112 minutes

The last thing that alcoholic detective Al Pacino needs as he goes through a midlife crisis is a serial killer who lies his/her naked male victims face down on the bed and puts a bullet behind their ears while the record player pumps out the old 1959 Phil Phillips 45rpm classic *Sea of Love*, over and over.

Will the case take Al over the edge that he is already precariously balancing on? Will the stunning blonde chief suspect (Ellen Barkin) fuck him to death before he solves the mystery? Will a detective he works with, who is married to Al's ex-wife, end up putting a bullet in him for pestering them at all hours of the night when he's fallen down the eye of a Jim Beam bottle? Will the serial killer get him?

It's almost enough to get Al off the turps but when he teams up with another hard-drinking cop (John Goodman) that doesn't seem possible as they lead each other through one drunken escapade after another in the pursuit of evidence to nail the Sea of Love Killer.

Sounds corny? It isn't. It's anything but. This is hard-core, racy drama at its best and there's not a boring or cornball moment in it. And don't tell your friends who the serial killer is. Let 'em guess.

17/ *Copycat* (1995) 125 minutes

Now here's a serial-killer movie with a difference. A serial killer who copies other serial killers. That's right. In this highly entertaining, but somewhat dubious, murder spree we have a psychopath on the loose who is re-enacting the murders of such infamous bygone American serial killers as Son of Sam, Ted Bundy and the Hillside Strangler.

Our killer re-enacts the murders down to the last detail and, in the process, terrorises agoraphobic psychiatrist Sigourney Weaver, who is a world authority and lecturer on serial killers. Sigourney's terror of leaving her home is justified in that she was attacked and strangled half to death by a demented hillbilly serial killer (Harry Connick Jnr) in a public toilet and, even though he is locked away forever, she fears that he will come back and get her. And what with a re-enacting serial killer on the loose ... guess what happens?

If you don't look too intensely at the plot, and just ignore the holes that you could drive a jumbo jet through, then this could be the movie for you.

18/ *The Bone Collector* (1999) 117 minutes

Welcome to the world of mega-high-tech serial-killer catching. And somehow director Phillip Noyce plausibly pulls it off without his hero, serial-killer super-sleuth extraordinaire Denzel Washington, the NYPD's leading forensics expert, laying a finger on the villain.

This is mainly due to the fact that Denzel is a quadriplegic confined to his bed at home, surrounded by nurses and so much computer and surveillance equipment that his electricity bill must eat up every cent of his medical insurance.

Mr Bone Collector conducts his grisly business in New York's nether world and with pouting policewoman Angelina Jolie standing in for him, Denzel guides her through an earpiece and watches her every move from a camera in her helmet as they pursue the latest in the seemingly never-ending procession of New York's periodical mass murderers.

No real surprises in this one, but it is cleverly made and very suspenseful. It also leaves you wondering if it really could happen. The policeman tracking down a demented serial killer from his bed, that is. Still, stranger things have happened. Professor Stephen Hocking is a classic example. If you watch *The Bone Collector* with this in mind it makes for a much more entertaining movie rather than sitting there picking holes in it, which is very easy to do.

19/ *Henry: Portrait of a Serial Killer* (1990) 90 minutes

Critically acclaimed as 'a film of ferocious, haunting power' and 'an unpleasant, unexploitative, and brilliantly directed portrayal of diseased minds', this squalid piece of work is based on just a few of the exploits of America's most prolific serial-killer Henry Lee Lucas who, in cahoots with redneck buddy Ottis Toole, murdered and raped the corpses of in excess of 150 men, women and children throughout America from 1960 to 1983.

What the movie doesn't tell us is that in between raping and killing and having sex with each other – they met as cell mates – the Texas good ol' boys also liked a little Southern ménage à trois with a chicken, a calf, Ottis' sister Beckie, or all three at once, and that as a kid Henry's prostitute momma beat him so bad that it gave him brain damage. Gee, really! Henry paid her back in 1960 by murdering her and raping her corpse.

But while Michael Rooker as Henry, Tom Towles as Ottis and Tracy Arnold as Beckie are perfectly cast as life's redneck losers, the real star of the show is murder itself and lots of it. To my mind *Henry* was grossly overrated but it will no doubt have its legion of fans of serial-killer movies.

20/ *To Catch a Killer* (1991)

This excellently produced tale about American serial killer John Wayne Gacy was also originally made for TV and ended up on video. Big man Brian Dennehy is superbly cast as real-life big man Gacy, a Chicago building contractor who gave generously of his time to public charities and often performed as Pogo the Clown at children's hospitals and benefits.

In the meantime Gacy was luring teenage boys to his home in Des Plaines, Illinois where he tortured, raped and strangled them and buried their bodies under his house. He was arrested in 1978 and found guilty of murdering 33 boys. Pogo the Clown was executed by lethal injection in 1994.

The movie portrays Gacy as he was in real life, an arrogant oaf who thought he could bluff the police because he was a respected member of the community. A must in any serial-killer video library.

INDEX

Another true crime title from The Five Mile Press

The Beat

A True Account of the Bondi Gay Murders

I.J. Fenn

In June 2001, 12 years after television newsreader, Ross Warren, disappeared following an evening out with friends in Sydney, a police operation was set up to reinvestigate the disappearance. What this new investigation uncovered was to prove far more interesting than the anticipated 'missing persons' case.

I.J. Fenn moves the story along with the pace of a detective thriller. The Beat is an ugly story about ugly people committing ugly crimes. This is a disturbing book, but you will not be able to put it down.

Another true crime title from The Five Mile Press

Outside the Law

Australian True Crime Stories

John Silvester, Andrew Rule & Others

A revised and expanded compilation of classic true crime stories from eight of Australia's foremost crime writers. John Silvester explores the Australian Mafia and the mystery of Donald Mackay, Andrew Rule looks at the Queens Street massacre, Vikki Petraitis examines serial killer Paul Denyer's horrific crimes, Greg Fogarty describes the intriguing Crawford family murders, Malcolm Brown covers the gruesome Ivan Milat murders, Jennifer Cooke examines the Anita Cobby murder, Murray Mottram describes the murder of a taxi driver by teenagers and Garry Linnell describes the life of an undercover cop.

Another true crime title from The Five Mile Press

Forensics

True Stories from Australian Police Files
Vikki Petraitis

Vikki Petraitis is one of Australia's most popular true crime writers. In this collection she tells stories from the police files in which forensics, as well as dogged determination, have played a major part in their resolution. They make for riveting reading.